THE PENTECOSTAL
MINISTER

SERMON
RESOURCE
MANUAL

THE PENTECOSTAL MINISTER

SERMON RESOURCE MANUAL

VOLUME 1

Floyd D. Carey and Hoyt E. Stone, Editors

Pathway
P·R·E·S·S

CLEVELAND, TENNESSEE 37311

Library of Congress Number: 87-072041
ISBN: 0-87148-721-7

INTRODUCTION

Fully convinced that the Pentecostal minister is unique not only in the style of his presentation but also in the force and content of his message, the editors believe a book of this nature is appropriate and that it has potential for contributing significantly to the effectiveness of one's pastoral and evangelistic ministry.

This is the first volume in a series of resource books to be selected, edited, and designed exclusively for Pentecostal ministers. The book divides conveniently into three sections: **Manuscript Sermons** which offer a total message with appropriate illustrations and guidelines; **Outline Sermons** designed to provide seed thoughts so that one can include personal illustrations and points; and a brief sample of **Teaching Outlines** by David Bishop which the editors trust will introduce a rather new "preaching-teaching" approach to leading a congregation into a more thorough understanding of the Word.

With few exceptions, these sermons have been purposefully solicited from men actively involved in the pastoral ministry. They represent congregations of different sizes and from varying social and geographical backgrounds. All contributors are Pentecostal. We believe the strength of the **Pentecostal Minister Resource Manual** lies in the variety of preaching styles and the wide range of subjects covered.

The pastor in today's world is beleaguered by demands from many publics. Nevertheless, he knows that first and foremost he must remember Christ's command to "feed my sheep." As editors we do not think for a moment, nor propose in any way, that a pastor lift these sermons from the printed page and serve them perfunctorily for congregational consumption. Such would impinge upon the very nature of Pentecostal preaching, emasculating the process, and moving God's man from the sanctuary of personal commitment and communion with God through the Holy Spirit.

The editors do feel, however, that the minister may at times find himself walking through a "desert place" in terms of ideas and inspiration, and thus offer these sermons as "seeds for thought." Perhaps, at these waters, through the reading of a message or the study of an outline, God's Holy Spirit will kindle such a fire in the soul that the minister will step forth boldly to plow a new deep furrow into the hearts of his own people.

Since the sermons are arranged primarily to express variety, rather than by subject or author, we suggest ready use of the contents pages. Also, each chapter heading is boldfaced, making it easy to flip to the numbered chapter or the designated page.

Pathway Press plans to produce a new volume each year. We welcome your comments and suggestions in terms of what will follow.

It is our prayer that this material might support you in winning people to Jesus Christ, in helping them to enjoy a fuller life in Christ, and in leading your congregation to experience the dynamics of the Holy Spirit on an everyday basis.

Floyd D. Carey and Hoyt E. Stone
The Editors

Table of Contents

Section 2, Outline Sermons

Section 3, Teaching Outlines

SOLD OUT

Ray H. Hughes

SCRIPTURE: Zechariah 11:12, 13; Matthew 26:15

INTRODUCTION

No man in human history had a greater opportunity for success and happiness than did Judas Iscariot. Yet, since his death, he has ranked at the top of the list among those who also betrayed the Lord. Luke called him a traitor. John the Beloved labeled him as a thief. And even Jesus Christ, the tender Man from Galilee, said, "It had been good for that man if he had not been born" (Matthew 26:24).

CONTRASTS OF LIFE

Let us discuss what Judas might have been over against what he was. The picture of Judas is a typical picture of many thousands of our day. Judas was honored to have his name included by our Lord among the Twelve. Had he not sold Christ for 30 pieces of silver, his name would have been inscribed in the multicolored foundations of the City of God. Whereas, today it is only a byword and a hissing among men.

In Bible days, the naming of a child meant a great deal more than it does today. In giving names to their children, the parents expressed their wishes and desires. The name *Judas* means "the praise of God" or "confessor," which is evidence that his parents had a great desire that he would glorify God and magnify His name.

He who had every opportunity to praise God became the son of perdition, went to a suicide's grave, and caused a potter's field to be purchased with his blood money. Judas might have been one like the Apostle Peter who, as he passed by the multitudes, they were made whole. Instead, his life has cast a shadow of reproach through which no noble person dares walk.

In the days of Judas Iscariot, the name Judas was one of the most popular. Today, no mother dares name her child "Judas' because of the stigma. He might have been the praise of God, but he became the curse of hell. In the lines of Whittier, "Of all the words of tongue and pen, the saddest of these it might have been."

THE DESTINY OF A SOUL

Judas was not compelled to sin, nor predestined to be lost. The prophecy of the psalmist David concerning this betrayal and the foreknowledge of God did not affect the free agency of Judas. He acted entirely of his own will. Judas, by transgression, fell and went to his own place—that is, the place of his choosing, which is hell.

No man is born to be lost, for it is God's will that all men be saved and come to the knowledge of the truth (1 Timothy 2:4). He is "not willing that any should perish, but that all should come to repentance" (2 Peter 3:9). And, again, "For God hath not appointed us to wrath, but to obtain salvation by our Lord Jesus Christ" (1 Thessalonians 5:9). Judas alone was accountable for his sin.

Judas was a man of opportunity. He had close and constant fellowship with the Lord. He had even been ordained of the Lord to heal the sick and to cast out devils. He was a bosom friend of the Lord, for at the Last Supper John sat on Christ's right hand and Judas on His left. For three years, he had listened to the music of His Master's voice; he had been guided by the light of His countenance; but now he had listened to the siren voice of the world.

2

In the light of all of these opportunities, the Bible said, "And they covenanted with him for thirty pieces of silver" (Matthew 26:15). This was according to the prophecy of Zechariah, "And I said unto them, If ye think good, give me my price; and if not, forbear. So they weighed for my price thirty pieces of silver. And the Lord said unto me, Cast it unto the potter: a goodly price that I was prised at of them. And I took the thirty pieces of silver, and cast them to the potter in the house of the Lord" (Zechariah 11:12, 13).

SOLD OUT CHEAP

Judas betrayed the Lord for a paltry sum, but when remorse seized his soul, he returned to the priests and made a confession, "I have betrayed innocent blood." Typical of the world, they said, "What is that to us. See thou to that."

When one lives for the world and its creature comforts, feeds his body at the expense of his soul, and the whole world bows before him and beats a path to his door, yet, there comes a time when human hands cannot render assistance. Those who have bargained with you in the sale of your Christ will turn again and rend you.

Jeremiah said, "All thy lovers have forgotten thee" (30:14). Cyrus the conqueror, who for awhile thought he was making a fine thing out of this present world, wrote his own epitaph for his tombstone: "I am Cyrus. I occupied the Persian Empire. I was king over Asia. Begrudge me not this monument."

In afteryears the world plowed up his grave.

William Blane describes the remorse of this scene in these words:

> Thirty pieces of silver burns on the traitor's brain,
>   Thirty pieces of silver, oh, it is hellish gain.
> "I have sinned and betrayed the guiltless," he cried
>   with fevered breath
> Then cast them down in the temple, and rushed to
>   a madman's death.

Judas tried the world and found that it was an unsatisfactory portion. He sold out cheap.

This has been the story of many men through the ages. Achan, the troubler of Israel, sold his soul for the yellow glint of the golden wedge, the white sheen of the silver shekels, and the bright colors of the Babylonish garment. He sold his soul for the accursed thing.

Balaam sold his soul for the promise of a house full of money. Peter wrote, "Which have forsaken the right way, and are gone astray, following the way of Balaam the son of Bosor, who loved the wages of unrighteousness" (2 Peter 2:15). Then in the words of Jude, verse 11, "Woe unto them! for they . . . ran greedily after the error of Balaam for reward."

Esau sold his soul for a mess of pottage. Ahab sold himself to carry out the wicked deeds of his evil wife. His devotion to evil outweighed his devotion to God. The Scripture says, "But there was none like unto Ahab, which did sell himself to work wickedness in the sight of the Lord, whom Jezebel his wife stirred up" (1 Kings 21:25). Some men barter their souls as though they were trinkets purchased in a toy shop. Isaiah said, "Ye have sold yourselves for nought" (52:3); that is, sold out for nothing.

You are possibly saying to yourself, "If I had been in Judas' place, I would not have sold Christ. I would have stood for Him." The fact remains that you and multiplied thousands are guilty of the same crime that Judas committed. Christ is still being sold—sold for silver and for many things of less value than silver. Anything, whatever it may be, that stands between you and your God and causes you to refuse to yield yourself to Him, is the price for which you are selling Jesus Christ.

EMPTINESS OF SIN

Judas received 30 pieces of silver but never received benefit from it. Man soon discovers that, with God left out, the world is empty and must cry forth as Solomon, "Vanity of vanities, all is vanity" (Ecclesiastes 1:2), which simply means, "Emptiness of emptiness; all is emptiness."

When a man faces eternity without God, he realizes what a fool he has been to be enchanted by this world. T. Dewitt Talmage said, "Many of you have tried the garden of this world's delight. You have found it has been a chagrin."

There comes a point in human existence when all earthly values fail. If all of the wealth of the Federal Reserve System were put in the pocket of your shroud, when you stand before

4

God you would not be able to pay five cents for your redemption. Many people have sold out to the devil and have nothing to show for it but remorse, guilt, a wrecked life and a blasted past.

A philosopher once said, "Every man has his price." He meant that there was a price for which any man would sell his soul under certain circumstances. This statement is not altogether true, but the masses of our day can be placed in this category.

For what are you selling your soul? Think about the words of this poem:

> It may not be for silver,
> It may not be for gold,
> But still by tens of thousands
> Is this precious Savior sold.
>
> Sold for a godless friendship,
> Sold for a selfish aim,
> Sold for a fleeting trifle,
> Sold for an empty name.
>
> Sold where the awful bargain,
> None but God's eye can see.
> Ponder my soul the question,
> Shall He be sold by thee?
>
> Sold and a weeping angel
> Records the fatal choice.
> Sold but the price of the Savior
> To a living coal shall turn.
> With the pangs of remorse forever,
> Deep in the soul to burn.

If you have sold yourself for silver, remember, "He that loveth silver shall not be satisfied with silver." (Ecclesiastes 5:10). Ezekiel wrote, "Their silver and their gold shall not be able to deliver them in the day of the wrath of the Lord; they shall not satisfy their souls" (Ezekiel 7:19). Though you may not have sold Christ for silver, what have you accepted in exchange for your soul? "For what shall it profit a man, if he shall gain the whole world, and lose his own soul?" (Mark 8:36).

THE PRICE OF A SOUL

No man has ever gained the world, but Christ said in effect, "If a man could gain the whole world and yet lose his own soul, there would be no profit." It would be a bad transaction.

There are some who, like Pilate when he was convinced that Jesus Christ was a faultless man, heard the cry of the crowd, "If thou let this man go, thou art not Caesar's friend" (John 19:12), and so, for a godless friendship, they forsake the friend that sticketh closer than a brother.

If you are selling Christ for godless friendships, remember: Alexander the Great conquered the known world in his day. After his death, he remained unburied for 30 days because no one would shovel him under.

The highest honor that could be paid a man in the days of Rome was to be made an emperor; yet, out of 63 emperors, only six of them died a peaceful death. If you have sold your soul for a name of fame, the Bible says, "The name of the wicked shall rot" (Proverbs 10:7). If you have sold your soul for a selfish aim and seek to spare yourself at the expense of Christ, the Bible says, "He that loveth his life shall lose it" (John 12:25).

Friend, is it well with your soul? Do you have perfect satisfaction about your future? Did you know that when all of your real estate is gone and friends have deserted you, there is a soul within you that will spend eternity somewhere?

"There is a life that always lives; there is a death that never dies."

If you are not prepared to meet God, your soul is ever dying, yet never dead. It will be ever burning but never consumed. It will be ever agonizing but never relieved. Consider your soul and turn your feet to Calvary today, for nothing but Christ shall be able to satisfy you in the day of death.

If you live for this world, all you will ever receive out of life is your board, clothing, endless worry now, and endless anguish in the world to come.

OUR GIFTS TO CHRIST

Floyd J. Timmerman

SCRIPTURE: Psalm 116:12

INTRODUCTION

The greatest gift ever made was by God himself in the person of His Son, Jesus Christ. We read of it in what is called the golden text of the Bible: "For God so loved the world, that he gave his only begotten Son, that whosoever believeth in him should not perish, but have everlasting life" (John 3:16).

Not only did God give His Son but the Son gave His life, and we are reminded in our Lord's own words, "Greater love hath no man than this, that a man lay down his life for his friends" (John 15:13).

Quite obviously, God is a giving God, a loving God, a God of mercy and grace. How marvelous indeed are His expressions to each of us!

Normally, in human terms, when we receive a little gift from some friend or loved one, at Christmas or on a birthday, we like to show our appreciation. But so glorious indeed are God's mercies that we overflow with thanksgiving and join the psalmist in our text, asking, "What shall I render unto the Lord for all his benefits?"

Our blessings from God are so numerous and so rich that we are made to testify as the Apostle Paul, "O the depth of the riches both of the wisdom and knowledge of God! how unsearchable are his judgments, and his ways past finding out!" (Romans 11:33).

What we can give to God is small, so very small, when compared to what He has given us; nevertheless, we must not fail in presenting our gifts to Christ. Let us now give consideration to four gifts we *can* render unto Him.

OUR LOVE

Even in human terms, love is the greatest of gifts. More words are written on love, more stories are told about love, more people are inspired by love than any other subject in human language. It is the constant theme of our novels, our TV dramas, and our human aspirations.

It is surely significant that Paul lists love as the first manifestation of the fruit of the Spirit: "Love, joy, peace, long-suffering, gentleness, goodness, faith, meekness, temperance" (Galatians 5:22).

Important as well is the fact that love is twofold, reaching first toward God and then toward our neighbors. When asked of a lawyer, "Which is the great commandment?" Jesus answered, "Thou shalt love the Lord thy God with all thy heart, and with all thy soul, and with all thy mind" (Matthew 22:36, 37). This is the first and greatest commandment, Jesus said, but the second is related, "Thou shalt love thy neighbor as thyself" (v. 39).

Adam Clarke puts it succinctly, "Our Lord shows us that the whole of true religion is comprised of us loving God and our neighbor."

All gifts are worthless and unacceptable unless accompanied by, and given from, a heart of love. True love has no limitations, no boundaries. Love cannot be purchased; it is always freely given.

No wonder the Scriptures place so much emphasis upon our love for God.

OURSELVES

Along with our love—in fact, in full confirmation of our love—we must give ourself as a vessel for His use. Paul writes, "I beseech you therefore, brethren, by the mercies of God, that ye present your bodies a living sacrifice, holy, acceptable unto God" (Romans 12:1).

In light of all His great gifts to us, how can we do less? Paul faced this question, adding the observation that such is our "reasonable service."

When a young man enters the army, he is trained and schooled in the hardships of military life. He holds none of his strength in reserve. He gives all. Our spiritual Commander, Jesus Christ, calls today for those who will bring all their powers into subjection and serve without reservation in the army of the Lord. There has never been a time in history when the cause of righteousness needed consecrated people more than it does today. Let us yield ourselves unto the Lord (2 Chronicles 30:8).

What better gift to bring to Christ than a yielding of our total selves to His will, saying with the Apostle Paul, "Neither count I my life dear unto myself" (Acts 20:24). Unless He is Lord of all, He is not Lord at all.

Thus we offer ourselves—a gift unto Christ.

OUR LOYALTY

The wise men who saw Christ's star, upon the occasion of His birth (Matthew 2:1-12), present a lesson in loyalty worthy of note. Not only did they pursue their journey with diligence, against great odds, but they refused the bribes of an earthly king, their loyalty firmly anchored in God himself. Others were unseeing, others refused to believe, but the wise men grasped a promise. They clung to God's Word.

We will never find Him, or serve Him, if we do not believe His Word.

The wise men were not satisfied just to find Him and leave. They recognized His divinity and they worshiped Him reverently, whom even angels bow before: "Let all the angels of God worship him" (Hebrews 1:6); and of whom David wrote, "Worship the Lord in the beauty of holiness" (Psalm 29:2).

What is more, they verified their love and worship through presentation of gifts—gold, frankincense, and myrrh, some of earth's most valuable treasures. They gave to Christ their very best.

We must do no less. Christ must be first in our life.

OUR TALENTS

In one form or another we each have special and unique talents. Our talents are not the same. They may not be equal in number or variety, but they are gifts, or graces, from the Creator and we must consecrate them to God.

When Henry Wadsworth Longfellow was a young man, he expressed himself in a letter to his father: "I am not sure as yet for what my talents fit me, but I am determined to be eminent in something."

I truly believe God has endowed each of us with capacity, with potential, with talent to become eminent in something. That eminence may not appear to men of this world but it will certainly register on God's perfect scale of values. The beautiful thing about giving what we have—our talents—to God is seen in what they then become under His leading and the direction of His Holy Spirit. Every Christian soon discovers himself, in the power of Christ, doing more and becoming more than he is personally capable of doing or becoming.

Paul wrote to young Timothy, his son in the Lord, "Neglect not the gift that is in thee" (1 Timothy 4:14). Nor must we either neglect our gifts or use them selfishly. Life is more than earthly existence, more than that which is presently seen: it is also the laying up of treasures in heaven. If we use our talents for His glory, we will have the smile of God upon us in this life and, at death, we will hear Him say, "Well done, thou good and faithful servant: thou hast been faithful over a few things, I will make thee ruler over many things: enter thou into the joy of thy lord" (Matthew 25:21).

CONCLUSION

All we have and all we are comes from God. "In him we live, and move, and have our being" (Acts 17:28). Therefore, let us rejoice and be glad, serving Him to the best of our ability every day.

THE CHRISTIAN'S BODY

Delbert D. Rose

SCRIPTURE: 1 Corinthians 6:19

INTRODUCTION

There was something amazingly wonderful and special about the body of the Lord Jesus Christ. What was it? Did it radiate with light as He walked among men? Could it be in two places at one time? Did a halo hover over His head? No, it was none of these things.

Was it different from the bodies of other men? Not really. Just like our bodies, it was "fearfully and wonderfully made." His body had two feet, two hands, two ears, a nose, a mouth and one heart.

Yet it was different.

What was special about the body of the Lord Jesus Christ? It was special because the Son of God assumed it to dwell among men. It was through a body indwelt by the Holy Spirit and dedicated to the will of God that Jesus carried on His ministry. The body of our Lord was also special inasmuch as it was not tainted by sin. There was no sin in Him, neither was there guile found in His mouth. At the time of His birth the power of the highest overshadowed Mary and the infant Jesus was born sinless.

In similar fashion, every Christian's body is special too. No, we were not conceived without sin. Neither do our bodies glow in the dark. They cannot last very long without food and water. They cannot jump 10 feet into the air or skip 30 feet. Neither can they pass through closed doors or be in two places at the same time. But, they are special. Apart from being fearfully and wonderfully made, our bodies belong to the Lord. This is what makes them special.

Jesus has bought us with a price, the shedding of His own precious blood. When you became a Christian by trusting in the atoning death of Jesus Christ on the Cross, the Holy Spirit entered into your body. At that moment your body became the temple of God. So your body is sacred. That is what makes it special.

What does Paul say about our bodies? How are we to use them? How can we best glorify God in them? Can we use them or abuse them, as the case may be, as we please? In our text, Paul answers these questions for us:

"What? know ye not that your body is the temple of the Holy Ghost which is in you, which you have of God, and ye are not your own? For ye are bought with a price: therefore glorify God in your body, and in your spirit, which are God's" (1 Corinthians 6:19).

Paul's words suggest four things:

FIRST, PAUL'S WORDS SERVE AS A REMINDER.

"What? know ye not?" This expression is used by Paul eight times in this first letter to the Corinthians. Again and again he had to say to them, "Didn't anyone ever tell you about these things? Haven't you been informed? Don't you know it's wrong to pit one preacher against another, wrong to organize yourselves into cliques and be constantly at war with each other? Don't you know that such spirits are disrupting the harmony of the church and creating deep feelings of hostility? Don't you know that drunkards, fornicators, adulterers, and sex perverts shall not inherit the kingdom of God? Don't you know that your body was purchased by the precious blood of Jesus Christ, that you are indwelt by the Holy Spirit, and that God wants to use it for His Glory?"

Could it be that the Christians at Corinth did not know better and had to be informed? After all, they had been saved from gross heathenism, dreadful superstition, and loose moral living. Perhaps they really didn't know how to behave as Christians.

Or it could have been that the Corinthians were ignoring certain information given them. They knew what was expected of them but they were doing nothing about it. They were not living up to their potential in Christ. They were not growing because they were not obeying Christ. I am convinced this was their problem. They were living too close to the world. They were being attracted by its allurements. Their separation was not complete. The world, the flesh, and the devil still had a hold on them.

Sometime ago I read of a woman who was 45 years of age and had the body and voice of a child. Spiritually speaking, the Corinthians were like that. Their souls had not kept pace with their age. They had been Christians for years, but they had been stifled in their growth. Paul wanted to feed them with the meat of God's Word, but he had to feed them baby food instead. They had not grown up as Christians. They refused nourishment. Consequently, they were underdeveloped as believers in Christ.

So Paul had to remind them that their bodies were special and were to be sacred unto God. Since the Holy Spirit had been deposited into their lives, all their faculties were meant to be holy unto the Lord. They were to be submissive to Him. They were to be set apart for His glory and honor.

SECOND, PAUL EMPHASIZES THAT WE ARE A RETAINER.

"What? know ye not that your body is the temple of the Holy Ghost which is in you?" One commentator says, "A temple is a house or dwelling of God, a building erected and set apart for the worship of the true God."

In the Old Testament God instructed Moses to build the tabernacle in the wilderness. He was to carefully follow the blueprint of God. Nothing was to be left out. There was something about the tabernacle which would distinguish Judaism from all other religions of that day. What was it? There was a supernatural occupant in the tabernacle. Other religions merely had man-made counterfeits; Judaism had the real thing. The presence of God actually indwelt the tabernacle. This is what made it a temple, a special place of worship.

The Temple of Solomon superseded the tabernacle. After its completion, Solomon dedicated it in these words, "Behold, the heaven and heaven of heavens cannot contain Thee, how much less this house that I have builded" (1 Kings 8:27). Solomon wisely realized that his beautiful edifice had limitations. He knew that God was bigger than anything he could make. Nevertheless, the Temple was dedicated to God and in a very special way it became His dwelling place. At its dedication the Shekinah Glory filled the house. God was there! Both of these structures "housed" the presence of God.

So Paul reminded the Corinthian Christians that their bodies were temples of God. They understood him. Their heathen city had many shrines which housed man-made gods. Here was a new conception of life, the body as a shrine of God. It was no longer a sacred building, it was a sacred body. They were carrying around in their bodies the presence of the Holy Spirit. No matter where they went or what they were doing, consciously or unconsciously, they took God with them.

Our bodies ought to be yielded up to God and set apart for His use and possessed, occupied, and inhabited by the Holy Spirit.

THIRD, PAUL MENTIONS THAT WE ARE RECEIVERS.

"What? know ye not that your body is the temple of the Holy Ghost which is in you, which ye have of God?" The body of every believer becomes, at the moment of regeneration, the temple of the Holy Spirit. He comes to indwell us and make of our bodies sacred habitations.

Christ gave His life for our salvation, that all who receive Him should be saved. And when we believe He claims us as His own—what a glorious moment!

And the secret of it is He places His Holy Spirit within us, making us new creatures—with new desires, new motives, and new interests. Indeed, old things have passed away and

14

all things become new. The Spirit of God now resides within us.

As recipients of His Spirit we are under His control. We are no longer slaves to the flesh. We have the power to overcome the intrusions of the adversary. We refuse to yield to his distractions, lest we grieve the Holy Spirit.

It is so easy to allow habits, practices, and ways of life to control and master us; but the Spirit we have received provides the strength to master them. We are no longer enslaved to the appetite of the flesh, our instincts, or desires. We now yield ourselves to the One who can do exceedingly, abundantly, above and beyond what we can even begin to imagine or think.

True enough, there are those who will insist that purity is a sign of weakness and suggest that we are inferior in terms of our manhood. But, remember, you are the temple of the Holy Spirit and must not grieve Him.

Some time ago I was reading of an aged saint who was being borne to his burial. He had been very poor, and with great haste they were moving his coffin to the grave, when suddenly the old minister said, "Tread softly. You are carrying a temple of the Holy Ghost."

The Holy Spirit abides in us to glorify Christ, our Savior. He takes the things of Christ and makes them meaningful to us. He leads us in our daily living that we may grow in the grace and the knowledge of our Lord. And as we yield our lives completely to Him, He fills us with His glory.

FOURTH, PAUL SPEAKS OF US AS REVEALERS.

"What? know ye not that your body is the temple of the Holy Ghost which is in you, which ye have of God, and ye are not your own? For ye are bought with a price; therefore, glorify God in your body."

Here we have the purpose for which we are indwelt by the Holy Spirit. Our bodies are special because they are indwelt by the Holy Spirit; they have been purchased by the precious blood of Jesus, and they are meant to glorify Him.

Paul had to remind the Corinthians that their bodies were sacred because they were using them in immoral ways; prostitution, fornication, adultery and even that which is contrary to nature. Venus was the principal deity worshiped in the

15

city of Corinth. She was a goddess of love, of licentious passion. The people of the city were devoted to her.

One can imagine the results. Her shrine appeared above those of the other gods; and it was a law that one thousand beautiful girls should officiate as public prostitutes before the altar of the goddess of evil. Even Christians were being influenced by the wickedness of the city. They too were guilty of sex abuses.

Paul is saying, "Glorify God with your body." The Greeks, however, looked down on the body. Among them was the proverbial saying, "The body is a tomb." To them, the important thing was the soul, the spirit of man; the body was a thing that did not matter. Being of this persuasion meant you could do as you pleased with the body.

If the soul is all that matters then what a person does with the body is of no significance, they argued. After all, if a Christian is the freest of all people, then is he not free to do what he likes? In other words, if the body is filled with certain instincts, why not yield to them? It is made for the sexual act, and the sexual act is made for the body; therefore, let the desires of the body have their way just as you do when you feed the stomach in response to hunger.

Paul makes it clear their concept is totally wrong. Man as a whole will not pass away. He is made for union with Christ in this world and a still closer union hereafter. This being the case, a body which belongs to Christ has been literally prostituted to the one to whom the sex sin has been committed. He proclaims that, of all sins, fornication is the one that affects a person's body and insults it.

So, Paul is pleading to save the Corinthians in body and in soul. Sex sin contaminates the temple of God, that body which is destined to union with Christ. Our Christian bodies are sacred, because God's spirit dwells in us. It is the temple of the Lord and must not be used to satisfy its own lust, but is to be set aside for the glory of Christ. This means we must keep it clean and pure. We must practice holy living.

Remember, your body belongs to God. "Present your body a living sacrifice unto God."

16

CONCLUSION

The feet that led you in sin should now be directed in the paths of righteousness, to the house of God and the place of prayer. The eyes that once looked upon things which violated the law of God should now be directed to the Savior. The ears that once listened to impure things should now be eager to hear the Word of Life. The hands that once were swift to shed innocent blood should now be engaged in the service of the Lord. The tongue that once talked so loosely and glibly should now be singing His praises and telling others of His great love. The heart that was set upon earthly things should now be embracing the things of Christ, and sharing His love to men everywhere.

Christ Himself has exhorted us to let our light so shine before men that they may see our good works and glorify our Father which is in heaven.

"Oh that a man would arise in me, that the man I am would cease to be."

Yes, we are the temple of the Lord, may we conduct ourselves in such fashion that others will know that His Spirit resides within.

To God be the glory, honor, and praise, now and forever more!

CLAY PEOPLE

Carl H. Richardson

SCRIPTURE: Genesis 3:19; Jeremiah 18:1-6; 2 Corinthians 4:7

INTRODUCTION

Ever felt like a grasshopper?

Unimportant, inferior, low-down?

Israel felt that way when Moses' spies reported back from their excursion into the Promised Land. They said, "And there we saw the giants, . . . and we were in our own sight as grasshoppers" (Numbers 13:33).

These people were impressed with the land, a land flowing with milk and honey, a land of unbelievable fertility, a land of incalculable promise. They were also impressed with the inhabitants of the land, so impressed in fact that they were whipped before they started.

The princes of Israel were overwhelmed with their own inferiority. It was inevitable that they projected inferiority upon the inhabitants. They said, "We were in our own sight as grasshoppers, and so we were in their sight."

This was not really true, as subsequent events revealed, but it highlights the double deception of an inferiority complex. The man who trusts in himself sooner or later feels like a grasshopper in his own sight, and he thinks everybody else feels the same way about him. As long as circumstances are all right, he makes out; but when life tumbles in, he crawls. The confidence he has is self-confidence and is sheer illusion.

What a difference in the person who has God-confidence! He's invincible because he counts on the resources of God, not on his own weak, limited assets. He's certain of victory because he's absolutely sure of the victor! Paul wrote, "I can do all things through Christ which strengtheneth me" (Philippians 4:13).

Just what are you? Are you an accidental, evolved, compilation of male and female genes? Some people think so! Are you an animal? With blood and organs and breath? With instincts and muscular reactions? No less and really no more than an ape in the African jungle? Some people think so! Are you a lonely, isolated universal happening? A blob soon to dry? A ripple soon to cease? A speck soon to be blown away? Some people think so!

But what are you? Really and truly!

Ask your doctor. He'll tell you one thing. Ask your science professor. He'll tell you another. Ask the chemist and he will tell you something else. But ask God and God will tell you that you are the creation of His hands. You are the fruit of His labor. You are the apple of His eye. You are the pride of His heart. You are the choice object of God's eternal love.

Just like each of us, the prophet Jeremiah wrestled with this whole concept of man. What is he? Where is he going? Why the dilemma of life? Jeremiah was especially disturbed that God's people had deaf ears and hard hearts. They would neither listen nor heed the warnings Jeremiah preached day after day.

God spoke to Jeremiah: "Go down to the potters house, Jeremiah. Watch him work. Learn a lesson" (see Jeremiah 18:2).

Numerous songs have been written and many sermons preached about the potter and the clay. It remains yet a beautiful lesson.

Pottery is a science of man rather than of manufacturing. The potter himself is the most important element. The clay next. God said: "I am the potter. You are the clay."

Picture it in your mind. The potter is seated on the ground, with a mass of clay nearby, a vessel of water by his side, and in front of him the potter's wheel. After moistening and softening the clay, he puts it on the horizontal wheel, and then with the wheel turning, he touches the revolving lump of clay and begins to shape the vessel. Sometimes, when the vessel is near completion, the potter discovers a serious flaw. But because the clay is still pliable, the potter is able to form the vessel again and place the clay once more on the wheel, where he forms a new vessel.

Ever hear someone say, "Mr. Jones is a self-made man." I've heard it and I know what is generally meant, but it's not really true. There are no self-made men. We are all the work of God's hand. "It is He that hath made us, and not we ourselves."

THE ORIGINAL PLAN

Long before the house you presently dwell in was erected, the house existed in the mind, in the thoughts, of an architect or builder. Also, long before the world existed in material form, long before you became flesh and blood, you existed in the mind of God.

God is knowledgeable. In fact, He knows all things. God also wills. He decrees. He plans. Not only has God planned what you presently are, but God is planning what you are capable of becoming. God knows the precise processes needed to make you a vessel of honor.

At this very moment I can almost hear someone asking, "What if I'm to be a vessel of dishonor?" I'd like to answer such a question with a question of my own.

Do you want to be a vessel of dishonor? Is your heart set on evil? Have you no desire at all to be worthy? If not, then that's exactly what your life is going to be: a vessel of dishonor. However, don't mark God off. God sets even vessels of dishonor up before the world as examples, and God uses even the evil schemes of the devil for contrasting and then beautifying His own plan.

If you desire the good, if you desire beauty, if you desire perfection, God has a plan. He is the potter. He is the master workman. He is able to perfect that work already begun in you. And He will perfect it if you yield to the artistry of His hands.

THE BASIC MATERIALS

Clay is a mixture of common earth and silica. It is the presence of that silica which makes clay something more than common earth. So with the story of man. Man's story begins with thunder and ends with glory. Man begins with dust, but breathed upon by God's Spirit, he becomes a living soul.

There are, however, some steps by which God prepares the basic elements making up your personality. Let's note some of them as they relate to the potter's craft.

Clay, first of all, must be crushed. You, too, must be made pliable in the hands of God. The crushing process is not pleasant. Life is often painful beyond description. But remember, until the lumps have been removed, until the foreign elements are screened out, until you have been sifted, you are not suitable material for the potter's skill.

I'm sure that quite often there are those of us who wish for the potter to get on with the work. We want perfection and artistry now. At times, we may even try to move the plan along, as Moses did, but God demands a crushing in the wilderness first.

The potter can make no use of clay which is too moist. He thus squeezes out excess water. One of the most difficult of all life's lessons is this matter of excess. Zeal is good but it must be tempered. So many of our virtues pervert themselves when permitted to run wild. God has methods for squeezing out the excesses.

A man impatient and critical of today's youth can suddenly learn kindness when his own son, or his own daughter, is beset with temptation.

Life can squeeze out a lot of excesses.

Customarily, the potter isolates the clay, hiding it away for a time, so that it might acquire its true texture. This isolation process is always important.

"What I can do for God seems very insignificant," some folks say. Or, "My little part would never be missed." But don't ever despair. It could well be that the dark corner where you are now isolated is only preparation for a spot in the sun. Isolation has proven spiritually helpful to many people. Moses spent forty years in the wilderness. Elijah often walked and talked with God in the solitude of the desert. John the Baptist discovered faith in the mountains. And Saul of Tarsus isolated himself with God prior to stepping forth to turn the Gentile world upside down for Christ.

Don't fret over moments spent alone with God. Let them temper your soul. Let them bring out your true nature. Tomorrow, next week, next year the potter may set you forth as a fit example of His art.

THE CREATION PROCESS

Once the clay is prepared, once the basic materials are ready, then the potter creates. Then, and only then, does God take us in His hands for molding on the spinning wheel of life.

It is fascinating to watch a pile of raw clay take shape in the potter's hand.

First, you observe the spinning wheel. Then, the master's hand: smoothing, lifting, shaping, forming. The wheel turns fast. Miraculously the pottery takes shape. A vessel tall, a vessel short, a vessel with narrow neck and spout, a vessel with handle. Each an individual piece. Each standing alone. Each a work of art.

So is your life . . . and mine . . . a unique creation. Note it, the clay plays but a minor role in the process. We are just submissive to Him, not charged with creative responsibility. Did not Christ Himself say, "Come ye after me, and I will make you to become fishers of men" (Mark 1:17)?

John was a work of the Master's hand. He lived past a hundred years. On Patmos he saw the heavens opened and God's glory revealed. He was, indeed, a prince among men.

But let's not forget that James, too, was a vessel of honor unto God. He preached but a few sermons, worked but a short while, and died on Herod's chopping block. God fashioned both. In no way would we be justified in thinking John to have been better loved then James. They differed only in their allotted roles.

So it is with us!

THE TRIAL BY FIRE

Green pottery, or freshly created pottery, must yet be fired. Otherwise, it is useless.

Our faith too must be tried as by fire. It's the furnace of life that tempers us. It's the rocks and stones of the road which put toughness into our feet. It's the action, the pain of muscles reaching to their full capacity, the strain of lungs gasping for air that makes us strong and creates stamina for the race ahead.

John Wesley came to America because he visualized himself a missionary to the Indians of Georgia. He returned to England a miserable failure, disheartened, discouraged, ready to give up. Then out of that fiery trial, even out of that failure, John Wesley received a vision that sparked revival throughout the entire church world.

The Bible declares: "I will bring [them] . . . through the fire, . . . and will try them as gold is tried" (Zechariah 13:9).

THE FINISHING TOUCHES

Do you ever ask yourself, what really makes a life beautiful? A good question, isn't it.

Surely we know it isn't money that makes life beautiful. The rich, too, are plagued with ulcers, nervous disorders, alcoholism, and unhappiness.

Success doesn't necessarily make life beautiful. Executives, starlets, athletic champions—these, too, drink cups of bitterness.

Really, when you get right down to it, only God the Master Potter can beautify our lives. It is He who must give us those finishing touches that make for real living.

After the clay has been prepared, after the vessel has been formed, after the fire has made it strong, then the Master picks up the brush and adds color—color as beautiful as the rainbow, soft as a rising sun.

But God wanted Jeremiah to learn yet another lesson on his visit to the potter's house. This time Jeremiah is commanded to take a potter's vessel, one that has been finished and baked in the fire, one that has been made beautiful in color. Our impression is that this vessel can never be changed. It is not like the other vessel that had been marred but was still soft and workable.

God, through Jeremiah, pronounces judgment upon the people because "they have hardened their necks, that they might not hear my words" (19:15). At the conclusion of these words of judgment, Jeremiah breaks the potter's vessel to tiny fragments on the rocks. And God said: "Even so will I break this people and this city, as one breaketh a potter's vessel, that cannot be made whole again" (Jeremiah 19:11).

I have heard the crash of those broken vessels—heard them in the cemetery, littered with the fragments of last chance and squandered opportunity, heard them in the tragedies of sin that has overtaken men and women in the prime of life.

I have good news. God the Master Potter can pick up the pieces and remake your broken vessel anew. Regardless of your past sins or neglects or failures, the precious vessel of life can be transformed and remolded and refashioned through repentance and faith. In a single moment of time, the marred failures of a lifetime can be transformed.

CONCLUSION

Clay people? Earthen vessels? Created from dust and returning to dust? Yes! But you can have this treasure of eternal salvation just for the asking. You belong to God. From the Old Testament the Lord says: "All souls are mine" (Ezekiel 18:4).

God is not searching for golden vessels, or silver vessels, or ornamental vessels, but He is searching for clean vessels to fill with His Spirit and power.

The good news is that the Master Potter can pick up the pieces and make your broken life anew.

LAUNCH OUT INTO THE DEEP

Paul J. Eure

SCRIPTURE: Luke 5:1-7

INTRODUCTION

Luke paints the scene so as to make one imagine a typical seashore . . . sand gleaming in the sun . . . water dark blue against a lighter sky . . . two fishing boats drawn up, with sails down and wrapped . . . men on shore, moving tiredly about, repairing nets.

There is a crowd of people pressing so near that the Master stands at the water line.

The Lord solved His problem by using Simon's boat as a pulpit. This separated Him from the people, placing Him high so all could see. With water and wind behind Him, an amphitheater effect was created, thus carrying His voice to the far side of the crowd.

In all likelihood the fishermen themselves paused to listen. We do not know the subject of that day's teaching; but once He had finished, Jesus quietly turned to the fishermen and said, "Launch out into the deep."

Fascinating words . . . those. They have been quoted often,

preached on, used for inspiration under varying circumstances. Nonetheless, let us note truths from them once again.

GOD NEVER GIVES FOOLISH COMMANDS

Jesus said to Simon, "Launch out into the deep, and let down your nets for a catch" (*New King James Version*).

This is a command that may have sounded foolish indeed to a fisherman who had toiled all night. Simon was the expert. He was the fisherman; Jesus of Nazareth was a carpenter.

Not only was Simon the fisherman but we have every reason to believe he was a very skilled fisherman. We know for sure that he had been raised on the Sea of Galilee and that he knew those waters as few other men. Simon knew and understood fish. He knew their habits, their spawning beds, their likely feeding places.

More pressing, in light of this drama, Simon understood that there were times when fishermen did not catch fish. He was tired. He had fished all night and had caught nothing.

The command seemed so foolish to him that even when Luke recorded the incident years later, he noted that Simon made excuses. "Master," he said, "we have toiled all the night, and have taken nothing" (v. 5).

Is not the lesson obvious? How easily we determine that God's commands are foolish, irrational, without meaning. We may not say so, but deep in our hearts, we begin to doubt— concluding that the Master really does not understand the situation.

WE HUMANS ARE PRONE TO MAKE EXCUSES.

It seems to be our nature to make excuses. We see from the human perspective, from the limited horizon, from the natural point of view; and so, like Simon, we presumptuously tell the Master just what the facts are.

Simon was saying, "Lord, we've been out there all night. There are no fish in those waters. We have already tried. Our muscles ache. We are tired. Besides, Lord, the sun is well up. Fishing is always poor during the heat of the day. If you can't catch fish during the night, especially during the early morning hours when they come near the surface for feeding, then surely you can't catch them now."

We too have our litany of excuses. We put forth our human efforts and then say, "Lord, I tried." We look at the places where others have tried unsuccessfully and we conclude, "There are no souls to be saved in that burned-out area." We have tried that before; it didn't work. He was once a member of the church, but he didn't last. On and on we go . . . human reactions . . . faithless answers . . . comments and attitudes which fail to take into consideration the person of Jesus Christ.

On another occasion Jesus told the disciples to find food for the multitude (Luke 9:13-16). They had similar excuses: "Lord, they are too many. We have but a few loaves and fishes. It would take a great deal of money and we have but little." The bright spot in this story, of course, lies in the fact that Simon Peter's faith follows on the very heels of his doubt. Simon's faith may have been small but there was something there, a lesson to each of us today.

FAITH REMAINS A POSSIBILITY

It is difficult to explain, this matter of faith—where it comes from, how it comes, just precisely when it comes to us. The Apostle Paul understood that faith is a mysterious mixture of that which is human and that which is divine when he spoke of saving faith:

> "For by grace are ye saved through faith; and that
> not of yourselves: it is the gift of God: not of works,
> lest any man should boast" (Ephesians 2:8, 9).

According to this passage we must conclude two things: First, God is the prime mover in this matter of faith, His grace being ever-present to help and to assist us. And second, faith is not without the human element, the human response, and we must play our roles as well.

Could it have been the Lord's presence there on the boat? The very dominance of Divinity? Simon, making his excuses but at the same time looking into the face of Jesus, must have realized, "There is something different about this man, something compelling, something which belies the fact that He would command foolishly?"

Who really knows?

What we do know, for the Bible tells us, is that Simon's faith came through. It came on the heels of doubt. It came in spite of doubt . . . unexpectedly . . . surprisingly . . . almost as if forced from him by the very power of Christ's presence.

"Nevertheless, Lord, at Your command, I will."

For Simon and for us, faith remains a possibility. To forget this truth leads to despair. Hope may be dim; the possibilities may seem utterly beyond all expectations; but we must not give up. We must look to the Master's face, look into His eyes and see beyond the human.

FAITH CAN BRING THE UNEXPECTED MIRACLE

Simon launched out. In all likelihood he moved with casualness, not greatly excited, but willing to obey the Master. The Sea of Galilee is not a large body of water. On a clear day, from the center of the lake, you can always see the shoreline. It did not take long to reach deep water. And there, Peter lowered his nets.

Fish!

Simon felt the tug of the net. His helpers took a firmer grip and they pulled together.

More fish! So many fish that Simon called for help! Two boatloads of fish!

Does not the story remind us that ours too is the responsibility of launching out? moving out into the deep? doing what the Master commands?

Not excuses, but action—that's what we need in today's world! I'd like to suggest at least three ways each of us can launch out:

1. *We can give ourselves to fervent prayer.* Too easily we forget the power of this mighty weapon, or we grow disheartened and give up on the miracle. It ought not to be.

One pastor recalls a saint in a church he pastored. She was not flashy or talented in many ways, but she literally burned with a passion for souls. She prayed often and occasionally she prayed through the entire night for the church and the salvation of souls. In my opinion that church is strong and flourishing today largely because of this sister's prayers.

From seeking God and interceding for others, the missionary Adoniram Judson developed great calluses on his knees. These were discovered at his death. Dave Wilkerson started with prayer and God has led him into a multifaceted operation which ministers to thousands of troubled youth and drug addicts. John Wesley traveled thousands of miles on horseback with the gospel, literally changing the face of the world in terms of religious impact. But back home was a mother on her knees praying for her son and for the lost.

Yes, we can and we should give ourselves to prayer.

2. We can make ourselves and all our resources available for the Lord's service. What God expects from us first of all is willingness to serve. It is upon this battlefield of the human will or on the field of submission that victory is either won or lost. A rich young ruler, confronted with this dilemma, turned sadly away. We must not. We must submit and say yes to the Master. All we have and all we are capable of becoming let us give to the Lord.

Christ yet has ways of taking our gifts and turning them into miracles. Whether we drop a net in strange waters or turn over a few pieces of bread and some fish or bring a friend to hear His words—each such simple act is an act of faith and submission, and it can be basis for a miracle.

Does not life prove that so often, when we least expect it, God does the seemingly impossible. I remember so many times in my ministry, after praying and working with people for months, sometimes for years, and quite often when I was really not expecting it, that person came forward with a commitment. Marvelous is God's grace. We must make all our resources available.

3. We must live out our faith. It is not enough to say, "Yes, Lord, I'm sure there are fish somewhere in the lake." Jesus wants us to "launch out." He wants us to put faith into action.

I remember the story of a new convert who decided to test the effectiveness of prayer. Kneeling at the church's altar he prayed for God to give shoes to a little girl he had seen barefoot that morning. Some time later he drove by her home to see if she had her new shoes.

This routine went on for a number of days. Still no shoes. Finally, again at the altar the man said, "God, I'm giving You one more day. If You do not give that little girl some new shoes by tomorrow, I'm going down to the store and buy them for her myself."

Faith must be put into action.

Ira Stamphill tells of visiting a young minister who pastored a small congregation. He noticed especially the man's prayer life and his persistent labor. Within a few years the man had a church of more than a thousand members. Faith must be put to work.

God has something for each of us. If we can't pilot the ship, then we can prepare meals for the crew. If we cannot swim or fish, then we can mend the nets. We each have a task to perform in the Kingdom, and God will help us to do it well.

CONCLUSION

Let us summarize. God never makes foolish commands. We humans are prone to make excuses. Faith remains a possibility. Faith can bring the unexpected miracle if we pray, if we make ourselves and our resources available, and if we put our faith into action.

God is still blessing and caring for His church. A Pentecostal revival is sweeping our world, bringing to our attention such miracles as that of Dr. Paul Yonggi Cho's church in Seoul, Korea, with a half million members. There are other great churches; but more importantly God is working in all our communities, giving us opportunities such as we have never known before.

Let us launch out into the deep. We are on the verge of ever greater miracles, in Jesus' name.

HOW CLOSE TO BEING SAVED ARE MY LOVED ONES?

Bobby Rose

SCRIPTURE: Romans 10:8-11

INTRODUCTION

Every true Christian has concern for the salvation of loved ones. For some, it is hard even to imagine them being saved. So we raise the question: how close are your loved ones to salvation?

FIRST, IT DEPENDS ON THEIR SPIRITUAL INPUT.

We may expect the public school to teach our children right from wrong, but they offer a thirty-hour week of evolution, situation ethics, narcotics, smoking, sex education, godlessness, no prayer, and no Bible. The schools will not do it.

We may expect friends or society to instill in our loved ones a desire for God but they offer violence, free sex, immorality, murder, rape, adultery, divorce, cursing, abortions, and drug addiction. What hope is there with this world?

We may even think the church will train our loved ones in the ways of God, but the church cannot undo in four or five hours all those evils set forth by thirty hours of TV watching. Besides, no one can reasonably expect the church to fully train a child in the ways of God with only four or five hours per week.

Spiritual training must come from within the home. Parents must train up their children. Talk about Him who died for you.

No one has any more influence in your life than the person you marry. Most husbands will determine if their wife goes to heaven or hell. Most wives will take their husbands to heaven or to hell with them. You hold life and death in your hands.

Most people have more than one person who has great influence on their lives. Just the right word at the right time may make the difference. A life that has a different set of values, that is lived by a different set of rules, will catch the attention of unsaved family members and just could be that positive force which brings them to God.

SECOND, IT DEPENDS ON YOUR INTERCESSORY PRAYER LIFE.

Prayer changes things. Intercessory prayer is this: a believer who through grievous concern and love touches the heart of God until He sends the Holy Spirit to deal gently or forcefully with that lost loved one finally bringing him/her to Christ.

Prayers prayed by teary-eyed, love-filled, passion-consumed, desperate, willing-to-die saints will touch God's heart and move the Holy Spirit.

THIRD, IT DEPENDS ON THE ATMOSPHERE IN GOD'S HOUSE WHEN YOUR LOVED ONES ATTEND.

Far too many attend God's house out of habit or sense of duty. Long before we arrive at the door of God's house, we should begin praying for an outpouring of the Holy Ghost to meet every need represented at each service. We should ask God, "What kind of spiritual contribution can I make to the service?" And we should ask what He expects us to receive from Him.

CONCLUSION

Your loved ones are not far, just off shore. As the end draws near, let us do everything possible to win them to Christ.

JESUS IN THE STORM WITH US

Julius Roberts

SCRIPTURE: Matthew 14:22-36 and Psalm 29:1-11

INTRODUCTION:

Christian faith is secure only when we recognize and live daily with the assurance that God is *always* with us, even in the storms of life.

Most of us are acquainted with the story recorded in Matthew's gospel where Jesus walked upon the water and came to His disciples in the midst of a raging tempest. We have heard the facts of the story since childhood. Nevertheless, there are further truths to be explored.

Let us note the background, the setting for this story.

Our Lord was approaching the high point of His ministry. It was at this time that He performed many miracles, including the feeding of a multitude with but a few loaves of bread and two fish. He was becoming popular with the people and a source of concern to religious authorities. Persecution was abroad in the land. King Herod had just put John the Baptist to death.

Matthew notes the significance of this cruel death with a twofold statement. He tells us Herod heard of the fame of

Jesus and reacted with, "It is John the Baptist come to life again." He also tells us that, when Jesus heard the news of John's death, He departed into a desert place to pray, to meditate, and to be alone with His thoughts.

This was surely a moment of personal pain in our Lord's own heart. Jesus loved John the Baptist. They were first cousins, boyhood companions who, quite likely, had spent many hours together growing up.

It was at this precise moment and time that Jesus ordered His disciples to get in the boat and go over to the other side. Rather than go with them, Jesus stayed behind to dismiss the crowds and for the more personal reason of private prayer and communion with His heavenly Father.

The disciples set forth, under direct orders from the Master, aboard a ship headed for troubled waters.

Is it not so with us? Do we not daily step forth to meet the unknown, the unexpected? The greatest of joys? The most sudden and unexpected of storms?

WE MUST LEARN TO RECOGNIZE JESUS.

The disciples had lived with Jesus. They knew Him in a very personal and intimate manner. Yet from this incident we understand there was a moment when they did not recognize Him.

Does it happen with us? Are there those times, those unexpected circumstances of our lives in which we simply do not recognize the Master's presence?

After all, is it not easier to be conscious of God when in church? Perhaps easier to be aware of Him when on our knees in prayer, or when engaged in those obvious Christian duties such as witnessing or ministering to the sick?

But what of the night? What of the darkness? What of the lonely moments, the totally personal struggles, the times when our hearts yearn to reach out and touch someone else and there is no one there? What of the trying times? What of the storms? Are we then able to recognize Jesus?

The disciples did not! They were too wrapped up in the struggle of the moment. They saw the tossing waves. They felt the threat of death. They heard the wind, saw the lightning, felt the pelting rain. But they did not recognize the Lord.

So I emphasize: We must *learn* to recognize God.

Life has a way of teaching us. Life has a way of reminding us. Just when we think all is running smoothly, all is well, all is under control; then comes the startling realization that storm clouds are blowing over. Just as we think we have solved the last problem, or taken care of the last pressing need, that's when the mailman arrives, or that's when the telephone rings, or that's when we discover a child is sick. No matter how often we have been down the road, there are yet surprises. We still have more to learn.

Such is life.

The disciples were about to learn the greatest lesson they would ever receive, the truth of Jesus in the storm. They knew Jesus already as the supplier of their needs. They had witnessed Him pay taxes with money from a fish's mouth. They knew He could multiply loaves and fishes, that He spoke words of life, that He had power over the works of the devil. They knew Him as a great teacher. Still, never having met Jesus in a storm, they did not recognize Him. All too often we make the same mistake.

We believe Jesus for our salvation and for the forgiveness of our sins. We look to Him as the supplier of all our needs. We trust Him to bring us into glory one day. But when everything is falling apart, we find it difficult to see Jesus.

We can't seem to believe that He would allow a storm to teach us how to trust Him. We are never quite sure He is nearby when things really get rough. The ship is now tossing. It appears to be sinking, winds are blowing. Everything is going contrary and it seems all hope is lost. The Bible says:

> "And in the fourth watch of the night Jesus went unto them, walking on the sea. And when the disciples saw Him walking on the sea, they were troubled, saying, It is a spirit; and they cried out for fear. But straightway Jesus spake unto them, saying, Be of good cheer; it is I; be not afraid" (Matthew 14:25-27).

WE MUST LEARN TO COPE WITH OUR FEARS.

Fear!

It is a destructive force that plagues each of us at certain times. Of course, some fear is normal. It helps us survive certain dangers.

For example, the fear of walking out in front of a car, or the fear of falling off a tall building—these are normal fears. They function for a noteworthy purpose.

Let us look at a dictionary definition of *fear*: "an emotion excited by threatening evil or impending pain, accompanied by a desire to avoid or escape; apprehension; dread; uneasiness about a thing; horror; alarm; terror; dismay and fright." Most of us have known fear in these varying shades of meaning.

But fear is also a spiritual force. It can actually destroy us if we yield to it.

Fear is not of God. God is not the author of fear. God does not send fear upon His people. He made all things. He sustains all things. He holds the key to all things. He is in charge of all things.

God Himself knows no fear. What could there be for Him to fear? The Word of God proves that He has nothing to fear. Therefore, His children really have nothing to fear. Note these words: "God hath spoken once; twice have I heard this; that power belongeth unto God" (Psalm 62:11). Jesus tells us, "All power is given unto me in heaven and in earth" (Matthew 28:18). Thus, why should we—His children—be afraid?

What I am trying to get across is that Jesus has done all these things before us and yet we do not really see Him in the storms of life. Many in the church family have seen God move in their lives in such a way that no one but God could have done it, yet we have trouble following Jesus all the time. We seem to forget that the Scriptures tell us, "The steps of a good man are ordered by the Lord: and he delighteth in his way" (Psalm 37:23). The psalmist goes on to say, "Though he fall, he shall not be utterly cast down: for the Lord upholdeth him with his hand" (v. 24).

If the steps of a good man are ordered by the Lord, and if God upholds the good man with His hand, then He must be here with us all the time! He has never been far away. We have never been out of His sight. When all *seems* to be going wrong, He yet has control.

We are so often like the disciples, not one of whom recognized Jesus when He came walking on the water. It could be that we believe and expect Jesus to be at the Samaritan well, or in the Temple driving out the money changers. We expect Him one day to be at the right hand of the Father, to make us kings and priests. But never do we expect Him to be with us in the storm!

For the disciples, that storm was just an act of nature, an unexpected disaster, a tragic accident of fate, an unwanted and unnecessary trial, a lonely and fearful journey into despair. It was a night to be forgotten.

If we could only remember: "He maketh the storm a calm, so that the waves thereof are still" (Psalm 107:29); and "There shall be a tabernacle for a shadow in the daytime from the heat, and for a place of refuge, and for a covert from the storm and from rain" (Isaiah 4:6).

Paul tells us, "In Him we live, and move, and have our being" (Acts 17:28). Again he says, "God has not given us the spirit of fear; but of power, and of love, and of a sound mind" (2 Timothy 1:7).

With God living in us, fully, there is no room for fear. We must discover in Him and through His Holy Spirit the power to cope with fear in all its many expressions.

WE MUST LEARN TO TRUST GOD IN THE DARKEST HOUR.

The storm which came upon the disciples came suddenly. They were put upon quickly. And there was no thought on their part that Jesus was nearby, watching over them.

If we are to speculate as to their thoughts, or their fears, in their moment of sudden danger, we may well imagine their reaction as being similar to our own. One of the disciples may have thought, "This is the work of the devil. He wants to kill us because of all those good things we have been doing." Yet another may have thought, "Where did we go wrong? Which one of us has sin in his life? God must be angry with someone on this ship." Yet another may have reacted, "Why us? We're doing what Jesus told us to do. We're not out of His will. Why this sudden storm. Jesus told us to get on board this ship. Why is this happening?"

All of us come eventually to those darkest of hours, to those lowest of moments, and we tend to despair. But let it not be! We must trust Him in the darkest hour.

The Bible says that "in the fourth watch of the night," just before dawn, at the worst possible time, when all hope was fading, Jesus came. He came unexpectedly and He came with miraculous power and demonstration.

How difficult it must have been for Jesus to wait on the edge of that storm, loving them so much, feeling every pain they felt, wanting so much to keep them from getting hurt, yearning after them as a father for his children in trouble. Yet, Jesus knew they could never fully know Him or trust Him, until the full fury of the storm was upon them.

Only when they had reached the limit of their endurance would He reveal Himself. Jesus knew that the ship would never have gone down, but if it had, they would be saved. Now their fear would have drowned them more quickly than the waves beating on the ship.

Let us always remember this: Jesus can calm a sea of trouble in our lives at any time, simply by speaking the word. But all this comes through faith. We must have faith in the Lord. There is peace in time of trouble. Jesus had told them to go, so why could they not have trusted His words. Why not command the sea in Jesus' name to be calm? Could not the promises have been put into practice? After all, He tells us, "All things asked in prayer . . . ye shall have."

Yet these things cannot happen in our lives until we have learned to recognize Jesus is in the storm with us. These things cannot happen until we have received faith to ride out the storm, until we have learned to be of good cheer even when the ship appears to be sinking.

It is imperative that we recognize Jesus in the storm, the darkest hour.

WE MUST ALSO RESIST THE NEGATIVES, THE GHOSTS OF LIFE.

Not only was it true that the disciples failed to recognize Jesus, but they thought Him to be a spirit, a ghost, something imaginary and unreal. The thought of Jesus being so near, so much a part of what they were experiencing—this did not even enter their minds.

I fear here is where our problem really lies. We are not able to see Jesus in our troubles; instead, we see ghosts. We become fearful and imagine what is not real at all. But the psalmist reminds us, "The Lord sitteth upon the flood; yea, the Lord sitteth King for ever" (Psalm 29:10).

Normal anxiety or reasonable fear becomes compounded when we get carried away with wrong thinking. The disciples faced a new fear when they imagined ghosts, when they saw what was not, but failed to see what was. It seems that one of them might have remembered the Master's promise, "I will never leave you, nor forsake you." It seems that one might have said, "Jesus sent us ahead of Him and we are in His will and everything is all right." Or that someone would have shouted out, "Hey, that is Jesus. He's right here with us."

But no, they said, "It's a ghost."

There was a simple lesson to learn from this storm. It was not some mystical, deep, earth-shattering lesson. Jesus wanted the disciples to learn trust in Him . . . at all times. He wanted them to maintain their cheer, joy, and peace, even in the darkest hour. That is what He wants of us. He does not want us to see ghosts, or spirits, or imaginary things. He wants us to trust Him.

Is it not true that we have different types of ghosts, different types of imaginary enemies? What about the ghost of wasted time? the ghost of grudges? the ghost of compromise? the ghost of covetousness? of hypocrisy? of lying? There may be many other things that we have promised the Lord we would or would not do and we just have not been faithful to our promises. Ghosts of the past come floating before us when the storm blows in.

These thoughts are from the devil. They are negative. We need to bring our thoughts under control through the Holy Spirit. When we have broken promises, then we must repent and ask God's forgiveness. Jesus wants to be with us, even in the storm. We must confess, repent, and welcome Him to be there, thus acknowledging His presence.

Truth is, no matter the storm, God is not angry with us. The ghosts are not real. The storm has not come because of failure on our part. This is God at work, seeking to reveal Himself in His saving, keeping, preserving power. The storm has a purpose. It could be to bring us to complete rest and trust in Jesus Christ as a present help in time of trouble.

Jesus is always there.

CONCLUSION

So what are our lessons? (1) We must learn to recognize the Master under all circumstances. (2) We must learn to cope with our fears, to handle them, rather than have them paralyze us. (3) We must learn to trust in the darkest hour. And (4) we must resist the negatives, the ghosts of life.

God does not wish His children to be filled with worry and anxiety. Jesus is always with us . . . in power and in glory. Our storms of life may be sickness, disease, pain, or loss; but Jesus is in the midst of the storm. His hands are raised to help. His voice is near to command.

Let us not despair.

OVERCOME

Alex Thompson

SCRIPTURE: *1 John 5:4*

INTRODUCTION

It is exciting to realize we are privileged to live at the end of this dispensation, when the conflict between Satan and his demons and Christ and His saints is fast moving toward a climax. The Word of God describes this period in the history of mankind as being in two different spheres, both of them critical.

THE WORLD TODAY

We read the description of world conditions in general from Paul's second letter to Timothy:

> This know also, that in the last days perilous times shall come. For men shall be lovers of their own selves, covetous, boasters, proud, blasphemers, disobedient to parents, unthankful, unholy, Without natural affection, trucebreakers, false accusers, incontinent, fierce, despisers of those that are good, Traitors, heady, highminded, lovers of pleasures more than lovers of God; Having a form of godliness, but

denying the power thereof: from such turn away.
For of this sort are they which creep into houses,
and lead captive silly women laden with sins, led
away with divers lusts, Ever learning, and never
able to come to the knowledge of the truth. Now
as Jannes and Jambres withstood Moses, so do these
also resist the truth: men of corrupt minds, reprobate
concerning the faith (2 Timothy 3:1-8).

This passage in the letter of the Apostle Paul to Timothy,
with its indisputable, detailed description of the conditions
of society toward the close of this twentieth century, bears
the unmistakable stamp of divine revelation. Surely the extent
and the accuracy of these prophecies must convey a positive
and a challenging message to the Christian church! Let us
hear it loud and clear. Time is running out.

In spite of and in contrast to these terrible conditions in
the world, there are times and places where revivals occur
and the power of God's Holy Spirit, working through the lives
of converts, brings a change in the conditions of society.

As long as this dispensation lasts and so long as God's
people give themselves to prayer, the possibility of such revivals
must be ever with us. We have witnessed such revivals in
our time in Korea, in South America, in Africa, and elsewhere.
May we never lose sight of the overriding desire of the Father:
"For God so loved the world that he gave his only begotten
Son, that whosoever believeth in him should not perish, but
have everlasting life" (John 3:16).

WHERE THE CHURCH STANDS TODAY

While that is how the world looks, what about the church?

When we read the messages to the seven churches of Asia,
we understand they were directed not only to those specific
congregations mentioned but also to us as in terms of prophetic significance. We turn to the last of those seven letters,
the message to the church at Laodicea, and discover a description that can be found in these last days within the Christian
church:

And unto the angel of the church of the Laodiceans
write; These things saith the Amen, the faithful and
true witness, the beginning of the creation of God;

> I know thy works, that thou art neither cold nor hot: I would thou wert cold or hot. So then because thou art lukewarm, and neither cold nor hot, I will spue thee out of my mouth. Because thou sayest, I am rich, and increased with goods, and have need of nothing; and knowest not that thou art wretched, and miserable, and poor, and blind, and naked: I counsel thee to buy of me gold tried in the fire, that thou mayest be rich; and white raiment, that thou mayest be clothed, and that the shame of thy nakedness do not appear; and anoint thine eyes with eyesalve, that thou mayest see. As many as I love, I rebuke and chasten: be zealous therefore, and repent (Revelation 3:14-19).

The seriousness of this message is seen in John's description of "one like unto the Son of man, clothed with a garment down to the foot, and girt about the paps with a golden girdle. His head and his hairs were white like wool, as white as snow; and his eyes were as a flame of fire; And his feet like unto fine brass, as if they burned in a furnace; and his voice as the sound of many waters. And he had in his right hand seven stars: and out of his mouth went a sharp twoedged sword: and his countenance was as the sun shineth in his strength" (Revelation 1:13-16).

DANGERS FACING THE CHURCH

Such language conveys strong warnings against complacency.

First of all there is the dangerous condition of lukewarmness which corresponds to inactivity and neutrality in the Christian life.

The church is in danger of trying to accommodate everyone and in the process losing its effectiveness and thereby becoming lukewarm. There is only one way by which a person can become accepted into the body of Christ and that is by the experience of the new birth.

Furthermore, there is the danger of the church diluting its principles so that they become obscure and the position neither hot nor cold.

What a sad accusation against the church—the body of Him who left heaven's glory to take the form of a servant in order to give us eternal life—that it should come to where its earthly possessions are considered its wealth. How awful the condemnation in this passage—"wretched, miserable, poor, blind and naked." This sounds almost as bad as the world itself.

After offering cures for these maladies, the Lord in His message to the church brings the matter back down to the individual with the words, "If any man hear my voice. . . ." The whole exercise is summed up in, "To him that overcometh."

ON BEING AN OVERCOMER

When we talk of overcoming, we indicate the process of facing temptation without succumbing. This is where the light shines through all the gloomy descriptions of our time: "For we have not an high priest which cannot be touched with the feelings of our infirmities; but was in all points tempted like as we are, yet without sin" (Hebrews 4:15).

He who tells us the answer is overcoming is the same One who has overcome and taken that victory into his own high-priestly ministry. Wherefore, as we read, "Let us therefore come boldly unto the throne of grace, that we may obtain mercy, and find grace to help in time of need" (v. 16).

Seeing He was tempted in all points as we, it behooves us to give attention to our Lord's temptations, especially those specifically recorded in the Bible (Matthew 4:1-11). They must surely incorporate the fundamental means by which the devil seeks to cause Christians to fall. By identifying these areas of temptation, we are thus in a better position to recognize the subtle efforts of the enemy.

PRINCIPLES BY WHICH WE OVERCOME

The first of our Lord's temptations was to turn stones into bread in order to satisfy his legitimate hunger. Having just completed a period of fasting and prayer, one might think this suggestion a fair proposition.

This experience of Jesus took place just as James explains temptation (James 1:14). Man is always tempted in terms of his desire; the enemy offers enticement but it is the yielding thereto that becomes sin. The Son of God and the Son of Man overcame the temptation to use His rightful power to perform miracles for His own satisfaction.

This experience classifies for us a sphere of temptation with which the devil is constantly busy, enticing us to misuse what we have in Christ Jesus, whether it be power, gifts, or liberty in the Holy Spirit. Paul particularly warns us about misusing our liberty, "But take heed lest by any means this liberty of your's become a stumblingblock to them that are weak" (1 Corinthians 8:9). Peter also wrote, "As free and not using your liberty for a cloke of maliciousness, but as servants of God" (1 Peter 2:16).

As the Son of God, Jesus Christ could have dealt with the devil purely on the level of His divinity but He chose to accept the challenge as Son of Man. Therein He won for us a victory and at the same time revealed to us the key for victory in this sphere of temptation.

God's Word is the answer; and we Pentecostals appreciate strong emphasis on the ministry of the Holy Spirit in bringing to our remembrance the relevant verses of Scripture.

Maybe we need to ask whether the quotation, "Because thou sayest, I am rich, and increased with goods, and have need of nothing," has something to do with the misuse of power the gospel has brought into our lives. With the power of God, there comes great responsibility. He that overcometh the temptation to misuse it for personal gain and benefit will sit with Christ in His throne.

The second of our Lord's temptations was to cast Himself down from the pinnacle of the Temple, implying a demonstration to the world that He was really the Son of God. Jesus Christ did not and does not need to prove He is the Son of God. No matter what anyone thinks, says, or does, that is who He is. Jesus' reply to the devil was to state the fact, "It is written, thou shalt not tempt the Lord thy God."

In other words, it was God in Christ Jesus whom the devil was tempting and there was no need of this physical demonstration. Incidentally, tradition claims this was something told as an anticipated manifestation of the Messiah.

John reminds us, "Behold, what manner of love the Father hath bestowed upon us that we should be called the sons of

God" (1 John 3:1), and in the next verse, "Beloved, now are we the sons of God."

Here lies another fundamental sphere of temptation: to doubt, or to question the fact that we are children of God by the new birth.

To succumb to this temptation and to fall into this state of doubt robs us of strength and spiritual vitality, for it is this blessed assurance of sonship that creates in us the peace, joy, and love which characterizes Christian living.

Writing to the church at Rome, Paul states, "Now the God of hope fill you with all joy and peace in believing, that ye may abound in hope, through the power of the Holy Ghost" (Romans 15:13). Then again to the Galatians, he writes, "The fruit of the Spirit is love, joy, peace . . . " (Galatians 5:22).

I know of a lady, who at one time was plagued by the devil in this area of temptation, and who says that in prayer the Lord graciously gave her a vision of a tombstone in the clouds with her name on it. How she rejoiced in the wonderful confirmation of the scripture, "For ye are dead, and your life is hid with Christ in God" (Colossians 3:3).

The only hope for our world in its awful state of degradation is to meet the Lord Jesus and to recognize Him as the Savior. And the only way people are going to meet Him is through an introduction by someone who knows Him personally.

At the time of His ascension, Jesus exhorted His disciples to tarry until they were endued with power from on high. They would then be witnesses unto Him.

If we today are to be effective witnesses for the Lord, we dare not doubt the reality of our sonship nor the indwelling, anointing presence of the Holy Spirit.

The third fundamental area of danger in relation to the battle plans of the enemy is revealed in the Lord's temptation of Satan's offer of the kingdoms of the world, something which was, though in a different sense, the highest goal of Jesus Christ. Jesus would not consider such an offer. It was a shortcut, something purely superficial, as an alternative to God's way.

Here, the devil was seeking to tamper with God's great plan of salvation through the substitutionary sacrifice of Jesus, a plan which meant that henceforth there should be no other name than Jesus given among men whereby we must be saved (Acts 4:10-12).

When we consider the waves of spurious theology rolling through the church, then we know this area of temptation is real indeed. It calls for positive withstanding of the enemy. In face of the gigantic problems in our world—starvation, persecution, revolution, illiteracy—there comes the temptation to find a shortcut; but let us realize there is no alternative to the gospel of Christ.

The gospel alone will meet the need of the whole man—body, soul and spirit. The gospel places the emphasis where it belongs, on right relationship with God. To bring that about requires a mediator, and there is only One who has lived without sin, died without blame, and risen again to fulfill that office.

Alternative gospels leave men wretched, miserable, poor, blind, and naked (Revelation 3:17). The way out is through a personal encounter with Jesus as He knocks and seeks admission to our hearts.

CONCLUSION

The call to overcome is very real and vital in these last days. John sums it up for us: "For whatsoever is born of God overcometh the world: and this is the victory that overcometh the world, even our faith. Who is he that overcometh the world, but he that believeth that Jesus is the Son of God?" (1 John 5:4).

Through all the chaos, hostility, and violence of our world, the light we see bursts into glorious radiance in the words of Jesus: "These things I have spoken unto you, that in me ye might have peace. In the world ye shall have tribulation: but be of good cheer; I have overcome the world" (John 16:33).

SANCTIFICATION

Floyd J. Timmerman

SCRIPTURE: 1 Thessalonians 4:3

INTRODUCTION

The doctrine of sanctification is one of the most misunderstood teachings recorded in the New Testament. This is due, in large part, to the fact that it deals with consecration and holiness.

If regeneration has to do with our nature, justification with our standing, and adoption with our position, then sanctification has to do with our character and conduct. In justification we are declared righteous in order that through sanctification we may become righteous. Justification is what God does for us; sanctification, what God does in us. Justification puts us into a right relationship with God; sanctification exhibits the fruit of that relationship—that is, a life separated from a sinful world and dedicated unto God.

Sanctification is a biblical doctrine. The word is found in its various forms at least four hundred times in the Old Testament, to say nothing of the many references to it in the New Testament.

THE MEANING OF SANCTIFICATION

The words "sanctify," "saint," "hallow," and "holy" all come from the same Greek root *hagizo* or *hagiazo* (ha-geed-zo). In the New Testament sense, the word means "to place in a relation to God answering to His holiness."

In the Old Testament, the root word is *kadash* (ka-dash) which means "to cut or separate." In either case, sanctification has to do with separation, and this separation is subsequent to, or because of, something else. The sanctified person or thing has been chosen first and then separated. Therefore, sanctification, or being set apart, is subsequent to regeneration.

Two thoughts are prominent in a definition of *sanctification*: separation from evil, and dedication unto God. *Separation From Evil.*

It is evident from scriptures that sanctification necessitates a turning away from all that is sinful and defiling to both soul and body. Note:

> Sanctify now yourselves, and sanctify the house of the Lord God . . . and carry forth the filthiness out of the holy place. . . . And the priests went into the inner part of the house of the Lord, to cleanse it and brought out all the uncleanness. . . . Then they went in to Hezekiah the king, and said, We have cleansed all the house of the Lord (2 Chronicles 29:5, 16-18).

> For this is the will of God, even your sanctification, that ye should abstain from fornication (1 Thessalonians 4:3).

> Teaching us that, denying ungodliness and worldly lusts, we should live soberly, righteously, and godly, in this present world (Titus 2:12).

> But as he who hath called you is holy, so be ye holy in all manner of conversation (1 Peter 1:15).

> Having therefore these promises, dearly beloved, let us cleanse ourselves from all filthiness of the flesh and spirit, perfecting holiness in the fear of God (2 Corinthians 7:1).

The life of separation, wrought by the experience of sanctification, challenges the believer to forsake the patterns of the world and to follow the pattern of holiness with Jesus Christ as the model.

Paul had a word for the Galatians and us when he wrote:

> Now the works of the flesh are manifest, which are these; Adultery, fornication, uncleanness, lasciviousness, Idolatry, witchcraft, hatred, variance, emulations, wrath, strife, seditions, heresies, Envyings, murders, drunkenness, revellings, and such like: of the which I tell you before, as I have also told you in time past, that they which do such things shall not inherit the kingdom of God (Galatians 5:19-21).

He spoke of his past life and old habits:

> Among whom also we all had our conversation in times past in the lusts of our flesh, fulfilling the desires of the flesh and of the mind; and were by nature the children of wrath, even as others. But God, who is rich in mercy, for his great love wherewith he loved us, Even when we were dead in sins, hath quickened us together with Christ, (by grace ye are saved;) (Ephesians 2:3-5).

This separation expresses itself in outward cleansing and inward holiness. Sanctification, as a condition of the heart, affects every facet of the Christian's life. It is the heart of the Christian faith, the theme of the Holy Scriptures, and the purpose of God for His people.

It is possible to profess sanctification by subscribing to legalistic and ceremonial codes without possessing sanctification of the heart. True sanctification will affect the entire nature of man, while Pharisaism merely affects the overt expressions of that nature. One theologian stated this:

"Pharisaism and holiness are not the same. Holiness is purity of the heart and nature. Pharisaism is an outward system of legalism. Holiness flows out of a pure heart of love that is full of forgiveness. Pharisaism flows out of a heart of law that is ready to measure, criticize, condemn, judge, and punish." *Dedication Unto God*

Note this passage of scripture:

> And when a man shall sanctify his house to be holy unto the Lord, then the priest shall estimate it, whether it be good or bad: as the priest shall estimate it, so shall it stand. And if he that sanctified it will redeem his house, then he shall add the fifth part of the money of thy estimation unto it, and it shall be his. And if a man shall sanctify unto the Lord some part of a field of his possession, then thy estimation shall be according to the seed thereof: an homer of barley seed shall be valued as fifty shekels of silver (Leviticus 27:14-16).

From this it is evident that whatever is set apart from a profane to a sacred use, whatever is devoted exclusively to the service of God, is sanctified. So it follows that a man may "sanctify his house to be holy unto the Lord," or he may "sanctify unto the Lord some part of a field of his possession" (vv. 14, 16).

So also the firstborn of all the children were sanctified unto the Lord (Numbers 8:17). Even the Son of God himself, insofar as He was set apart by the Father and sent into the world to do God's will, was sanctified (John 10:36). Whenever a thing or person is separated from the common relations of life in order to be devoted to the sacred, such is said to be sanctified.

THE TIME OF SANCTIFICATION

From the Church of God "Declaration of Faith," the article on sanctification states that we believe in sanctification subsequent to the New Birth (regeneration).

A number of questions relating to time present themselves when considering the doctrine of sanctification.

1. *Why are regeneration and sanctification not comprehended and completed in a single act? That is, why two distinct works?*

It is impossible to say what God may or may not do. His Word, however, clearly reveals that He does not justify and entirely sanctify by a single work of grace. Doubtless the sinner does not realize his need of sanctification. His guilt

51

and condemnation at first occupy his attention and only later does he come to see his need for further cleansing.

Justification and sanctification deal with different phases of sin: the former with sins committed, or sin as an act; the latter with sin inherited, or sin as a principle of nature. It appears to be impossible to fully discover the latter condition without having experienced the former.

Then, too, these works of the Spirit are in one sense directly opposite—the one being an impartation of life, the other a crucifixion or death.

Finally, the experience of sanctification is obtained by faith which may be exercised only after meeting certain conditions, including entire consecration. Such conditions cannot be met by one who is in an unregenerate state.

2. What length of time must elapse between regeneration and sanctification?

This depends wholly upon the experience of the individual. This progressive work may be cut short and finished at any moment. Sanctification occurs when the intelligence clearly comprehends the defects of the present state, and when faith comprehends the power and willingness of God to sanctify us wholly, and to do it now.

3. Where does growth fit into the picture?

Luke tells us that even Jesus, who knew no sin, grew in a manner similar to the growth of other men (Luke 2:52).

Peter tells us, "Grow in grace, and in the knowledge of our Lord and Saviour Jesus Christ" (2 Peter 3:18).

The Christian must study, pray, witness, and consistently use what he has to improve his effectiveness as a Christian. This growth has nothing to do with sin; sanctification does. As the weeds are rooted out around a rosebush that it might flourish and grow, sin is rooted out of a man's life that love might abound and that he might bring forth "fruit unto holiness" (Romans 6:22).

Fruit is a result of something that is already there. A person cannot grow in grace, if he does not have any grace to grow in. One grows *in* grace, not *into* grace; also, one grows *in* sanctification, brings forth fruit, but does not grow *into* sanctification.

52

The whole problem reverts to a difference between *purity* and *maturity*. *Purity* is the cleansing from sin, while *maturity* implies an increase of knowledge, and alludes to such things in a similar category which are continuous and progressive. If one accepts the correct definition of sanctification, there is no way of making entire sanctification a thing of growth.

In stating a position thus far, we have denied the progressiveness of entire sanctification. In so doing we refer primarily to God's work, because the experience itself is totally God's work. The progressive state of sanctification is, for the most part, the work of man. And, according to the Scriptures, salvation is by faith and not by works, thus precluding any acceptance of credit on man's part for obtaining any blessing —"but for the grace of God!"

In what ways, then, is it sound doctrine to consider sanctification as being progressive?

First, at the time of conversion (regeneration) a process of initial sanctification takes place. That is, during the regenerate work of God, guilt and pollution are dissolved. God imparts, through His grace, a seed of life, which designates a beginning of the process of becoming sanctified.

Second, we must consider man's gradual preparation for the instantaneous act by God. That is, an individual becomes consecrated and, through his own volition, he step-by-step separates himself from worldliness and unchristian practices.

Third, when sanctification is bestowed as a second definite work by God, it requires a continuous fulfillment of righteous living in order to keep it. Consequently, the probationary elements of salvation necessitate that man constantly progress in his living.

To recap on the important stress on the time of sanctification, let us end on this thought: Regeneration considered in itself is a perfect work. It is the bestowal of divine life and, as an operation of the Spirit, is complete in itself. But regeneration is only a part of the grace embraced in the New Covenant. Only in this sense may it be said to be incomplete. Regeneration is also the beginning of sanctification, but only in the sense that the life bestowed in the New Birth is a holy life.

We are not to infer from this that the mere expanding of this new life by growth will bring the soul to entire sanctification. Sanctification is an act of cleansing, and unless inbred sin be removed, there can be no fullness of life, no perfection of love. In a strict sense, regeneration is not purification. Initial sanctification accompanies regeneration, but the latter is something more than the finishing touches of the former.

THE MEANS OF SANCTIFICATION

We can only properly appreciate the nature of sanctification by taking into account the means and agencies which God employs to stamp His image upon the hearts of men.

Like other aspects of the believer's salvation, sanctification is accomplished in a twofold way. There is a role which only God can play and there is an assigned responsibility for man.

Sanctification has its origin in the work of the Father, "And the very God of peace sanctify you wholly; and I pray God your whole spirit and soul and body be preserved blameless unto the coming of our Lord Jesus Christ" (1 Thessalonians 5:23). The original cause is the love of God: "Herein is love, not that we loved God, but that he loved us, and sent his Son to be the propitiation for our sins" (1 John 4:10).

God's love is expressed perfectly in the work of His Son Jesus Christ: "Christ . . . loved the church, and gave himself for it; That he might sanctify and cleanse it with the washing of water by the word" (Ephesians 5:25, 26).

The meritorious or procuring agency for sanctification is the blood of Jesus Christ: "If we walk in the light, as he is in the light, we have fellowship one with another, and the blood of Jesus Christ his Son cleanseth us from all sin" (1 John 1:7).

The active agent and efficient cause of sanctification is the work of the Holy Ghost: "But we are bound to give thanks always to God for you, brethren beloved of the Lord, because God hath from the beginning chosen you to salvation through sanctification of the Spirit and belief of the truth" (2 Thessalonians 2:13).

We are saved by the washing of regeneration and the renewing of the Holy Ghost (Titus 3:5); we are said to be elected through sanctification of the Spirit (1 Peter 1:2); and, we are chosen to salvation through sanctification of the Spirit and belief of the truth (2 Thessalonians 2:13).

It is the triune God—Father, Son, and Holy Spirit—who does the work. God the Father planned it; God the Son provided it; God the Holy Spirit performs it.

The specific instrument through which God works is truth—the Word of God. John wrote, "Sanctify them through thy truth; thy word is truth" (John 17:17).

The Holy Spirit acts through the instrumentality of the Word. Thus Peter writes, "Ye have purified your souls in obeying the truth" (1 Peter 1:22); and St. John declares that "whoso keepeth his word, in him verily is the love of God perfected: hereby know we that we are in him" (1 John 2:5).

On the human side the conditional cause of sanctification is first by faith which centers in Christ's redemptive work: "To open their eyes, and to turn them from darkness to light, and from the power of Satan unto God, that they may receive forgiveness of sins, and inheritance among them which are sanctified by faith that is in me" (Acts 26:18).

When, therefore, we speak of sanctification as being wrought by the Father, or by the Son, or by the Holy Spirit—whether we speak of it as by the blood, or through the truth, or by faith—we refer merely to the different causes which enter into this glorious experience.

True faith is accompanied by a complete dedication of life: "I beseech you therefore, brethren, by the mercies of God, that ye present your bodies a living sacrifice, holy, acceptable unto God, which is your reasonable service. And be not conformed to this world: but be ye transformed by the renewing of your mind, that ye may prove what is that good, and acceptable, and perfect, will of God" (Romans 12:1, 2).

And with dedication there must be a submission to divine discipline: "For they verily for a few days chastened us after their own pleasure; but he for our profit, that we might be partakers of his holiness. Now no chastening for the present seemeth to be joyous, but grievous: nevertheless afterward it yieldeth the peaceable fruit of righteousness unto them which are exercised thereby" (Hebrews 12:10, 11).

CONCLUSION

Sanctification is brought about in the life of the believer by his separating himself deliberately from all that is unclean and unholy, and by presenting, continually and constantly, the members of his body as holy instruments unto God for the accomplishment of His holy purposes. Thus by these single acts of surrender unto holiness, sanctification soon becomes the habit of the dedicated life.

The experience of sanctification is not attained through mystical feats, nor through strict legalism, nor mental acumen. A proper concept of holiness terminates in the obvious— whatever belongs to a pure and righteous God must correspond with His nature, and be responsive to the uses of a pure and spiritual service.

It matters little whether or not Christianity makes men rich; but it does matter that it make them truer, purer, and more noble. A character of this nature can only come about through a definite, instantaneous work of grace known to us as sanctification.

What physical health is to the body, holiness is to the soul. A sanctified life is a natural process unless retarded by tradition, prejudice, or pride. In the final analysis, man will get no higher than his concept of God.

A SURE HERITAGE

Guy P. Duffield

SCRIPTURE: *1 Peter 1:1-5*

INTRODUCTION

On the eighteenth of July, A.D. 64, during the reign of that tyrannical emperor, Nero, the great fire of Rome took place in which three quarters of the city was consumed. It has been usually thought that Nero caused the fire and that while he watched from a balcony, he played on his violin. Whether he started it or not, the blame was put on the Christians and great persecutions arose against them.

The two Epistles of Peter were written under the shadow of these persecutions, which spread throughout the empire. Jesus had said to Peter:

"Simon, Simon, behold, Satan hath desired to have you, that he may sift you as wheat: But I have prayed for thee that thy faith fail not: and when thou art converted, strengthen thy brethren" (Luke 22:31, 32).

This precious Epistle, from which our text is taken, may be considered a marvelous fulfillment of that word spoken to Peter by our Lord. "When thou art converted [or turned back], strengthen thy brethren." It is addressed to "the strangers scattered." These were Christian Jews and Gentiles who were scattered out of the land of Palestine, a scattering often referred to as the "Diaspora."

In a very special sense, every Christian in every age is a stranger, a foreigner, and a pilgrim.

"These all died in faith, not having received the promises, but having seen them afar off, and were persuaded of them, and embraced them, confessed that they were strangers and pilgrims on the earth. . . . And truly, if they had been mindful of that country from whence they came out, they might have had opportunity to have returned. But now they desire a better country, that is, an heavenly; wherefore God is not ashamed to be called their God: for he hath prepared for them a city" (Hebrews 11:13-16).

As Christians, this world is not our home. We should not be at all surprised if we feel like strangers in a world of sin. In fact, there is something drastically wrong with a Christian who does not feel like a stranger among those who do not know the Lord.

Though it is surely true that the Christian does not feel at home here below, and is often misunderstood by those who have not experienced the miracle of salvation, Peter shows us here that we are (1) chosen of God, (2) children of God, (3) heirs of God, and (4) kept by the power of God.

Let us now examine each of these four marvelous positions and relationships.

CHOSEN OF GOD (1 Peter 1:2)

"Elect according to the foreknowledge of God the Father." The world may reject the children of God, considering us strange and deceived, but it is blessed to know that we are chosen of God. This doctrine of predestination has probably caused more disagreement among conservative theologians than any other facet of spiritual truth. It is doubtful if any of us fully understand it in its completeness; principally because it rests entirely in the hands of Almighty God, and His ways are continually far above our ways.

Election is "according to the foreknowledge of God the Father." Paul makes it quite clear that we were chosen *in Christ* "before the foundation of the world." In His great foreknowledge, God looked ahead and saw us in Christ Jesus. He did not choose us outside of Christ, but in Him. How did we get there? Through faith in Christ.

Thus, we are "elect according to the foreknowledge of God the Father, through sanctification"—or separation—"of the Spirit, unto obedience"—the obedience of faith—"and sprinkling of the blood of Jesus Christ." Each member of the Godhead—Father, Son, and Holy Spirit—had a part in our salvation.

CHILDREN OF GOD (verse 3)

"Blessed be the God and Father of our Lord Jesus Christ, which according to his abundant mercy hath begotten us again unto a lively hope."

He "hath begotten us again." We are "born again." We are in the family of God. We are not merely the recipients of His pity. We have been brought into the loving, privileged relationship of His fatherly love. Such a miracle could only happen because it was "according to his abundant mercy."

What a glorious hope we have through this marvelous relationship! Our first birth was disappointing. We were "dead in trespasses and sins . . . by nature the children of wrath" (Ephesians 2:1, 3), but now we are new creatures in Christ Jesus. Peter goes on to say that we have been begotten again "unto a lively [living] hope by the resurrection of Jesus from the dead."

The two disciples who were on their way to Emmaus on that memorable first day of the week after Jesus' crucifixion were met by the Lord, though "their eyes were holden that they should not know him." They answered Jesus' question, "What manner of communications are these that ye have one to another . . . and are sad?" with the words, "Art thou only a stranger in Jerusalem, and hast not known the things which are come to pass there in these days?" Jesus said, "What things?" They replied, "Concerning Jesus of Nazareth . . . our rulers delivered him to be condemned to death. . . . But we trusted that it had been he which should have redeemed Israel" (Luke 24:16-21).

Their hope was a dead hope. But after He had been revealed to them as He broke bread in their home—and they knew that He had risen from the dead—theirs became a living hope. Thank God, those who know Him today are alive in Christ Jesus and have a living hope—they themselves are alive in Christ Jesus!

HEIRS OF GOD (Verse 4)

"To an inheritance incorruptible, and undefiled, and that fadeth not away, reserved in heaven for you."

The passage in Romans 8:16, 17, joins these two thoughts most gloriously: "The Spirit himself beareth witness with our spirit, that we are the children of God: And if children, then heirs; heirs of God, and joint-heirs with Christ." It must be a remarkable experience for one unexpectedly to receive notice that he has been named in someone's will, and has suddenly become the heir to a vast fortune of this world's goods! This is nothing compared to the inexplicable joy that comes to one of God's children when he realizes that he is an heir of God's eternal riches—yea, even a "joint-heir with Christ."

If one of my brothers and I were named as joint heirs in a will, it would mean that neither of us could receive one penny more than the other. The Bible says that we are joint heirs with Christ. Could that possibly mean we will share on an equal basis with our Lord Jesus Christ in the heavenly inheritance?

The fact that we are named as heirs of God proves once and for all that we are in the family of God—that He has really accepted us in the Beloved One (Ephesians 1:6). Paul says, "If children, then heirs."

Peter now proceeds to describe, in a fourfold way, this blessed inheritance which is ours.

It is an everlasting inheritance. It will never end. So many of life's joys last for such a short season. You have all experienced the delights of a two-week vacation. Then, as the second week began, you realized that your pleasant vacation was already half over, and you could hardly enjoy the last few days because of the realization that it was all to end so soon. We will never have those moments of regret as heirs of God, for our enjoyment of God's great provisions will never end.

Nothing impure will ever enter therein. Part of our eternal inheritance will be the privilege of dwelling in that celestial city which John saw coming down from God out of heaven, and he tells us, "There shall in no wise enter into it any thing that defileth, neither whatsoever worketh abomination, or maketh a lie" (Revelation 21:27). So many of earth's beauties and pleasures are marred by the presence of sin. Moses turned his back on all that Egypt held for him, as the son of Pharaoh's daughter, because he esteemed them as "the pleasures of sin" (Hebrews 11:25).

A minister and his wife who have traveled rather extensively in evangelistic and conference work often find themselves visiting in a new city. If they have an hour or so to spare, they enjoy driving through the area of the city where the most beautiful homes are built. They revel in the grandeur of the architecture, the beauty of the wide, spreading lawns, the lovely flowers and trees. It is a delightful way to enjoy the beauty at someone else's expense. On many of these excursions the loveliness of the scene has been spoiled as they have realized that within those gorgeous mansions, among some of the most affluent circumstances, live men and women whose lives are blighted with sin and unhappiness.

Thank God, ours will be an undefiled inheritance.

Ours is an inheritance that does not fade away. The most beautiful of earthly scenes soon begins to fade when we view them again and again. A visitor distinctly remembers the first time, in his adult life, he saw the glory of the cascading waters of Niagara Falls. As he stood there on the old, high-level bridge and watched the sheer grandeur of the scene of so much water falling from such a height and over such a wide expanse, as he watched the clouds of mist rising and the little ship, *The Maid of the Mist,* making her perilous way up to the very foot of the falls, he thought to himself, *I could stay here forever and watch this thrilling sight.*

He spent a long while trying to take it all in, but after being there for several days, he found he could pass the same scene with only a passing glance. Somehow, familiarity had caused its charm to diminish.

I am sure this will never happen in relation to my spiritual inheritance in Christ. It is an unfading inheritance and will never cease to bless and thrill with an ever-increasing experience of heavenly delight.

Ah, but someone is thinking, *Will I ever reach that blessed time? Others will, but maybe I will never make it.* Listen to Peter's last word of description which he holds out to every

61

redeemed child of God. This inheritance is not only incorruptible, undefiled and unfading, but it is also reserved in heaven for you.

Reserved in heaven for you. No probate court will ever be able to take it away from you. No inheritance tax will ever deplete this great legacy. It is reserved for you. I believe your name is already recorded in the Lamb's Book of Life as the eternal heir of that bequest.

A minister tells of growing up in Toronto (Ontario), Canada, in the early twenties and before that, he was captivated with the accomplishments of the Edmonton Grads and their fabulous coach, Percy Page. The Edmonton Grads was a girls' basketball team from a teacher-training college in Edmonton, Alberta. Percy Page had established a dynasty of championship basketball teams, much like John Wooden did years later at UCLA. This team of girls, constantly changing through graduations, were women's world champions for some 16 years or more. They traveled throughout the world and continued their dominance. They even played one complete game when the opposing team did not score a point.

What a delight it was when he discovered one Saturday, as he arrived in Edmonton to hold some evangelistic meetings, that the Edmonton Grads were to play a team from Tulsa, Oklahoma, for the women's world championship that very night, in the downtown arena! He asked a friend of his if he would like to go see the Grads play. He agreed, and with unmingled delight they made their way down to the arena and purchased general admission tickets for the sum of 50 cents each. (Money was scarce in those days.) The building seated some eight thousand and there was a large crowd present when they arrived. They made their way around to the seats in the end of the arena, where they were supposed to sit—a long way, it seemed, from the basketball court.

As they went around to the area they noticed a lot of empty seats with a much better view. So, because they were empty, they occupied two of them. They had not sat there very long before he felt a tap on his shoulder, and an usher informed them they were sitting in someone else's place. They had reserved tickets. Slightly embarrassed, they made their way to some other empty seats nearby.

Only a short time later, he felt another tap on his shoulder, and again an usher called their attention to the fact that some other people had reserved tickets for the places they were occupying. Really embarrassed this time, they decided they had better go around to the area indicated by their tickets.

Oh, my friends, I am glad that my place in heaven has been reserved for me—purchased by the precious blood of the Lord Jesus Christ, and no big angel is ever going to tap me on the shoulder and tell me that I do not belong there. My place is "reserved in heaven" for me.

Someone says, "But suppose I cannot hold out to the end against Satan and his wiles?" Hear Peter's last encouraging statement.

KEPT BY THE POWER OF GOD (verse 5)

"Who are kept by the power of God through faith unto salvation ready to be revealed in the last time." The inheritance is being kept for us; and we are being kept for the inheritance.

For what are we being kept? "Unto salvation."

Here it is being looked at in its glorious and eternal nature. Salvation includes a double idea. We are made safe, but also we are made sound. We are rescued from the deadly peril, but we are also cured of the deadly disease of sin. It is not enough to rescue a drowning person from the devastating flood and then leave him shivering in the cold. Our redemption provides everything that is needed for a complete salvation —salvation "ready to be revealed" in all its abundant fullness.

By what are we being kept? "Kept by the power of God."

Peter had earlier made the mistake of thinking that he could keep himself when Jesus warned him that before the cock would crow twice he would deny Him thrice. But now he had learned that he could only be kept by the power of God.

Literally, what Peter said was this: "guarded IN the power of God"—surrounded by the power of God. "As the mountains are round about Jerusalem, so the Lord is round about his people" (Psalm 125:2). "The name of the Lord is a strong tower: the righteous runneth into it, and is safe" (Proverbs 18:10). "The angel of the Lord encampeth round about them that fear him, and delivereth them" (Psalm 34:7). "Hid with

Christ in God" (Colossians 3:3). Our only means of security is to keep ourselves in the keeping power of God.

A father and a daughter went for a walk in the park when she was just two years old. He put out the forefinger of his right hand, and her little hand was just big enough to circle it. As they walked along the gravel path, she was looking at the flowers and trees and a little dog, not paying any attention to where she was walking. Soon she stumbled on the path; her little hand slipped off his big finger and down she went in the gravel. Fortunately, she had on a snowsuit so she did not hurt herself. But he realized that something more was needed if she was not to fall again. So when she took hold of his finger, once more he found that he could circle her wrist with his thumb and little finger. It was not long before the same thing happened. Childlike, she was not paying attention to where she was walking and again she stumbled and her little hand slipped off his finger; but this time she did not fall to the ground. With his thumb and little finger encircling her wrist he was able to hold her tightly and keep her from falling.

If my being kept depended on my holding on to God, I am sure I would have been distracted by the things sof this world and wou ld hmave fallen many times—my hand slipping its hold on Him. But God is there with His great hand of love holding on to me, so that I am kept from falling.

Through what are we kept? "Through faith."

This is absolutely necessary on our part. He alone can keep us, but we must look to Him in faith. As you must open the window to let in the air, raise the blind to let in the sunshine, and eat your food to gain nourishment, so you must trust in order to be kept. Make no mistake: It is not your faith that keeps you, it is His power. But it is by your faith that you constantly lay hold of His keeping power.

CONCLUSION

We are favored above all people, for we are *chosen of God*; we are *children of God*; we are *heirs of God*, and we are *kept by the power of God!*

REDEEMED FROM THE CURSE OF THE LAW

E. J. Reynolds

SCRIPTURE: Galatians 3:13, 14

INTRODUCTION

This passage of Scripture brings together the spiritual principles involved in our salvation from sin—Christ, by being made a curse for us, has redeemed us from the curse of the law. This passage also sets forth our spiritual and moral state before we were redeemed by Christ—we were cursed. And it sets forth our present spiritual state as redeemed people—we are blessed with all the blessings of Abraham and have received the promised Holy Spirit. Let us think about these various and related truths one by one.

REDEEMED FROM THE CURSE

The text says we who belong to Christ are redeemed from the curse of the law. The law spoken of here is specifically the Ten Commandments. The moral requirements of the Ten Commandments represent the universal law of God and were incorporated into the larger legal code we commonly refer to as being the law of Moses. Since the law represents God's moral demands of man, we should understand that the curse of the law is the divine condemnation which comes upon mankind for breaking God's moral law. The Bible declares that every person has broken God's law: "For all have sinned, and come short of the glory of God" (Romans 3:23).

Because all have sinned, until we are redeemed by Christ, all are under the curse of the law. Every person is condemned by the law, "for by the law is the knowledge of sin" (Romans 3:20). Since no person can give perfect obedience to God's law, "by the deeds of the law [by doing the law] there shall no flesh [person] be justified in his [God's] sight" (3:20). So, every person who is unredeemed by Christ is under the curse or condemnation of the law. Cursed by our own violations of God's moral law—this is our spiritual state apart from redemption in Christ. The law cannot redeem us; it exposes the fact we are sinners and makes us aware of our need of the Savior, Jesus Christ. "Wherefore the law was our schoolmaster to bring us unto Christ, that we might be justified by faith" (Galatians 3:24).

We are redeemed from the curse of the law, the condemnation for our sins, by faith in Jesus Christ. "There is therefore now no condemnation to them which are in Christ Jesus. . . . For what the law could not do [that is, redeem man from sin], in that it was weak through the flesh [the weakness of the law was that sinful man breaks God's law], God sending his own Son in the likeness of sinful flesh [as a man], and for sin, condemned sin in the flesh [condemned sin by his own holy life and death in a human body]: That the righteousness of the law [perfect obedience to God's law] might be fulfilled [realized, made a fact by the imputation and impartation of Christ's righteousness] in us, who walk not after the flesh [the sinful nature], but after the Spirit" (Romans 8:1, 3, 4).

CHRIST WAS MADE A CURSE FOR US

Jesus Christ was not cursed because He was hanged upon the Cross. He was hanged upon the Cross because He was cursed by the law for bearing our sins. The statement, "Cursed is every one that hangeth on a tree" (Galatians 3:13) is quoted from the passage in Deuteronomy 21:23. In ancient Israel, people were not killed by crucifixion, but the dead bodies of those executed for some capital offense were exposed upon trees or crosses as a sign of the curse of God which was upon them for their sin—"for he that is hanged is accursed of God" (v. 23).

The fact that Jesus was crucified, hanged upon a tree, was an indication of the curse upon Him for our sins. The Prophet Isaiah understood that men would regard Jesus Christ as being cursed of God for sin. Isaiah prophesied,

"Surely he hath borne our griefs, and carried our sorrows: yet we did esteem him stricken, smitten of God, and afflicted. But he was wounded for our transgressions [our violations of God's law]" (Isaiah 53:4, 5).

The language of the New Testament, describing what happened when Jesus was made a curse for us, is very strong and mysterious. The Bible says, "For he [God] hath made him [Christ] to be sin for us, [Christ] who knew no sin; that we might be made the righteousness of God in him [in Christ]" (2 Corinthians 5:21). The language is strong in that *God made Christ to be sin for us.* That is, when Christ died for our sins upon the Cross, all the sin of the human race was brought together in the person of Christ. There, God was able to judge all sin for all time by regarding His Son as the representative of all sinners.

The mystery of this language is that Christ who knew no sin, "became sin for us." Although Christ "did no sin, neither was guile found in his mouth," yet, "his own self bare our sins in his own body on the tree" (1 Peter 2:22, 24). In some mysterious way, Christ became totally identified—as one—with our sinfulness in order that we might become as one with the righteousness of God. Christ was made a curse for us. He accepted the curse of the law for our sins in order that we might become righteous by faith in Him.

BLESSINGS THROUGH JESUS CHRIST

Because Christ was made a curse for us, who were cursed by the law, now we are blessed. Christ turned the curse into a blessing for us. What is the nature of our new blessed status in Jesus Christ? All the blessings of Abraham are upon us; that is, all the blessings promised to Abraham because of his faith in God are extended to all who believe in Jesus Christ.

Since the blessings of Abraham come upon us by faith in Jesus Christ, we must ask, What are these blessings? These blessings have to do primarily with Abraham's relationship with God and his justification by faith. Of course, the blessings God pronounced upon Abraham included promises of land to his heirs, and promises of greatness for his descendants. However, Abraham saw these temporal blessings as being representative of God's eternal kingdom and family. The Bible says of Abraham, "He looked for a city [community of believers] which hath foundations, whose builder and maker is God" (Hebrews 11:10).

Abraham and the other patriarchs of Israel lived by faith in God and fixed their hope upon things eternal. The Bible says of them, they "confessed that they were strangers and pilgrims on the earth," and "they desire a better country, that is, an heavenly" (vv. 11:13, 16). The divine blessings upon Abraham were essentially "spiritual blessings" which also resulted in material and physical blessings for him and his descendants. These blessings had to do primarily with bringing Abraham into a right relationship with God because of his faith in God. "And he [Abraham] believed in the Lord, and he [the Lord] counted it to him [gave him credit for it] for righteousness" (Genesis 15:6). This passage is cited in the New Testament in these words: "Abraham believed God, and it was accounted [credited] to him for righteousness" (Galatians 3:6).

Now what is the significance of all this? That Abraham was made righteous in the same way that Christians are made righteous—by faith in God. "For by grace are ye saved through faith; and that not of yourselves: it is the gift of God" (Ephesians 2:8). When we believe God—that is, when we accept by faith His provision of salvation through Christ —the blessings of Abraham come upon us. We are justified and made righteous by faith. We are no longer under the curse of the law or the condemnation of God. We are blessed. We are made right with God and we have the divine favor which is bestowed only upon those who are redeemed from the curse of the law. The blessings of Abraham embrace all the blessings of the Christian life—"all spiritual blessings in heavenly places in Christ" (1:3).

RECEIVING THE SPIRIT THROUGH FAITH

The New Testament leaves no doubt that the personal experience of the indwelling of the Holy Spirit was extremely important to the early Christians. When some of the Christians at Galatia were tempted to depart from Christ, the Apostle Paul inquired of them, "Reccived ye the Spirit by the works of the law, or by the hearing of faith?" (Galatians 3:2). No, we do not receive the Holy Spirit into our life by perfect obedience to God's law—we break the law of God. We receive the Spirit in the New Birth and regeneration by faith in Jesus Christ to save us from our sins. We receive the baptism in the Holy Spirit by faith in Jesus Christ who promised to give us the Spirit.

To anyone who reads the Book of Galatians, chapter 3, it is obvious that some of the Galatians were either defecting or being tempted to defect from Christ. What was the nature of this defection? It appears that false teachers had come among the Galatians, teaching them that they could be justified in the sight of God only by keeping the law of Moses. Acceptance of this teaching would have meant that the Galatians were no longer depending upon Christ for their salvation. Instead, they would have turned to trying to save themselves by works of righteousness. Thus it was that the Apostle Paul reminded the Galatians that the law cannot save because all have sinned and all are cursed by the law.

Our redemption from sin and our reception of the promised Holy Spirit come by faith in Jesus Christ. Christ became a curse for us upon the Cross so we could "receive the promise of the Spirit through faith" (Galatians 3:14).

CONCLUSION

Christ is all we need to be redeemed from sin and the condemnation of sin. Faith in Christ is all we need to transform our life so that we are made righteous by God. Jesus Christ is made to us all we need.

IF GOD DOES NOT

Harold O. Downing

SCRIPTURE: Daniel 3:13-25

INTRODUCTION

A leading churchman said recently Americans have become so tense and nervous it has been years since he has seen anyone asleep in church. Even among the ranks of those who believe faith in God is the answer to life's crises, there are days when faith battles hard to maintain its foothold.

We do not always understand the circumstances in which we find ourselves. Indeed, there are times when even God seems hidden from view. We ask hard questions; there seem to be no answers.

Our Lord said it would often be this way. He told His anxious disciples, "A little while, and ye shall not see me: and again, a little while, and ye shall see me, because I go to the Father" (John 16:16). Though He spoke literally of His crucifixion and resurrection, His statement seems to be a spiritual reality in our lives as well.

For each of us there are those "little whiles" during which God lets us glimpse something of His powerful purposes, when He seems to draw back the veil and permit us to see what He is doing and how He is doing it. When this occurs, our enthusiasm runs high and our faith is strengthened. There are other "little whiles," however, when these things are hidden; when, like Job, no matter where we look, we cannot seem to find Him (Job 23:1-9). All we see is affliction and adversity. It is then that faith has its greatest opportunity.

FAITH RECOGNIZING GOD'S POWER

Surely one of the greatest biblical accounts of faith operating in adversity is found in the story of God's deliverance of three young men from a fiery furnace (Daniel 3).

Imagine the circumstances. Shadrach, Meshach, and Abed-nego found favor with the Babylonian king Nebuchadnezzar. When the Babylonians in Nebuchadnezzar's court became jealous of the privileges these men received, they sought to discredit them, devising what seemed to be the perfect plan. Knowing Shadrach, Meshach and Abed-nego would never break Jehovah's command, "Thou shalt have no other gods," the jealous Babylonians told the king of their refusal to bow to his golden image.

Furious, King Nebuchadnezzar ordered the three Jews to worship the idol or else be thrown into the furnace. But in the midst of such affliction, the faith of these young men was exercised in a marvelous way, a way that stands as an example to us that we might possess their faith and so prove triumphant in the darker "little whiles" of life.

First of all, they expressed faith in the ability of God to deliver them. Notice their response: "If we are thrown into the blazing furnace, the God we serve is able to save us from it" (v. 17, New International Version). Shadrach, Meshach and Abed-nego knew their God was the One who had all things under His control. They knew the Lord God Jehovah who said of Himself: "Behold, I am the Lord, the God of all flesh: is there any thing too hard for me?" (Jeremiah 32:27).

They knew the same God who promised Abraham a son though he was old. They had faith that the God who brought that son into being could certainly deliver them from the furnace of their affliction. This faith was not merely assent to the belief that God can do anything, but rather belief in His ability to do a particular thing which is of specific concern.

Do we, in the midst of our own crises and turmoil, believe in God's ability to do *specifically* what is needed? Are we willing to trust Him?

Not only did these young men have faith in God's ability to rescue them, they also had confidence in His *willingness* to deliver. They said, "And he *will* rescue us from your hand, O king." Belief in God's willingness to deliver is an entirely different thing from believing in His ability to do so.

There are many people who believe God *can* work who do not necessarily believe He *will* work on their behalf. The Bible tells us God is love. Therefore, knowing Him means being assured He loves us and will always act in a lovingly consistent way for our greatest good.

This does not always mean He will deliver us in the manner we imagine. In fact, at first it appeared these three were not going to be delivered at all. Yet, they stood firmly on what they knew to be true of their God—not only that He was able, but also He was personally concerned for them and therefore willing to act on their behalf. God miraculously delivered them from the fiery furnace.

Today, just as He did then, God performs miracles in response to faith—miracles that pierce the hardness of unbelief, strengthen the faith of believers and bring many to Himself. God is exalted through such miraculous interventions.

But it is at this point where so many of us run into trouble in our own lives. We believe in the omnipotence of God . . . that He *can* rescue. We also believe in the loving desire of God to give what is good. Therefore, we dare to believe he *will* rescue.

FAITH CONFRONTING THE DILEMMA

But if He doesn't, what then? For every person who is healed of cancer, for instance, there are others who are not. For every individual who prospers financially, there are those who do not. For every deliverance *from* the furnace, there are those who seem to be left in it. What about them?

First, we must take into consideration possible hindrances to miracle-producing faith such as sin in our lives or unbelief and doubt in our hearts. Once we have examined ourselves thoroughly, however, and can find no such hindrance, then

72

we must answer the question, "If not, what then?" by accepting the sovereignty of God.

Notice the final words of the Hebrew boys to their king. After they had expressed faith that God could and would rescue them, they went on to say, "*But* even if he does not, we want you to know, O King, that we will not serve your gods or worship the image of gold you have set up." These words did not express doubt in God; they revealed faith in His sovereignty. Even if He did not rescue them as they believed He would, they would still trust Him. That was faith!

This affirmation that God is sovereign and may not always do as we expect or wish Him to is the missing ingredient in much of today's teaching on faith. And because it is missing, many sincere believers are left to conclude they are second-class citizens in God's kingdom solely because their faith has not resulted in miraculous deliverance.

After preaching a similar message some time ago, I watched a woman from the congregation come forward to speak with me. She looked at me and said, "This is the first time I've been able to understand that I am not a second-class Christian." She was in a wheelchair. For many years she had been made to feel there was something wrong with her faith, that she was but a stepchild to God because she had not been healed. Accepting God's sovereignty in her situation enabled her to realize God had not failed, and neither had she. If we lean on this as the crowning point of our faith, we will be well on the road to spiritual maturity.

It is undoubtedly true that God is glorified through miracles and supernatural visitations, but must we conclude the faith which produces such is the only kind of faith that brings Him honor? Can those who are not healed, those who do not prosper materially bring Him just as much glory? Isn't it possible the faith which *endures* rather than being delivered, the faith that submits wholly to God in the face of adversity, can bring as much if not more joy to God's heart? Such arises from a more selfless love.

I knew a saintly woman who had borne the pain of crippling arthritis for 40 years. She contracted the disease at age 22. Her husband subsequently left her. Having lost the use of her hands and feet completely, she was forced to move in with her brother. During our last conversation she spoke of the manner in which the enemy would seek to torment her while she was confined to her bed.

"I cry out to the Lord," she said, "and He drives that evil presence from the room."

She told me of a recent prayer in which she had reminded God of the deliverance He had provided Moses by taking him in death after he had suffered in the wilderness for 40 years with the Israelites. Comparing her own situation to his, she had said, "Now, God, I have suffered in my own wilderness for 40 years—without complaining. Would you please take me home, too?"

The next time I saw her, I was preaching her funeral. God honored her request. She passed from this life not in defeat but in victory, for she trusted God in the midst of an affliction from which she was never rescued. Hers was a faith that *endured* the furnace and surely it brought glory to God in that it produced a sweet perseverance of character, a humble submission that belongs only to those who know He is sovereign.

FAITH ACCEPTING A HIGHER WILL

We in the Church need to get away from the idea that deliverance from trial is necessarily the highest form of spiritual blessing. Such an attitude is entirely alien to the New Testament, and certainly it was not the attitude of the Lord we follow.

Hebrews 11 is perhaps the most famous Bible chapter on the subject of faith. It is known as the "Hall of Faith" for it contains a record of those who were heroes in the lives they lived before God. Verses 32-35 of this chapter list for us those heroes of the faith who were supernaturally delivered from trial and affliction, those who through faith "stopped the mouths of lions, quenched the violence of fire, escaped the edge of the sword." We read of those who were miraculously healed, for "out of weakness they were made strong."

None of this is surprising to us. This is how we envision those whose faith is pleasing to God.

But if we continue to read, we find another group of heroes, and the results of their faith may be somewhat surprising:

Others were tortured, not accepting deliverance; that they might obtain a better resurrection: And others had trial of cruel mockings and scourgings, yea, moreover of bonds and imprisonment: They were stoned, they were sawn asunder, were tempted, were slain with the sword: they wandered about in sheep-skins and goatskins; being destitute, afflicted, tor-mented (vv. 35-37).

Those heroes of faith who were delivered are here listed side by side with those who apparently were not, and yet verse 39 tells us, "And these *all*, having obtained a good report through faith. . . ."

Did those who were rescued from affliction obtain a better report for their faith than those who were not? No. The scripture here clearly teaches that *enduring* faith is equal to or greater than *escaping* faith.

Has God left us when we have exercised our faith in clear conscience and yet remain in our own particular fiery furnace? Or could it be He is allowing us an equal or greater opportunity to glorify Him by leaving us there?

Paul wrote, "For our light affliction, which is but for a moment, worketh for us a far more exceeding and eternal weight of glory" (2 Corinthians 4:17). We often think the affliction to which Paul refers must be something as severe as martyrdom or intense persecution. But any affliction which drives us to God and is faced by us with a spirit of submission and love toward Him works in us His purpose—that glory which only eternity will reveal. God is exalted in the faith that endures and produces patience, beauty of spirit, and humble devotion to Him.

It is with faith that we must respond to the dark and troubling "little whiles" of our lives. As did Shadrach, Meshach and Abed-nego, we can assert confidently, in the midst of any situation, God is *able* to deliver. We can rest assured that He is *willing* to deliver, and then, as the fireproof insur-ance of our faith within the furnace, we can boldly proclaim as they did, "If He does *not* deliver us, we will yet live and praise Him."

CONCLUSION

Whether ours is a faith that brings escape *from* the fire, or endurance *in* the fire, we have the firm promise of Scripture that the other "little while" of which Jesus spoke will someday come and we will see Him as He is.

If God does not, what then?

Only this: we say with Job, "Though he slay me, yet will I trust in him" (Job 13:15), and with the Hebrew boys, "Even if God does not choose to remove us from the furnace of our affliction, we will never bow down to another."

Such faith will see us through the questions and anxieties of life's hard places and produce in us an eternal weight of glory.

"In *all* these things we are more than conquerors" (Romans 8:37).

FRINGE BENEFITS

Robert Varner

SCRIPTURE: Numbers 15:37-40

INTRODUCTION

Forgetfulness. It is a persistent human weakness. We forget things we shouldn't. A husband forgets his wedding anniversary and faces some uncomfortable moments with his wife. A mother forgets to pay a bill and the collector shows up at the front door. A son forgets to mow the grass and has to suffer the reprimand of his father.

We are forgetful. The distresses and pressures of living may even cause us to forget who we are and the privileges we have as children of God. Some things are best forgotten, but God does not want us to forget His faithfulness or the benefits we have as His people.

GOD GAVE ISRAEL A REMINDER

During Israel's exodus from Egypt, divine miracles reminded Israel of God's presence with them. They crossed the Red Sea on a dry path God made through the sea. They were led by a pillar of cloud in the daytime and a pillar of fire by night.

They rejoiced when God miraculously delivered them from the treachery of Pharaoh's army.

In the wilderness of Sinai, on the way to Canaan, Israel witnessed still more reminders of God's presence with them. They were fed daily with manna from heaven and drank water from a barren rock. They saw the power and presence of God revealed in clouds, fire, and thunder upon the top of Mount Sinai. They heard the Lord address the nation with an audible voice. They saw the earth open and swallow rebels who rejected Moses' leadership. All these were divine reminders that God was with Israel.

While they were still in the wilderness, God commanded Moses to instruct all the Israelites to sew threads of blue into the fringes of their garments. Why? The blue thread in the fringes of their garments would serve as a divine reminder to the Israelites.

The time would come when Israel would not have miracles to remind them of God's presence. In these times, when it might seem that God was very far away, the Israelites could look at the fringes of their garments and be reminded of the Lord's commandments and that they were God's people.

The purpose of the blue fringe upon the garments of Israel was stated in these specific terms:

1. "That ye may look upon it, and remember all the commandments of the Lord, and do them " (v. 39).

2. And, "that ye seek not after your own heart and your eyes . . . and be holy unto your God" (vv. 39, 40).

Stated in contemporary language, the blue fringe served to remind the Israelites of God's commandments so they would obey His commandments. And the blue fringe reminded them that they were God's people and were, therefore, not to merely follow their own desires in life. Instead they were to seek to fulfill the will of the Lord.

WE NEED TO BE REMINDED

We, no less than the ancient Israelites, need to be reminded of our relationship with God. Perilous times are here. Ungodliness, immorality, dishonesty, and violence are commonplace in our world. The pressures of living in this evil age have caused some Christians to forget who they are. While some suffer emotional distress, others suffer spiritual defeat and drift away from God. These things do not have to happen. We are gathered here in worship to be reminded of our relationship with God. He has given us His Word to live by and we are His people. If we will remember this, we have what we need to get us through these difficult times.

It could be said that every reminder of our relationship with God is a *fringe benefit*. Every reminder of our duties and privileges as believers in Christ is a *fringe benefit*. Think with me about ways in which the blue thread in the borders of their garments served Israel as *fringe benefits*.

FRINGE BENEFITS OF THE BLUE THREAD

Imagine a time long after the death of Moses. An army of Israelites have been badly beaten in their first encounter with the enemy. To the Israelite general, defeat seems inevitable. His forces have been reduced by death and injury and others have deserted out of fear. He is outmanned, outmaneuvered, and outfought. Already he has sent for the trumpeters to sound retreat. Suddenly, as he sits dejected, hopeless, the blue fringe of his garment catches his eye. He begins to think about what it means. It is a reminder that Israel belongs to God and must obey the Lord. It is a reminder that he must not lean to his own understanding, but trust in the Lord. Slowly his doubt and fears begin to melt away. Faith in God grows. The trumpeters arrive. A command is given—not "retreat" but "charge!" The battle belongs to the Lord and victory is won, all because of the blue fringe on the general's robe—*a fringe benefit*!

Again, imagine with me that a young Israelite man has wandered far from home and has fallen deeply into sin. He hits bottom and tears stream down his face as he thinks about pleasant times before he left his father's house. Reduced at last to eating husks with the swine, the young man still wears the blue fringed garment made for him in his father's house. As he prods himself laboriously to feed the swine to earn his own food, he begins to think about the blue fringe on his garment. He remembers the Lord and all the commandments of the Lord he has broken. He remembers that his father taught him that his life should be holy unto the Lord. As these thoughts race through his mind, he wonders if his father will forgive him and looks wistfully in the direction of his father's house. Words begin to form in his mind and he begins to talk out loud to himself: "I will arise and go to my father, and will say unto him, Father, I have sinned against heaven, and before thee, And am no more worthy to be called thy son: make me as one of thy hired servants" (Luke 15:18, 19).

And he arose and came to his father. And the father received him home with forgiveness and joy; because the young man was reminded—*a fringe benefit!*

THE BLUE FRINGE ON OUR GARMENT

We do not sew a blue fringe on our garments as the Israelites did, but in a spiritual sense it might be said we have a blue fringe to remind us of our relationship with God. It is the blue thread of God's love—grace, mercy, redemption—running through the whole Bible. It is the blue thread of assurance whereby the Holy Spirit bears witness with our spirit that we are children of God (Romans 8:16). In times of need, God's Word and God's Spirit remind us of our relationship with Him. The Word and the Spirit remind us that God has chosen us to be His people and to do His will. And because He has chosen us, we do not have to settle for defeat or failure.

Satan would like to destroy our self-esteem. He would like to lower our self-image until we see ourselves as slaves or bums. But we are not these if we belong to Christ. We are children of God—"a chosen generation, a royal priesthood, an holy nation" (1 Peter 2:9). Let us remember who we are.

We all pass through times when there are no spectacular or miraculous reminders that God is with us. We may feel that God is very far away. We are assaulted with doubts and fears and defeat seems inevitable. Turn again to God's Word. Discover again the blue fringe of God's faithfulness. Listen again for the assurance of the Holy Spirit. Reap the *fringe benefit.* Be renewed in your relationship with God.

TOUCH THE FRINGE OF CHRIST'S GARMENT

The time was over 1900 years ago. A frail Jewish woman was returning from a visit to one of Israel's top physicians.

He, like all the others she had seen, could offer her no hope. Her case was incurable and it was slowly draining away her life. As she walked home, she thought about a man named Jesus. She had heard from some that He was a great prophet, able to heal the sick and raise the dead. She made up her mind to find this Jesus and seek His help.

Days passed. One day the woman heard that Jesus was in town and would pass near her door. This was her chance. She would go to Jesus and appeal to Him to heal her. However, when she came to where Jesus was, He was surrounded by a large crowd. How could she ever get to Jesus? She would not try to speak to Him. She would simply press her way through the crowd until she could get close enough to reach out and touch the blue fringe of His garment. She did it! She pressed her way through the crowd. She reached out, with just one hand, and touched ever so slightly the fringe of His garment. Immediately she knew she was made well by the power of God. And Jesus knew it. He acknowledged her act of faith. She received a *fringe benefit*!

CONCLUSION

Do you feel your need of a *fringe benefit*? Jesus Christ still has the blue fringe on His priestly robe. It is there for all who need His help. It is there to remind us of God's promises and of our duties and privileges. Reach out to Christ. Receive your *fringe benefit* today.

TWO WAYS OF TITHING

Jack D. Smith

SCRIPTURE: Leviticus 27:30-34

INTRODUCTION

God allows us to make an investment in the kingdom of God, which has both earthly and eternal consequences. That opportunity is through tithing.

That fantastic opportunity is not unlike the good fortune that came to the widow when Elijah allowed her to give him a cake first and thereafter she and her starving son lacked for nothing at meal time. Or like the boy who gave his lunch and saw the Master's multiplication miracle and the enormous leftovers the satisfied thousands were too full to eat. Or the widow who gave the two mites, all she had, and having given them received both a commendation from Christ and an eternal memorial in the Bible.

Tithing is not only an investment with the greatest possible dividends, but it offers other benefits: a means of worship, a way of showing our gratitude to God, and an expression of our faith and obedience to the Word of God.

There are those modern debates on whether the so-called "New Testament Christians" should pay tithes. The argument holds that tithing is an Old Testament principle somehow replaced with a different concept in the New Testament. However, those who believe in the whole Bible know that "the tithe . . . is the Lord's" (Leviticus 27:30).

Dedicated Christians accept this scripture and fact without dispute. Those less dedicated will always look for loopholes in the Word of God.

Upon these statements, let me put forth a conclusion drawn from the practical observation of the tithing habits of many people. There are two methods of tithing: (1) tithing by convenience and (2) tithing by commitment.

THE TWO METHODS DESCRIBED

Tithing by convenience is when the person gives to God what he feels he can, if and when there is something left over. This kind of giving is capricious and inconsistent and leaves the giver with a feeling of guilt, defeat and inadequacy. Those are feelings, incidentally, which should be felt under these circumstances.

Tithing by commitment is based on the conviction that it is God's will to tithe, regularly and scripturally; and that such is beyond negotiation and compromise. This type of tithing puts God first. It expresses the conviction that the remaining 90 percent will accomplish more than the 100 percent without tithing.

Here is an examination of the two methods.

TITHING BY CONVENIENCE

Convenience tithing is not scripturally approved. God loves consistency. Many inconsistent tithers are well-meaning, hoping someday to do better. You have possibly heard that the road to hell is paved with good intentions.

The problem these Christians face is a common one in our society. Their hindrance is an insurmountable and often continuous pile of debt obligations. Generally, such excessive debt drains away the persons' income leaving them little or nothing to give to God.

Abuse of credit is a plague in our land and a curse from hell on church members. It is a scheme Satan perpetrated on Christians. Its design is to drain multiple millions away from the kingdom of God into the world's businesses, thus preventing souls from being blessed and saved.

Since tithing is God's way of funding the Kingdom, Satan will naturally mount a frontal attack to defeat that. Unfortunately, he is winning through many Christians, for that successful attack plan is to immerse the Christian into so much debt that by the time he goes to church he only has a dollar or less left over for God. It is sad to work all week and then go to church, where it counts the most, and be broke.

DEBT IS AN OBLIGATION

Let's look at debt for a moment. When you make a debt you also make an obligation for repayment. That obligation is a commitment.

Now isn't that interesting? Debt, often the defeat of Christians' good intentions, is based on the same principle as God's tithing system, commitment.

The truth is obvious. You will either commit your tithe (a tenth of your income) to pay debts or you will commit it to God's glory. It should be mentioned that we owe God far more than we could ever owe GMAC or J. C. Penny's or Mastercharge.

So finances involve commitment either way. We end up paying our tithes cheerfully to God or unknowingly to the devil. Pastors need to make this fact known to Christians.

THE WAY OUT

For those inundated with debt and unable to please God, there is victory. Let God heal your sick finances! Here are some steps toward victory over defeating debt.

1. No one is happy being under crushing debt. This should show you that it is wrong. The first step then is to stop making more debt than you can afford. Be determined to never exceed that limit again.

2. Planning is essential to good financial management. Make and keep a personal or family budget. You can find help if you do not know how to do this.

3. This next step is very important. Begin immediately to prayerfully and faithfully pay full 10 percent tithe. Tithing is

the only way God asked us to prove Him (Malachi 3:10). Trust God through tithing for your finances.

4. You may need to make arrangements with your creditors to clear up your debts. If so, explain to them what you are doing and what payments you can make to clear up your debt. When you reach an agreement with them, stick to it and make your word good. You will feel better for it.

5. Find ways to cut back on your spending habits. You can live on less! Happiness is being out from under that mountain of debt. Debt is a prison. Let God set you free.

6. When you pay off a charge account, close it permanently. When you pay off a credit card, destroy it and do not get any more of them. If you can not keep your checking account in balance, close it. Your goal is to reach a place where you live on a cash basis, not credit or overdraft. You will then be in control of your finances and God will be able to bless you even more.

7. Finally, if you have unusually high debts, consult a financial counselor. He will help you to arrange a plan and solve your problems.

Here is a great truth: Most of us do not need more money; what we actually need is more wisdom in managing what we have. And here is a scripture: "If any of you lack wisdom, let him ask of God, that giveth to all men liberally, and upbraideth not; and it shall be given him" (James 1:5).

If you want to please God and tithe He will help you do it.

TITHING BY COMMITMENT

Dedicated Christians neither stagger nor hesitate when it comes to obeying God in tithing. They know it is the Word of God and therefore, His will. Commitment, which is the make or break point in consistent tithing, has already been learned by them in many other habits of Christian living. They have and are developing this trait through holy thoughts and deeds, prayer, reading the Bible, faithful church attendance, Christian service, and the like.

Tithing is no special nor unusual requirement among God's standards. His yoke is easy and His burden is light (Matthew 11:29, 30). The dedicated Christian would no more miss tithing than he would miss prayer. He has found that tithing is worship, tithing is service, tithing is obedience. Christians find joy in tithing. That is why the Bible says we give cheerfully (2 Corinthians 9:7).

Tithing is spiritual yet it has earthly as well as eternal consequences. The hungry thousands were not fed until the boy gave his lunch. The church cannot grow without our support; the Kingdom cannot expand on earth without our commitment of tithes. The difference will be the souls saved or lost as a result of your tithing or not. We are the key, God uses us.

In Psalm 50 God tells us He does not need our money for Himself; rather, for the work of the Kingdom. Jesus founded the Church; we are to fund it.

Tithing does also have eternal consequences. Jesus taught, "Lay up for yourselves treasures in heaven, where neither moth nor rust doth corrupt, and where thieves do not break through nor steal: For where your treasure is, there will your heart be also" (Matthew 6:20, 21). I do not want to get to heaven and walk the streets of gold and be personally broke, having not laid up any treasures in heaven.

God makes it easy for us to tithe for He gives us victory over ourselves. We are our own worst enemy. Debt, which causes us to live on a lower level in life, is our own making but God heals our inner self, the source of our nervous quest to accumulate more things.

The greatest statement on material possessions in all the world is Jesus' statement, "But seek ye first the kingdom of God, and his righteousness; and all these things shall be added unto you" (Matthew 6:33).

Our quest is not really for more possessions or things in life but for happiness. Only God can give us that (John 14:27). Let us obey God in tithing and in all points so that we may be happy as He desires for us to be.

You can always afford to do God's will. He makes it possible (Philippians 4:13).

Even our government makes it more advantageous for us to give our tithes to God when we deduct what we give to the church from the income tax report. I would far rather know my money was going to support an American minister or missionary in a foreign land than to see it go to produce more guns and ammunition for heathen nations to use in their wars.

The devil wants your tithe, first to keep God from getting it, and secondly, to use for evil purposes. We actually owe our tithes to God, for it is He who blessed us, prospered us, provided food, rest, air, health, and strength for us to earn income. But God wants to use it for the ultimate good—the salvation of souls. He pays great dividends, on earth and in heaven (Hebrews 11:24-26).

CONCLUSION

Let me ask this question: What is most important to you financially? your car payment? house payment? charge account? or God?

If you have not made that decision, then you are faced with it regularly. The Christian's conscience and the Holy Spirit shows us what is right. We cannot ignore God and be at peace.

Do you want to have righteousness? One definition of *righteousness* is simply "being right." That is why Jesus taught: "Seek ye first the kingdom of God, and his righteousness" (Matthew 6:33). We must have righteousness in our lives to be acceptable before God. We cannot be right unless we obey Him in terms of finances.

I read a tract years ago. A man near death had a scary dream in which he stood before God and heard he was acceptable in everything except that he had robbed God of his tithe. When he awoke he called for the pastor and ordered his wife to write a check for all the back tithe. He wanted his record in heaven to be clear.

Is that story too strong? Or could it be that you owe God financial obedience and service which may bar heaven's doors? I would rather know that "there is *nothing* between my soul and my Savior."

Let us remember, we can do *all* things through Christ, who strengthens us.

Let us begin now to tithe faithfully. God will take care of the rest.

THE NEW LIFE IN CHRIST

Victor Pagan

SCRIPTURE: Ephesians 4:22-24

INTRODUCTION

"New life" is a very familiar term, especially to people from a Christian background. We talk about it as being a gift from God. Some think we now have this new life while others feel it is a promise for the future. Of course, there is always that happy medium—those who believe we begin the new life here and now and that we will continue it there and then.

However, it must be realized that the living of a new life requires some adjustments. Maybe, more than adjustments, it requires—learning, a lot of learning. That is probably one of the reasons for so much teaching in the Scriptures. God wants us to learn how to live and enjoy and benefit from this new life He has given us through Jesus Christ.

Too often we Christians forget that living the new life in Christ requires some action on our part.

I do not mean we help the Lord or that we earn our blessings. I write of some things we must do if we are to enjoy our relationship with Christ to the fullest extent.

The Apostle Paul mentions some of these things in our text verses.

PUT OFF THE OLD MAN

First we must "put off" the former conversation of the old man. The term *conversation* here really means "way of living." We are to get rid of all bad habits and sinful attitudes. Anyone may live a religious life, pretending to be an angel. But Christians who are born again, truly born of the Spirit, should be aware that it is exactly that—a brand-new life. It is another life.

The former life is corrupt. It is based on sinful desires. It is a life where thoughts come from a mind that is empty and vain; where ideas come from a darkened understanding. The Apostle describes the life of the old man as one being alienated from God, full of ignorance and with a blind heart. The old man has given himself to lasciviousness and to uncleanness with greediness.

As we may see from this description, our former life was ugly and worthless, to say the least. I do not understand how some people may still act proud of what they once were. We may have had money, fame, good looks, education, pleasure, or any of many other worldly commodities, and yet our lives had no meaning. There was no true joy in the heart, no peace of mind.

Trying to live the new life with the old habits is what keeps many people from fully enjoying the abundant life they now have in Christ.

There is the story of a rich man who one day, while riding his limousine downtown, saw a poor beggar on a street corner. The rich man immediately recognized the beggar, an old friend from his childhood. He stopped his limousine, called his friend and took him home with him.

The rich man instructed his friend to feel at home, took him to a room where some nice clean clothes were laid out on a bed, and gave him 20 minutes to be ready for supper. Twenty minutes later, sitting together at the table, the beggar squirmed with discomfort from the new clothes. The rich man was disturbed by an unsavory odor from the beggar's body.

"What did you do with the clothes you were wearing?"

The beggar unbuttoned his clean shirt and pointed to his chest where he was still wearing his old clothes underneath.

There was the problem.

I feel that some Christians have the same problem today. Not wanting to put off the old garment, the old life, they just clean themselves on the surface. From within they still spread the bad odor of hate, hypocrisy, gossip, and anger. That is why the Christian life feels like a straight jacket to them. They never seem to find the true value and beauty—the treasure if you will—which is a well-lived new life in Christ.

RENEW THE SPIRIT OF THE MIND

A second thing we must do is to renew the spirit of our mind. The mind is a battlefield, and the new life cannot be lived with an old mind. Thank God, we now have the mind of Christ.

To give us a hard time, it would seem there are two ways the devil attacks our minds. First, he keeps bringing back to our minds some of the things of the past—sins, ugly acts in which we were involved while living away from God. The devil is trying to tell us we are living a lie, that we were too mean and too bad to be forgiven. We should already know, of course, that making us doubt is an old satanic trick. Can we not remember Eve in the garden of Eden?

It is true that we were sinners of the worst kind. But it is also true, and even more, that the blood of Jesus Christ cleanses us from all sins. We must not let the devil confuse us. We must rebuke him in the name of Jesus. If God has forgotten our sins, there is no need for us to remember them. Yes, we are free indeed because the Son has made us free. We must set our affections and our thoughts on things above, forgetting all things which are behind.

Second, there is another trap. Let us be careful! When Satan cannot disturb us with the things of the past, he then tries to destroy us with anxiety for the future. The news and reports about the future make some people sick. Things are getting worse every day. People fear nuclear destruction, the AIDS epidemic, financial upheaval, wars and terrorists activities. They fear the Communist threat, political insecurity, and race confrontations. It is an endless list.

The real problem is that, with such turmoil in the mind, nobody can see the bright side of life. Such thinking affects the pattern of everyday conduct. It weakens and sometimes may destroy relationships with those around us. It will definitely affect our physical and mental health.

Such should not be with the Christian. We surely do not know the future but we do know the One that makes the future happen. Instead of despair and fear for the future, we need to fill our minds with hope and faith. We must keep going, we must keep on praising, singing, praying, witnessing until Jesus comes.

Writing to all the saints in Philippi, Paul recommended: "Whatsoever things are true, whatsoever things are honest, whatsoever things are just, whatsoever things are pure, whatsoever things are lovely, whatsoever things are of good report; if there be any virtue, and if there be any praise, think on these things" (Philippians 4:8).

PUT ON THE NEW MAN

The final recommendation of the Apostle is to put on the new man. It would seem that some Christians get off-balance on the principle of salvation by faith alone. They abuse the gift and grace of the Lord Jesus Christ in that they greedily and very actively seek all they can get personally from both God and man.

A grown and mature Christian, however, knows there is enormous pleasure in giving, in doing good works, and in the sharing of one's life. These virtues develop through putting on the new man.

A lot of people define the new life negatively, by the things they no longer do. They do not drink, nor smoke, nor commit adultery. They do not use foul language, nor many other things which were once a part of their lives. There are many secular people who do not do such things either, but they have no new life in Christ. Quite obviously there are some "do nots" which are associated with putting off the old man, but we cannot stand naked; we must put on the new man, which is created after God, in righteousness and true holiness.

What specific things are we instructed to do?

The list includes many aspects of human conduct: Speak the truth, be temperate, be sober, do your own work, give to the needy, talk in a manner which is edifying, minister grace, give liberty to the Holy Spirit of God, be kind, be tenderhearted and forgiving.

Doing these things will enhance our relationship with God. It will let our testimony shine within the community and it will bring the greatest of joy to our lives.

CONCLUSION

A middle-aged man decided to make a trip to a coast town and visit the beach. All his life he had heard of the beauty and the riches of the ocean. He wanted to see it for himself.

Arriving at the beach, the man discovered to his dismay that it was dirty and littered with sea weed, pieces of wood, and human garbage. How disappointing!

While the man stood there, thinking how he had been fooled about the beauty of the sea, a young man dressed out in his scuba-diving equipment, waded into the ocean, and soon passed from sight beneath the blue waters of the nearby reef.

A couple of hours later the young man was back, filled with awe and a sense of admiration and satisfaction for the beauty and pleasure he had seen while diving in deep waters.

Such is the case with Christians. Those who come but stay on shore in shallow water will never realize how great, how beautiful and wonderful is new life in Christ; but those who come and equip themselves—by putting off the old man, by renewing the spirit of the mind, and by putting on the new man—never cease to be amazed at the treasure and beauty found in Christ.

NEW DIMENSIONS OF LIFE IN THE SPIRIT

Joel D. Hobbs

SCRIPTURE: John 14:16

INTRODUCTION

These words taken from the Gospel of John are some of the parting words of Jesus to His disciples before His crucifixion. Jesus assured the disciples that He would personally intercede to the Father and request the coming of the Comforter. These seemed to be strange disclosures to the disciples, but it was a part of the fuller revelation of truth they were to receive.

The introduction of the Holy Spirit by Jesus implied that they were going to enter a new dimension of living. The Holy Spirit would no longer merely be "with" them, He would be "in" them (John 14:17). They would become the temples of the Holy Spirit. After His coming at Pentecost the Holy Spirit would usher the disciples into a new dimension of prayer, worship and victorious living. This coming would be powerful and would have a great impact on all believers.

Jesus introduced the Holy Spirit to His disciples as "another Comforter," thus implying personality. That the Holy Spirit is a divine person all Scripture gives testimony. He is called

"God" (Acts 5:3, 4) and He is joined with the Father and the Son in the baptismal formula (Matthew 28:19).

The Holy Spirit is presented to us in Scripture as eternal (Hebrews 9:14); omnipresent (Psalm 139:7-13); omniscient (1 Corinthians 2:10;) and omnipotent (Luke 1:35; Romans 15:19).

Many activities are ascribed to Him. It is said of Him that He strives with sinners (Genesis 6:3); He reproves (John 16:8); He teaches (14:26); He guides (16:13); and He glorifies Christ (16:14). With all the ministries of the Holy Spirit there are several that are especially precious to the believer. When His fullness comes to the believer, the believer is ushered into a new dimension of prayer, worship and victorious living.

A NEW DIMENSION OF PRAYER

Prayer is one of the most vital aspects of the Christian life. A prayerless Christian is unthinkable. Most believers are aware of the strength that comes through prayer. Jesus certainly knew the strength that comes through prayer; therefore, He urged His disciples to pray and He warned them of the weakness they would experience if they neglected prayer. "Also [Jesus] told them a parable, to the effect that they ought always to pray and not to turn coward—faint, lose heart and give up" (Luke 18:1, *Amplified Bible*).

With all the encouragement we receive from the Scriptures to pray, we sometimes feel so helpless, so barren of desire. It is at these times the Holy Spirit will come to our aid. Paul reveals this tremendous truth to us in Romans:

So too the (Holy) Spirit comes to our aid and bears us up in our weakness; for we do not know what prayer to offer nor how to offer it worthily as we ought, but the Spirit Himself goes to meet our supplication and pleads in our behalf with unspeakable yearnings and groanings too deep for utterance. And He Who searches the hearts of men knows what is the mind of the (Holy) Spirit—what His intent is —because the Spirit intercedes and pleads [before God] in behalf of the saints according to and in harmony with God's will (8:26,27; *Amp.*)

This passage reveals several important things:

1. Because of our spiritual and mental limitations we do not always know for what or how to pray.

2. The Holy Spirit comes to our aid and bears us up in this weakness.

3. The Holy Spirit makes intercession for us in unspeakable yearning and groaning too deep for utterance.

4. God who searches the hearts of men knows what the mind and intent of the Holy Spirit is.

5. The Holy Spirit's intercession is always according to the will and purpose of God.

We have seen that praying, empowered by the Holy Spirit, will accomplish several things.

1. *Praying in the Spirit will bring us edification or upbuilding.* This praying that brings edification can be in tongues or with our understanding quickened by the Spirit. It is believed by most Pentecostal scholars that Romans 8:26, 27 can be a reference to the Holy Spirit interceding for the believers in tongues. Most Spirit-filled believers have experienced times when the Holy Spirit did indeed pray through them, quickening their spirit.

This passage in 1 Corinthians 14:14 seems to confirm this, "For if I pray in an unknown tongue, my spirit prayeth, but my understanding is unfruitful." The *Amplified Bible* sheds much light on this verse and also verse 15, "For if I pray in an [unknown] tongue, my spirit and [by the Holy Spirit within me] prays, but my mind is unproductive—bears no fruit and helps nobody. Then what am I to do? I will pray with my spirit—by the Holy Spirit that is within me; but I will also pray intelligently—with my mind and understanding."

The human spirit thus quickened by the Holy Spirit is edified. To this both Paul and Jude agree: "He that speaketh in an unknown tongue edifieth himself" (1 Corinthians 14:4); "But ye, beloved, building up yourselves on your most holy faith, praying in the Holy Ghost" (Jude 20).

2. *Praying in the Spirit will keep our prayers in line with the will of God.* The passage in Romans 8:26, 27 emphasizes that the Spirit makes intercession for us according to the will of God. Praying according to God's will is one of the great prerequisites for answered prayer, "And this is the confidence that we have in him, that, if we ask any thing according to his will, he heareth us" (1 John 5:14). The Holy Spirit knows

the divine purpose and intention for us and His intercession is in keeping with this purpose.

3. *Praying in the Spirit will help us in those unknown urgings that we often feel.* There are times when we feel impelled to pray but we are not aware of a special need.

This happened to my wife and me while I was serving as a mission representative for the Church of God. We were in Nicaragua during the revolution and in a very dangerous situation. My daughter, who was in Cleveland, Tennessee, at the time, felt a special burden to pray for us. She was unaware of our danger, but the Holy Spirit, who is so faithful, moved her to intercession and we were delivered out of a situation that could have been tragic.

A NEW DIMENSION OF WORSHIP

The coming of the Holy Spirit brought a new dimension of worship and praise to the Father. One of the most startling statements of Jesus is recorded in the Gospel of John. Jesus made the statement that the Father was seeking "true worshipers." The worship of the Old Testament was centered around the Temple and a prescribed order of service and sacrifice. This worship degenerated into a formal performance. It could be done without heart and spirit. God sought a higher form of worship—worship that would be from the heart and not just from the head.

It was at the coming of the Holy Spirit that the heart of God could be satisfied with worship that was warm and meaningful both to Himself and the worshiper. The worshiper, moved and anointed by the Holy Spirit, could joyfully express praise and worship to God beyond his own emotional feelings. Worship of this nature is called for by the Father and is acceptable to Him. Jesus emphasized this, "But the hour cometh, and now is, when the true worshipers shall worship the Father in spirit and in truth: for the Father seeketh such to worship him. God is a Spirit: and they that worship him must worship him in spirit and in truth" (John 4:23-24).

Paul emphasized the fact that we have not truly worshiped until we have worshiped in the Spirit: "For we are the circumcision, which worship God in the spirit, and rejoice in Christ Jesus, and have no confidence in the flesh" (Philippians 3:3).

The *Amplified Bible* pictures this beautifully: "For we [Christians] are the true circumcision, who worship God in spirit and by the Spirit of God, and exult and glory and pride ourselves in Jesus Christ, and put no confidence or dependence [on what we are] in the flesh and on outward privileges and physical advantages and external appearances." Paul explains in 1 Corinthians 12:3, "No man can say that Jesus is Lord, but by the Holy Ghost."

It is essential to us as true believers that we come by the "Spirit into the temple," for it is only then that we will see God and express true worship to the Trinity.

THE NEW DIMENSION OF DYNAMIC LIVING

The Holy Spirit gives another dimension to the believer's life. He not only gives power in prayer and a sweet anointing for worship and praise, but He also gives us power for witnessing and a worthy walk. Our witness for Christ is only effectual if it is in the power of the Holy Spirit.

Luke urges this truth upon us in his Gospel and the Acts story. Luke records Jesus' command: "And, behold, I send the promise of my Father upon you: but tarry ye in the city of Jerusalem, until ye be endued with power from on high" (Luke 24:49). The endowment with power was absolutely essential. The *Amplified Bible* states, "But remain in the city [Jerusalem] until you are clothed with power from on high."

In His closing words to His disciples before His ascension, Jesus encouraged His disciples with the promise of the power of the Holy Spirit for witnessing: "But you shall receive power —ability, efficiency and might—when the Holy Spirit has come upon you; and you shall be My witnesses in Jerusalem and in all Judea and Samaria and to the ends—the very bounds—of the earth" (Acts 1:8, *Amp.*).

Acts 8 is a beautiful example of the Holy Spirit directing and empowering a believer for soulwinning. It should be the cry of our hearts that the Holy Spirit would empower us and lead us in effective witnessing.

The Holy Spirit not only gives us power for our witness but He also gives us power for our walk before the Lord. In Galatians 5, this walk before the Lord is spelled out. The chapter deals with the believer and the practices of the flesh.

It is amazing how much is said about the Holy Spirit and His ministry in the life of the believer as he confronts the works of the flesh. The flesh and its power is very real. The only answer to real victory over the flesh is a "walk in the Spirit."

The works of the flesh are listed in Galatians 5:19-21. You do not have to go to the most worldly place to see all of these manifestations of the flesh life—just observe where you worship. There are people who attend worship regularly who are not free from these practices. As a pastor I see enmity, strife, jealousy, anger and selfishness in my own congregation. I know the only answer to the needs of people in my congregation who fall into these sins is a deeper cleansing and more intimate relationship with the Holy Spirit.

Hear Paul's explanation and counsel in this section of Galatians:

> But I say, walk and live habitually in the (Holy) Spirit—responsive to and controlled and guided by the Spirit; then you will certainly not gratify the cravings and desires of the flesh—of human nature without God. For the desires of the flesh are opposed to the (Holy) Spirit, and the [desires of the] Spirit are opposed to the flesh (Godless human nature); for these are antagonistic to each other—continually withstanding and in conflict with each other—so that you are not free but are prevented from doing what you desire to do. But if you are guided (led) by the (Holy) Spirit you are not subject to the Law.

> And those who belong to Christ Jesus, the Messiah, have crucified the flesh—the Godless human nature —with its appetites and desires. If we live by the (Holy) Spirit, let us also walk by the Spirit.—If by the (Holy) Spirit we have our life [in God], let us go forward walking in line, our conduct controlled by the Spirit (5:16-18; 24-25, Amp.).

It is only as we we walk in the Spirit that we can demonstrate this truth: "There is therefore now no condemnation to them which are in Christ Jesus, who walk not after the flesh, but after the Spirit. For the law of the Spirit of life in Christ Jesus hath made me free from the law of sin and death" (Romans 8:1, 2).

CONCLUSION

The Holy Spirit is indeed our Comforter and as we allow Him to perfect His work in our lives we will grow into true Christlikeness. Our prayer life will be strengthened and made effective. Our worship will be enriched as we gather with the believers to give praise to the Father. And last, we will be empowered and strengthened in our "inner man" to face the temptations of the flesh and reign victoriously over them.

Our prayer should be, "Come, Holy Spirit and fill this temple that I, empowered by Thy presence, may enter these new dimensions of prayer, worship, and victorious living."

THE MAN GOD USES

B. L. Kelley

SCRIPTURE: 1 Corinthians 1:22-29

INTRODUCTION

This text tells me what kind of a man God uses. It is evident that God's measuring rod is different than ours. He has the ability to look inside and see what we cannot see. Notice especially how many times the Apostle Paul uses the words "but God has chosen."

It is apparent that God does not choose men for their wisdom as men count wisdom, or at least wisdom from a human standpoint. God has chosen what the world calls foolish to shame the wise. God has chosen what the world counts poor and insignificant. He is the only One that can take what the world cannot see and put their strongest to flight. Verse 29 says, "that no flesh should glory in his presence." So there is no place for human pride in the presence of God. I am vitally interested in the kind of a man God uses.

A quick glance through history will reveal that the men God chose and used were different from the norm.

John Wesley, founder of the Methodist Church, was such a man. It is said of him that he rode 20 miles a day for 40 years; preached 40,000 sermons; wrote 400 books. In those early days of John Wesley's ministry, one man wrote that he seemed to pray all the time.

There is a story told about Wesley that gives the impact of his ministry. An English nobleman traveling through the countryside in England stopped to ask a peasant, "Why is it that I can't find a place where I can buy a drink of liquor in this wretched village?" The peasant replied, "Well, you see, my lord, about a hundred years ago a man named John Wesley came preaching in these parts."

In the early days of the American frontier, the Methodist church had the foresight and devised a plan to reach the settlement on the edge of the wilderness. They started what is called the "circuit-riding preacher." The circuit rider normally had a swaybacked horse given to him by a farmer. His library consisted of a Bible, hymnbook, and the Methodist discipline. One writer said that the preachers in that day had only one text and it never grew stale: "Behold the Lamb of God that taketh away the sins of the world."

Peter Cartright was described in Clarence Edward McCartney's book, *Sons of Thunder—Pulpit Powers of the Past*, as rough, masculine, courageous and crude, but at the same time gentle, kind, humble and considerate toward the men and women to whom he preached. William Warren Sweet, a historian, said that "the old pioneers wanted a preacher that could mount a stump, a block or an old log, or stand in the bed of a wagon without notes or manuscript; quote, expound, and apply the Word of God to the heart and conscience of the people." Such a man was Peter Cartright.

It was a custom in those days that when night would fall they would stop and build a campfire to spend the night. Peter Cartright was traveling the Cumberland Mountains when he came upon a small community, and in one of the lodgings there was a dance. He went inside and as he stood there, a young lady asked him if he would like to dance. The whole company seemed pleased at the act of politeness of the young lady shown to a stranger. He took hold of her hand, went over to the fiddle player and said, "For several years I have not undertaken any matter of importance without first asking the blessings of God upon it." Then Peter Cartright knelt there on the floor and began to pray. He said, "You ought to have seen the consternation which at first seized this young lady when she realized what I was doing." She tried to get away but he held her tight. It wasn't very long until tears found their way down her cheeks and others also began to pray. This broke up the dance that night and a Methodist church was started in that community with 32 members—all because one man dared to be used by God.

It is said of D. L. Moody that he was preaching in the Fifth Avenue Church in New York City. The people of this cultural, refined, and sophisticated church were on the edge of their seat when Moody began to preach. He called Daniel "Dannal" and Gideon "Gedgen" and he pronounced *Jerusalem* in two syllables, but the writer said that he had not gone far in his sermon till they were sitting on the edge of their seats in waiting expectancy. Vance Havner summed it up in one sermon, that D. L. Moody had what made the difference—he dared to be used by God.

FIRST, GOD USES A MAN WHO IS NOT AFRAID

There is a fear that is good and the Bible speaks of this kind of fear many times (Deuteronomy 6:13-15; Matthew 10:28). But there is a fear that brings torment and causes one to pull away from obedience to God: "The fear of man bringeth a snare" (Proverbs 29:25). Everyone who has ever been used by God has had to conquer his fear of man and his fear of failure.

In 1 Samuel 17 we find the most unusual story of a young shepherd boy, probably in his mid-teens, who stood up to the giant Goliath, while all the armies of Israel hid in their tents afraid to show their faces. David had been sent there by Jesse, his father, to bring some parched corn and bread to his brothers who were with the army. As David brought the food to his brothers, the giant Goliath began to call insults to Israel. The Bible says that when the men of Israel saw the giant, they fled from him and were sore afraid.

But David said, "What shall be done to the man that killeth this Philistine, and taketh away the reproach from Israel?" David's older brother, Eliab, heard what David had said and with a sneer said, "Why camest thou down hither? and with whom hast thou left those few sheep in the wilderness? I know thy pride, and the naughtiness of thine heart; for thou

102

art come down that thou mightest see the battle" (1 Samuel 17:26, 28). David never let the accusation of his brother, nor the size of the giant, scare him. There are three reasons why David was not afraid:

1. David had spiritual insight. "Is there not a cause?" (1 Samuel 17:29). He had the spiritual insight to see that there was something greater going on there than just a giant. He detected that it was a struggle between good and evil, and that God needed a champion. David had the spiritual vision to see what needed to be done.

It is easy, in these turbulent days, to lose your spiritual vision; to be caught looking at the problem and the difficulty and not at the magnificent size of our Savior's power. In Revelation 3:18, the Lord said to the church at Laodicea, "Anoint thine eyes with eyesalve, that thou mayest see." It appears that many in the church need their eyes anointed so they may have a spiritual vision.

2. David had spiritual hindsight (1 Samuel 17:34, 35). He tells the story that while he was watching his father's sheep, there came a lion and a bear and they took a lamb out of the flock. David said, "I went out after him, and smote him, and delivered it out of his mouth: and when he arose against me, I caught him by his beard, and smote him, and slew him."

The giant Goliaths of this world have killed a lot of God's saints because they never learned how to handle the lions and the bears in their own lives. David learned what it was like to live a victorious life when no one was around and nobody was watching. When it came time for him to defend Israel, he was prepared.

3. David had spiritual foresight. He had the spiritual foresight not to try to use Saul's armor. That was not God's way for David. His trusty old slingshot that had served him well when defending his sheep would be sufficient for this task as well. He picked up five smooth stones, and while the Philistine, Goliath, looked upon David with disdain, he said, "Am I a dog, that thou comest to me with staves?" The Philistine cursed David by his gods. He said, "[you] come to me, and I will give thy flesh to the fowls of the air and to the beasts of the field. Then said David to the Philistine, Thou comest to me with a sword, and with a spear, and with a shield: but I come to thee in the name of the Lord of

hosts, the God of the armies of Israel, whom thou hast defied. This day will the Lord deliver thee into mine hand" (1 Samuel 17:42-45). And, indeed it happened! God uses a man who is not afraid of the devil's boasting.

SECOND, GOD USES A MAN WHO GIVES HIS ALL

God is looking for those who will be totally committed to Him. In John, chapter 6, the story is told that Jesus had gone over the Sea of Galilee and a great multitude followed Him because they saw the miracles that He did, and there were many there that needed help. Jesus went into the mountain and sat with His disciples, and when He lifted His eyes He saw a great company coming to Him. He knew they had been a long time in that region and needed nourishment. Jesus said to Philip, "Whence shall we buy bread, that these may eat?" He said this to prove him, for He himself knew what He would do. Philip answered Him, "Two hundred pennyworth of bread is not sufficient for them, that every one of them may take a little" (v. 5-7).

It is so easy to look at a problem and at our human supply and say that what we have is not sufficient to meet the need. There was a little boy there that Andrew, Simon Peter's brother, brought to the Lord. It is not uncommon for men to want recognition; to sit on the platform; to be seen of men; but Andrew was one of those persons that mingled with the crowd and found a young lad who had brought a small lunch with him. Certainly what he had was not enough for a crowd. But Andrew brought the little boy to the Lord.

Jesus took the five loaves and two small fish and blessed it and began to break it. He gave it to the disciples and each one of them distributed it to the multitude. When they got through, there were 12 basket fulls left.

Sometimes the Lord wants to bless us but cannot because we are still withholding part of ourself from Him. "Give and it shall be given unto you; good measure, pressed down, and shaken together, and running over, shall men give into your bosom. For with the same measure you mete withal it shall be measured to you again" (Luke 6:38). The reason God does not bless some people is because their measuring rod in giving to God is too little and too short. The Bible says that the Lord will bless in direct proportion to your gift.

104

It is this preacher's opinion that Jesus gave the remaining fragments to the little boy as a reward for what God had done for him. Someone asked me, "How do you know when you have given your all?" My answer is simple: When you have nothing left, when you can truly say that everything that you possess belongs to God, you have given your all. There are no secret corners of your heart that you are reserving for yourself. You open yourself up to Him when you say "It is Yours Lord—all is Yours."

THIRD, GOD USES A MAN WHO DOESN'T KNOW WHEN TO QUIT

One of the most interesting stories in the life of Israel is when they crossed over the Jordan and immediately ran up against the walled city of Jericho. It has been documented that four chariots could run abreast on top of the wall.

Israel was not prepared to knock the wall down, much less defeat Jericho. But Joshua got a word from the Lord to tell the people to start marching and to march once each day and seven times on Sunday. "Seven priests shall bear before the ark seven trumpets of rams' horns: and the seventh day ye shall compass the city seven times, and the priests shall blow with the trumpets. And it shall come to pass, that when they make a long blast with the ram's horn, and when ye hear the sound of the trumpet, all the people shall shout with a great shout; and the wall of the city shall fall down flat, and the people shall ascend every man straight before him" (Joshua 6:4, 5).

It is not hard to imagine that the people of Jericho found it amusing to see this host of people marching around the wall day after day. You can almost hear the laughter, "What do they think they are going to do—choke us to death with the dust from their trampling feet?" It is easy for us to want victory when we have only done half a job. We have only marched half the required amount. But we must march all the way if we are going to gain the victory.

A pastor tells of a lady who came to church one Sunday morning and told him that God had saved her husband the previous night. As he began to rejoice with her he thought, *What a miracle. Her husband was one of the meanest men I have ever met.*

The lady indicated that she and her husband had already gone to bed when she felt the bed shaking. She turned over and asked what was wrong. With tears dripping off on the pillow, he said he had been talking to the Lord. "Pastor, I never even got out of bed. I prayed him through right there."

The pastor asked her, "How long have you been marching around that wall? How long have you been believing for your husband?" He had been her pastor for a number of years. He knew that her husband had gone out on her, had broken the marriage vow, and had abused her. The lady indicated that for 20 years she had been believing God for his salvation. She had been coming to church alone and bringing her children, but that night the wall came down. I tell you, you will never get the wall down if you quit marching.

CONCLUSION:

A minister who served as state youth director in California, found the caretaker of the camp rather hard to get along with. Finally, one day he made a friend out of him and the caretaker shook his hand and said, "I want to thank you Pentecostals for keeping the 'amen' in religion." He had never been thanked for that, but for Pentecostals everywhere he said, "Thank you.'" The caretaker said, "You know what is wrong with our church?" Well, the minister had a pretty good idea but he wanted to hear what the caretaker had to say. He said, "We know how to march around the walls, we know how to line the priests up, we know how to play the ram's horn, we know how many times to march, but we are not getting many walls down today." Of course this struck the minister's interest and he asked why. He said, "Because we have forgotten how to shout." Then the minister remembered the words of the Lord to the children of Israel, when He said, "After you have completed 13 laps, then let the ram's horn trumpets sound and shout with a great shout, for the Lord has given you the city" (*paraphrased*).

The interesting thing is that the ram's horn and trumpet signal victory. The people shouted, but as yet, the walls were still standing. However, it was only after the Israelites began to rejoice at the victory that the collapse of the wall actually became a reality. So, don't give up, keep on marching. Heaven is near.

106

RENEWAL OF RELATIONSHIPS

Kenneth Hall

SCRIPTURE: 2 Chronicles 30:1-5, 11-13, 26

INTRODUCTION

The passage this text is taken from deals with a young man by the name of Hezekiah. Hezekiah was 25 years old when he was anointed king of Israel. Hezekiah did not inherit a kingdom that was free of problems. Financially, his rule was sound; politically, his rule was sound; it even had solidness in its relationship with the enemy countries that it had been at odds with. The reason why Israel had such a good relationship with their enemies or the alien countries was the same reason that Israel was in such poor shape spiritually.

Hezekiah's father, Ahaz, was a man who had turned his back on the spiritual needs of Israel. First of all, Ahaz had decided that the temple worship was not really needful any longer. He had closed the Temple down; he had taken all the sacred artifacts from the Temple and given them away to the Assyrian kings as presents to enhance his relationships. Not only had he closed down the Temple but Ahaz had decided there was no need for the Passover, the covenant meal of God's people. He had allowed the people to observe the Passover in just any way they pleased or not even to observe it at all.

He had just quietly led God's people away from their commitment to Jehovah God and their recognition of their dependence upon Him.

When Hezekiah became king, he looked at the total situation of Israel and diagnosed the need specifically. He looked at Israel and said, "We must return to our God."

When we consider renewal, we must look at ourselves and make sure our relationship with our God is more important than anything else. In fact, many people struggle with the acceptance of a renewal of relationship. They struggle with renewal because renewal is many times the product of change.

Change is difficult. People find it hard to change and move toward God and really find renewal for their souls. If you read in the Gospels (Matthew 9, Luke 7, Mark 2), you will find where Jesus spoke of renewal. Speaking of the traditions of the Pharisees and of the new Kingdom, Jesus said you can't put new wine into old wine skins. The old wine skins have no elasticity. With the fermentation process they will burst and ruin the new wine.

When we look at renewal, we must be flexible and we must be ready for change. We must be softened to the Spirit to know what is going on today, and we must be willing to receive what God has for us now. The Jewish people had found if they would bathe those wine skins in olive oil many of them would soften and could be reused. In fact, when the skins became very stiff, they would sometimes place them in a hot oil vat for days, letting them soak until they became soft, flexible, and pliable so they could be used for new wine.

That is what God is trying to say to us today—it is time to let the oil of the Holy Spirit soften us and let the touch of the Spirit give us what we need to be flexible and pliable for the spiritual renewal God is wanting to give His people.

Hezekiah had a design for renewal. A very specific design and that is what we want to study about in this sermon.

GOD'S HOUSE OF WORSHIP

The first thing Hezekiah did was to redefine the temple purpose. He sent the priest to the Temple with instructions that it be cleaned and made ready for worship. The second thing he did was to gather the people and sanctify the Temple.

They could not keep the peace of Passover because the Word said the priests had not sanctified themselves sufficiently. They were not ready for renewal. Until they were fully cleansed and purged, they were not ready to redefine their purpose and reunite themselves with the meeting place of God. We too must understand there can be no renewal without cleansing, without a new purging; no renewal until we are washed clean and sanctified holy through the blood of Jesus Christ—made to be totally His.

Not only did he cleanse the Temple, he also made the priests sanctify themselves sufficiently. The Word of God says "when he brought the people to the temple he sanctified them." He took the seven rams, seven lambs, seven bulls, and seven he-goats and he gave an offering of sacrifice so that the people could be cleansed and be made ready for renewal. Not only did he cleanse the people but he changed their attitudes toward their God.

Here, all of a sudden, Hezekiah is telling us it is time to recognize God as our source, God as our strength, God as our power, God is all we need. With this message, he says the first thing we are going to do is to praise God with an offering. The order of the day is to give an offering of praise and thanksgiving.

This is typical of renewal. When God's people are renewed, the first thing is to realign themselves with the purpose of the Temple. The Temple is the meeting place of God, the dwelling place of God, where God meets His people and we come face to face with Him. The Temple is a place of healing, a place of restoration, a place of strength, a place of power. It is a place where we go to God and give ourselves as a sacrifice unto Him, where we lay ourselves on the altar and are cleansed and made ready for service.

An attitude change is the primary factor. Many of us struggle with our attitude. We need a renewal of our attitude that is godly and that begins with thanksgiving and praise, one that recognizes God as source and strength. With such an attitude, renewal will be ours.

GOD'S COVENANT WITH HIS PEOPLE

The second thing Hezekiah did was to realign the people with their covenant. The Passover meal was the link to that covenant, the meal where they sat down with their families and commemorated their ancestors' miraculous deliverance from Egyptian bondage. All would eat the same meal, talking about the exile, reminding their children that Pharaoh said they were to be bound, but God said they were to be free.

The Passover meal was a symbol of the bondage God delivered them from and the freedom He led them toward in the Land of Promise. Because they lived in a Land of Promise, they were a people of promise. Because they were a people of promise, God had made for them a total provision.

God's total provision meant a cloud by day and a pillar of fire by night. It meant manna for food and water from a rock. It meant clothes that would not wear out and constant evidence of the presence and "watch care" of God.

The people in Hezekiah's day had forgotten this. Ahaz had destroyed the idea of their being God's people of promise. They had turned to materialism, to political structure, to allegiances with alien powers, to strange gods, and to a mixing of the blood line of Israel with heathen nations. They had tried in man's way to make peace with their enemies and God was reminding them one more time that He was the God of their provision. He is Jehovah, the one and only true God.

Today, we need realignment with our covenant, the one which begins at Calvary. Jesus is the source of our covenant. Satan couldn't stop Him. Death couldn't hold him. On the third morning He arose victoriously. Because He lives, so do we. We say with Paul, "Oh death, where is thy sting? Oh grave where is thy victory?"

In Christ we have a covenant greater than anything man could ever imagine. We do not lean on man's ingenuity but upon the eternal word: "Therefore, since we have a great high priest who has gone through the heavens, Jesus the Son of God, let us hold firmly to the faith we profess. For we do not have a high priest who is unable to sympathize with our weaknesses, but we have one who has been tempted in every way, just as we are—yet was without sin. Let us then approach the throne of grace with confidence, so that we may receive mercy and find grace to help us in our time of need" (Hebrews 4:14-16, *New International Version*).

Paul spoke of our covenant in these words "For you did not receive a spirit that makes you a slave again to fear, but you received the Spirit of sonship. And by him we cry "Abba, Father" (Romans 8:15, *NIV*). Thus we are His. We have a covenant with Him.

GOD'S PURPOSE FOR UNITY

The third thing Hezekiah did was to reunite the people with one purpose.

If there is any one thing God's people need today, it is unity of purpose. Satan has divided us and we have lost our direction. We have lost our thrust, our purpose. What happened with Israel in Hezekiah's day is expressed in these words: "Also in Judah the hand of God was to give them one heart to do the commandment of the king and the princes, by the word of the Lord" (2 Chronicles 30:12).

When I think of this "one heart," I am reminded of "When the day of Pentecost was fully come, they were all with one accord and in one place" (Acts 2:1). If we are going to be Pentecostal, we are going to have to have unity.

One man said that too many churches are frozen together instead of melted together by the fire of God. We need to have a oneness of God with a unity of purpose and vision, so Satan cannot destroy us, divide us, or defeat us. We are one in God; and in that unity we find purpose, we find strength, we find power and hope. In that unity we find the heart of God—one Body and one spirit.

GOD'S PLAN FOR WORSHIP

The fourth thing Hezekiah did for renewal was to realign the people with their worship. The Word says, "There was great joy in Jerusalem" (v. 26).

The key word here is *celebration*, (worship, praise, joy). We need a new celebration in our midst. In some places our worship means little more than going through the same old ritual we have been going through for years. We have learned how to sing, how to conduct our services, but our worship is no longer exciting and vibrant with the presence of God.

The psalmist wrote, "Lift your hands in the sanctuary, and bless the Lord" (Psalms 134:2). Bless ye the Lord of Zion who has made the heavens and the earth. Worship should be an exciting time.

When Hezekiah got ready to worship, he called on his Levite trumpet choir made up of over 300 people. As the people came to the Temple with their praise and thanksgiving offerings, all the choirs began to sing praises unto God and it absolutely charged the atmosphere. There was great joy in Jerusalem.

Today, there needs to be great joy in our churches, in our homes, in our lives; and the only way for joy to abound is when we let our celebration begin as a spirit of praise. Because He is God, He is our Source, He is our Strength, we have aligned ourselves with our covenant and we have been touched by His Spirit. David asked, "Wilt thou not revive us again: that thy people may rejoice in thee?" (Psalms 85:6). He was saying there has to be a renewal, there has to be a revival before there can be rejoicing.

The rejoicing and the revival follow the work of renewal. When we renew ourselves and our relationship with God, then once again we become the true people of God.

EXAMINE YOUR HEART

J. Dwight Burchett

INTRODUCTION

God wants all of us to look at ourselves and evaluate our hearts. After the spirit of conviction falls upon the church, it will be released by repentance. When there is repentance in the heart of the people, then there is great rejoicing and a lifting of the oppressive feeling in the congregation. Sometimes it is not necessarily pleasant to look at ourselves like we ought. Sometimes I don't like to see myself as God wants me to.

FORM OF GODLINESS

God gives us the picture of some people who exist in the last days (2 Timothy 3:1-10). Now let's look at some of the phrases: "Holding to a form of godliness," "although they had denied His power," and "always learning and never able to come to the knowledge of the truth." Then he says, "Avoid such men."

What does it mean to have a form of godliness. The word here is from *morphe*, which means "to have a form of godliness." This word is used over and over again in the New Testament, illustrating Jesus being in the form of God or Jesus being God. Morphe says that we are godlike, or we are in the image of God.

Now the derivative of *morphe* is used in verse 5 which is *morphosis*. That word means "an outward semblance or image of God"—not godlike, not part of the God person, not the God person but the image . . . in the semblance of God, but not godly. This implies a group of people that have the form of godliness, but there is no godliness within them.

Another word is *hypocrite*. The Bible says in verse 10, "You know My doctrines, Timothy. Not only do you know but those that you have ministered to know the teaching of the Word. As far as the world is concerned, they have a form of godliness. But nobody knows what's taking place on the inside of them."

Remember the king who had the gold vessels, the swords, the shields, the vials in the temple of the Lord? They were made of gold but the enemy came and took them, so the king made shields of brass and hung them in their place. Those new shields were not gold, they were counterfeit—a semblance of what it should be.

There are those here that know how to do godly things perfectly. There are some that have a form of godliness but are denying the power thereof. You are not letting God purify your hearts. You are playing games with God. On the inside you are dirty.

God gives a clear warning to such people. It is not just a formal confession. It is not just a religious deed. If we're just going to adopt a religious creed, let's go out and join some good social order and be religious about it. God said, "I'm calling you to holiness, to dedication, and surrender. Know that I am your God. I'm calling you to a heartfelt experience in Me. Quit playing with Me."

He said in the last days there is going to be a falling away. He adds that many will be outwardly rebellious, ungrateful, unholy. God is just as concerned about the man who looks godly on the outside but inside he's full of dead men's bones —vile, unkempt, unholy.

Nobody knows your backslidings as well as you. Nobody! Nobody knows the throes of indecision you're in at this moment. Even as you hear there may be a churning taking place on the inside because you say, "Well, the preacher doesn't know about me." "My wife doesn't know about me."

But you know about yourself and that's who God is talking to. He says, "Quit putting on a sham and playing the hypocrite." Get right with Him, get happy with Him, get in tune with Him.

PLAYERS IN THE GAME OF LIFE

Let's note these words:

> But whereunto shall I liken this generation? It is like unto children sitting in the markets, and calling unto their fellows, And saying, we have piped unto you, and ye have not danced; we have mourned unto you, and ye have not lamented. For John came neither eating nor drinking, and they say, He hath a devil. The Son of man came eating and drinking, and they say, Behold a man gluttonous, and a winebibber, a friend of publicans and sinners. But wisdom is justified of her children" (Matthew 11:16-19).

When I first studied that passage I thought God was saying they are playing in the market and have no time for God. That's not what He's saying at all.

Jesus has just gotten through talking about John the Baptist. What did you go out to see? A man dressed in soft clothing? Of course not. Those who wear soft clothing are in kings' palaces. They don't wear camel's hair. They don't eat locust and wild honey. When they went out to see this man, they went to see a man just as rugged, just as bold, just as courageous as any who ever lived.

Jesus then goes on to say that John the Baptist is least in the kingdom. Jesus compares this generation to children playing in the market place, who blow flutes, who play horns, who give invitations, but who won't take time for reality. They are too busy playing. They don't have time to look at the seriousness of their soul's worth. They don't have time for anything except for doing what they want.

They were "copping out"—a good expression of our day. We've got a lot of people "copping out." They don't want to get involved. They refuse to take part. They refuse everything Jesus offers.

The battle is not between you and the preacher, or you and your neighbor, or you and your parents. The battle is between you and the Lord. What are you going to do with Him? Invitations come. God pours out the supernatural so He can invite His people in. Some people won't even come with the supernatural, with the gifts of blessing that God extends to them.

A few generations ago, in the 1960s, we had the beatniks and all the others that were dropping out on life, pretending the world didn't exist. We still have to deal with reality. Christianity is the most important business in the world, and we can't ignore it. We are like people playing games—we don't want anybody to know what hand we are holding. The rules are keep your face somber, don't show emotion; nobody will ever know.

Scripture condemns any action of men seeking to justify their own acts of darkness. That's what this means. God laid His hand upon us and we must obey Him.

STRONG DELUSION

Don't be duped. Don't fall into delusion. Don't fall prey to some lying spirit that will destroy you. Satan has signs and false wonders that are contrary to God's signs and God's wonders; but you don't have to substitute and you don't have to fake it. There are genuine miracles for those who pay the price.

Some of you have a form of godliness but deny the power thereof, and it has hindered your growth. Or you may be like a child in the marketplace who has failed to comprehend that you live in a real world and that there's a real God Who is confronting you about your sins.

Delusion means mental strain; wrong opinion, error in morals or religion. It means deception. We sometimes comfort ourselves with the assurance that we are as good as someone else, but it is not a matter of whether we're as good as someone else. The question is one of righteousness in the sight of God. Have we surrendered our life to Him? We have too much of weighing ourselves with somebody else. Is God pleased with us? Ultimately, the spirit of delusion leads to reprobation (not knowing right from wrong).

A lot of people do not know right from wrong because they have erred from the Bible. They have listened to what this preacher says and what that preacher says, but they need to get back to the Word of God and start living according to what He says.

In 1 Kings 13 we have the story of what I'm talking about. God spoke to a prophet. The kingdoms were divided; the northern kingdom had built an altar in Bethel and was offering sacrifices on the altar there. God spoke to a prophet from Judah and told him to go up and preach the judgments of God. "When you go," God said, "don't turn to the right hand or the left. Go straight up there and preach what I've given you to preach. When you get through preaching, return to Jerusalem. Don't talk to anybody, don't go home with anybody, don't stop for anything."

The young preacher went up. He preached the message. Miracles were performed and the king invited him to go home with him. He said, "No, the Lord has commanded me not to go to anybody's home but to return back home as soon as the message is delivered."

The king understood and supposedly repented.

The young man had done everything like God had told him. Two sons of an old backslidden prophet, who had been at the meeting that day and had seen what God had done, took the message back home. In the old prophet there was a stirring. He thought, *If I could just have a little bit of time to talk to this young prophet.*

The old prophet went after the young prophet, found him under an oak, and invited him home. The young man told him what God said, but the old prophet told him an angel had canceled the former assignment and the Lord now said to come home with him.

Rather than listening to the voice of God, the young prophet listened to the alluring voice of an old backslidden prophet. The young man turned on his way, and he went back to the old prophet's house, contrary to the voice of God that had spoken to him in the spirit.

They sat down at the meal. I can just hear that old prophet begin to reminisce about the good old days—how God used to bless and how the power of God used to fall and how it's so different from today. In the midst of conversation, the voice of God rose up out of his spirit and he pointed his finger and spoke a prophetic word to that young prophet. "Because you did not obey God, on your road home today a lion is going to come out and kill you."

It wasn't a very popular word. The young man arose and went on his way and sure enough a lion jumped out and killed him. The old prophet heard about the young prophet that was killed and went and buried his body.

How many of you know that in hell there are going to be old preachers, young preachers, losing preachers, lying preachers right there with other people who have listened to the wrong message? I'm here to bring conviction if I possibly can. Under the power of God you'll repent and come back to God and do your first works over.

Some of you are building on quicksand. I don't know what God is saying to you right now, but you're building on superficial things. God knows your heart and you have a spirit of delusion. Jesus is the only way. Men will say, "This is the way, walk ye in it." They take you another way rather than through Jesus and through the blood. There are those who are saying, "This is an easier way." But there is only one way: that's God's way—holiness, righteousness, truth and peace.

CONCLUSION

The Bible says, "Judgment must begin in the house of God." Strong evaluation must begin right here today. One of the things that's confounding the world today is that they look at the church and the church is no different than the world. Our lives should be full of joy and peace. Our lives should be entering into a full dimension of glory, and they will when we truly know God.

You have to be honest with yourself and with God. If you repent, God will forgive. He says, "Whosoever will, let him come."

RUNNING OUT

Robert Frazier

SCRIPTURE: Galatians 5, 7

INTRODUCTION

Certain Judaizers were teaching that circumcision was necessary for salvation and were demanding observation of certain laws of Moses (Galatians 1:7; 5:10, 12; 6:12, 13). Paul rises to the challenge and offers an impassioned defense of the pure gospel and rejects attempts to "Judaize" Christianity. Paul levels the charge in the text against the Galatian Christians intending to bring them "back on track." Let's take a closer look.

"Ye did run well." Taken at face value, this statement was not intended sarcastically, but was meant to be complimentary. They had previously done a good job of following the prescribed track as outlined by Paul. An ancient account of the runner Pheidippides will help us to appreciate what the human body can do when it comes to running.

When the Persian fleet approached the plains of Marathon in 490 B.C., the Athenian Pheidippides set out for Sparta in quest of military aid. Despite the summer heat, he traveled 150 miles of mountain roads in 48 hours at an average speed of 3 miles per hour. His oxygen consumption, work output, energy stores, water metabolism, and cardiovascular function were sufficient to sustain him on this journey. His brain was adequately supplied with blood, and upon arrival, he acted diplomatically as a suppliant and orator.

Although the Spartans agreed to meet their treaty obligations, they postponed their departure until the end of a summer festival at the full moon six days later. Somewhat disappointed, he jogged back to Athens and then on to Marathon, where he helped to defeat the Persians.

The Galatians had made a good start. But they were hindered. "Who did hinder you?" Paul wants to know. The word *hinder* means "breaking up the road; placing an obstacle in the path." This same word is used in 1 Peter 3:7, "Likewise, ye husbands, dwell with them according to knowledge, giving honor unto the wife, as unto the weaker vessel, and as being heirs together of the grace of life; that your prayers be not *hindered*."

The prayers of a husband are hindered in getting through to God if he improperly regards his wife. On occasion, our good intentions encounter obstacles. Consider the fellow who was driving home from work listening to the radio announcer suggest that his listeners surprise their mates. "When you arrive home for dinner this evening," the announcer suggested, "instead of growling something like `When will dinner be ready?' why not surprise your wife with a little gift?"

The man thought that sounded like a good idea, so he stopped along the way for a bouquet of flowers and a box of candy. Instead of driving into the garage, he went to the front door and rang the bell.

His wife opened the door, saw him standing there wearing a radiant smile, holding out his gifts and declared crankily, "Listen, Buster, the baby has colic. The washing machine has broken down. Junior and another boy got into a fight today at school and were expelled. And now, as I might have expected, you make my day perfect by coming home drunk!"

It's possible that some of the greatest hindrances we encounter are from people with whom we are the closest. The Judaizers causing the most trouble were not monsters from another country, but people with whom they were familiar. Let's take a closer look at some specific hindrances to successfully running this Christian life.

HINDRANCES TO RUNNING

The first hindrance to be highlighted would be referred to as "running out of track," or failing to properly judge the race. This problem is beautifully illustrated in the following story by a father, writing in Issue One, *Evangelism* (Nashville Tidings, 1970).

> One day, a couple of years ago, I picked up one of my sons who was fourteen and competing in a track meet. As any busy father, I wasn't there, but probably should have been, when he ran the race. But I was there to pick him up.
>
> As he came out of the gate, I could see he hadn't won. You can tell the difference between a winner and a loser. That morning he had left, saying, "Daddy, I feel great. I had a good night's sleep, I'm on training and I'll really do well today."
>
> He normally doesn't do very well in track. I think he has won two races in ten years. And that day as he came to the car I could see that it hadn't gone well, so I thought we would get it over with and said, "Son, how did you do?"
>
> "The worst I have ever done. You see, Daddy, it's like this, I run the 330 and in the Junior High School where I go we train on a 330-yard track. Here today the 330-yard race was staked out on a 440-yard course. I misjudged the length of the race. I started off easy, saving myself. I started running real hard too late. The race was over too quick, and when the race was over, I had too much left. I hadn't used all I had."

It's not enough to be physically conditioned. We must keep our heads in the race as well. Paul wrote in Galatians 3:1, "O foolish Galatians, who hath bewitched you, that ye should not obey the truth?"

Just as the emotions of a cheering crowd generate a surge of adrenalin in runners, so can an emotional service and encouragement from fellow Christians give us strength for the short term. Yet, there must be more of a commitment to the Lord than that.

It has been said "The man who wants to lead the orchestra must turn his back on the crowd." In short, let's individually purpose to fully serve the Lord now, not saving ourselves for some future emotional burst of Christian service. Let's not "run out of track" by saving ourselves for later, only to have the Lord appear and interrupt all our good intentions.

Another hindrance to Christian service is "running out of gas." We can misjudge our own level of endurance. The writer of Hebrews 12:1 said it best—"Let us run with patience." The Christian's race is not a sprint, but a marathon. Learn to see yourself as working for Christ years in the future. William Cary's life is a wonderful encouragement here. To quote his own words:

> If, after my removal, any one should think it worth his while to write my life, I will give you a criterion by which you may judge of its correctness. If he give me credit for being a plodder, he will describe me justly. Anything beyond this will be too much. I can plod. I can persevere in any definite pursuit. To this I owe everything.

A final hindrance is what I would term, "running out of heart." In the final analysis, form and running technique must take a back seat to heart and desire. In Christian terms, can it be said that you prefer to serve the Lord above all else? Or does the following poem illustrate your true feelings?

> I'll go where You want me to go, dear Lord;
>   Real service is what I desire;
>
> I'll say what You want me to say, dear Lord—
>   But don't ask me to sing in the choir,
>
> I'll say what You want me to say, dear Lord—
>   I like to see things come to pass:
>
> But don't ask me to teach girls and boys, dear Lord
>   I'd rather just stay in my class.
>
> I'll do what You want me to do, dear Lord;
>   I yearn for the Kingdom to thrive;
>
> I'll give you my nickels and dimes dear Lord—
>   But please don't ask me to tithe.

122

I'll go where You want me to go, dear Lord;
I'll say what You want me to say;

I'm busy just now with myself, dear Lord—
I'll help You some other day.

—Author Unknown

CONCLUSION

Have you gotten "off track" in your Christian walk? Isn't it time you got back on track with your spiritual training? Let's do it now.

HOW FAR WILL LOVE GO?

David M. Griffis

SCRIPTURE: 2 Samuel 21:1-4; 1 John 4:7-11

INTRODUCTION

It is said that "love makes the world go around." Love is the motivational force behind fulfillment in living. As the redeemed of the Lord, we know that our redemption was provided through love. Love is God's nature implanted in us. It shines the brightest, endures the longest, carries the most hope, and remains forever.

In this Scripture lesson an unknown, unsung woman of low estate illustrates the power and far-reaching influence of love in a beautiful way.

ISRAEL WAS UNDER GOD'S JUDGMENT

Famine, the worst of all natural disasters, had struck Israel for three years in a row. Although we expect judgment to come to others, only when it comes to us do we begin to understand what it means. Modern religionists refuse to talk of judgment and even label as fanatics those who declare it's existence. The Scripture declares, however, that "judgment must begin at the house of God" (1 Peter 4:17). Amos, the prophet, stated emphatically, "Let judgment run down as waters" (Amos 5:24)!

At this time David is king. But he is not dancing before the Lord with all his might. The women are not singing about him killing his "tens of thousands." The widows of Ashdod are not trembling at the sound of his trumpets. The remnant of Rabbah are not looking on him in awe as he enters their city. David, the man after God's own heart, is ruling over a nation in trouble.

Famine has parched the fields of Israel. Chariot wheels stir up more dust than at any time in memory. Grain has been scraped from the barren crevices of the storage silos. Hunger is a constant visitor. Even the animals have that exhausted, crazed look in their eyes. The sons and daughters of Abraham are in a stupor. "Where is the rain and abundance of Jehovah?" they cry.

But God's chosen king, the sweet Psalmist of Israel, turns in desperation to the Lord. Godly men always inquire of the Lord in a time of great need.

At Ai, when 36 of Israel's best men were slain, Joshua fell on his face and inquired of the Lord.

On the hill of Moreh, with the Midianites "as thick as grasshoppers" in the valley below, Gideon placed a fleece on the ground and cried to the Lord.

Samson, his eyes hollow and his enemies making sport of his utter hopelessness, looked up and inquired of the Lord, saying, "Lord, remember me."

Elisha's inquiry of the Lord at Dothan, when the host of Syria had him surrounded was for God to open the eyes of his young servant and show him the real circumstances.

Godly men always inquire of the Lord, for He is an unfailing source. And when good men inquire, God gives an answer.

GOD REVEALED THE INJUSTICE DONE TO THE GIBEONITES DURING THE REIGN OF SAUL.

He who sees the fall of a sparrow and clothes the lily in beauty has never allowed the innocent to suffer without vindication. The Gibeonites had dwelled peaceably in Canaan since the days of Joshua. In Joshua 9:15, Israel had made a treaty with them, although the Gibeonite's forefathers obtained the treaty through craftiness, wisdom, and foresight. They even agreed to become "carriers of water and hewers of wood" just for the privilege of dwelling peaceably with God's people.

Saul, however, in his zeal to impress Israel and re-establish some of his own popularity, conspired to destroy the Gibeonites. He and his sons committed war crimes against these innocent people (2 Samuel 21:2, 5).

When David heard of this injustice, he sought out the injured Gibeonite leaders and asked them what could be done to satisfy justice and stay the wrath of God. The Gibeonites asked not for silver or gold, nor any punishment against Israel. They did want the the guilty to be punished by men of their own nation.

This meant that Saul's seven sons would be hung in Saul's own territory, Gibeah. Only the lame Mephibosheth, Jonathan's son, was spared because of the oath between David and Jonathan. At the execution of these sons of Saul, we see one of the greatest acts of love in the pages of Holy Writ.

THE STORY OF RIZPAH IS ONE OF THE GREATEST LOVE STORIES EVER RECORDED

Rizpah had been the concubine of King Saul, and two of the men hanged in Gibeah that day were her sons. She had once dwelt in a palace, but now she is a pauper. She once had the attention of the King, but now she remains silent. Her spirits sink as the sentence is read. Her heart is shattered as the horses leap forward and the ropes grip tightly the necks of her sons. She had held them as chubby-fisted babies. She had watched them grow as stouthearted boys. Now this mother is helpless to help the sons she loves. What Rizpah does, however, defies belief.

Rizpah takes a piece of sackcloth and spreads it on a rock near the hanging tree. The bodies are cut down and left to decompose; they are denied a decent burial in order to set an example. For 150 days, from the beginning of barley harvest until rain fell from heaven, Rizpah guards the remains of those seven sons of Saul. Her ears listened every night for the footsteps of the jackal or some other scavenger. Her sun-burned face scans the heavens so she can scare away the vultures.

The bones of the seven bleached white in the sun. To stand guard was her gift of love. To do what she did staggers the imagination. Only love could provide this kind of motivation. Only love could forge this kind of determination. Only love could furnish this kind of resolution. Only love could go this far.

When the news of Rizpah's act reaches David, he sends for the bones of Jonathan and Saul. With their bones and the bones of the seven, they conduct a stately burial ceremony at Zelah, near the sepulcher of Kish, Saul's father, "After that God was entreated for the Land" (2 Samuel 21:14).

HOW FAR WILL LOVE GO?

Love made Abraham go after Lot. Lot deserved no such consideration. Choosing the well-watered plain, he left his Uncle Abraham on the rocky hillsides. His tent was pitched toward Sodom and his family became infected with its licentiousness. But when Lot was taken captive by the fierce kings of the plain, Abraham risked life and limb, along with 318 of his choice servants, to rescue the nephew he loved.

Love caused Paul to speak up, for the runaway slave, Onesimus. He told Philemon, Onesimus' Christian master, that if he owed anything "just charge that to my account." He had begotten Onesimus in the Lord while he himself was a prisoner. Love made him plead for Philemon's understanding.

Love made Stephen's face shine like that of an angel as he prayed for the forgiveness of his own executioners. Love could not be stopped by pelting stones or gnashing teeth or wicked men. Stephen, because of love, did not hesitate to plead with the Father of all mercies to go the extra mile of love.

Love will go the extra mile. Love gives both the coat and the cloak. Love turns the other cheek; it prays fervently for its enemies. Love causes you to do good to those who despitefully use you.

LOVE'S LONGEST JOURNEY TOOK IT TO CALVARY.

Love had never taken a trip like the one it took when the eternal Son of God, butchered and bleeding, ascended the hill of the skull. There He was poured out like water for a dying, sin-sickened humanity. Every clout of the hammer, reinforced Dad's love. Every drop of blood and every bead of sweat showed His unfathomable love. As a spear opened up His side, a fountain of love was opened up "into the House of David for sin and uncleanness."

But love did not end it's journey at Calvary. Love "led captivity captive and gave gifts unto men." On the third day, God did not leave his soul in hell nor suffer his Holy One to see corruption. The Spirit who loves us, quickened His mortal body and raised the Son of Righteousness from the dead. The songwriter, must have understood this when he lifted his pen and wrote:

> Could we with ink the ocean fill,/ And were the skies of parchment made;/ Were ev'ry stalk on earth a quill,/ And ev'ry man, a scribe by trade;/ To write the love of God above,/ Would drain the ocean dry;

> Nor could the scroll contain the whole,/ Tho' stretched from sky to sky.

Love goes farther, reaches higher, delves lower, and sings sweeter than anything else. Tongues will one day cease, and knowledge will vanish as the morning fog, but love never fails and will remain forever.

ON THE VERGE OF
A MIRACLE

Terry Hart

SCRIPTURE: *John 5:1-8*

INTRODUCTION

I would like for us to take a trip to the city of Jerusalem. People have come to Jerusalem from all around Palestine to celebrate the giving of the Law at Sinai. This celebration is the Feast of Pentecost. Excitement fills the air as people renew old acquaintances.

However, where we are going today is not an exciting place. We are headed to the pool of Bethesda, a spring-fed pool located on the northeast side of the city, by the sheep gate. *Bethesda* literally means "House of Mercy," but there is absolutely nothing merciful-looking about this place. This place is a pitiful scene of misery and heartache.

Crammed all around this pool is a great multitude of impotent, blind, halt, and withered people who are just waiting for a miracle to happen. They are just waiting for the angel to come by and stir the water, so they can jump in and be healed. Some have been waiting for days, some for months, and some even for years.

In the midst of this great multitude of sick individuals, we spot a crippled man who has been waiting for his miracle for 38 long years. Little does he realize that today his waiting will be over—today he will walk again! He will meet Christ, the Great Physician, who specializes in the hopeless and the helpless—who forgives sins and heals the sick.

In this passage of Scripture, we see described for us a perfect picture of today's world—lost, spiritually sick, dying in sin, unable to help itself out of this dilemma. Let's examine four significant truths about this man's situation at the pool of Bethesda.

THIS WORLD IS FILLED WITH PEOPLE WHO ARE AFFLICTED BY SIN AND THEY CANNOT SAVE THEMSELVES.

There was a great multitude of afflicted people waiting by this pool for the miraculous moving of the water. Among them was this man who had been waiting for 38 years, on the verge of a miracle, but had never been healed. For 38 years he had been hoping and dreaming that a miracle would transpire in his life, and for 38 years he had been disappointed. That is a long time to wait. Thirty-eight years is about the average length of a man's productive life.

Each day he would sit and dream of the time when he would walk again. Then, he would awaken out of his dream and realize that it was no use. "I can never be healed. Even if the angel did stir the water today, someone would beat me to it. I'll never walk!"

For 38 years this man sat on the verge of the miraculous. He was separated from a miracle by only a step or two. So near and yet he was so far. He had become resigned to what he thought was his destiny in life. He was really just a spectator in life. He was utterly helpless to save himself!

Those lost in sin today find themselves in much the same situation this man was in. They are not physically crippled, but they are spiritually crippled by the effects of their sin. They are unable to lift themselves out of their situation. They wait idly by the pool of false hopes and dreams, hoping to find inner peace and eternal life, only to be disappointed time and time again! But just like this poor man, they finally give up in despair and resign to what they think is their fate in life.

JESUS ISSUES THE SAME CHALLENGE TODAY AS HE DID TO THIS MAN BY THE POOL OF BETHESDA.

Jesus said to this man, "Wilt thou be made whole?" In other words, "Do you want a whole life? Do you want to be healed?"

That's what Jesus says to those who are lost in sin, or to those who are in need today. "Do you want to be delivered from this crippling bondage of sin that has you bound? Do you want to be made whole?"

His invitation may be:

Come now, and let us reason together, saith the Lord: though your sins be as scarlet, they shall be white as snow; though they be red like crimson, they shall be as wool (Isaiah 1:18).

Or the words may be:

Behold, I stand at the door, and knock: if any man hear my voice, and open the door, I will come in to him, and will sup with him, and he with me (Revelation 3:20).

But always His words will be full of love and concern. He is a loving and merciful God.

However, many respond to Christ's challenge like this man —by offering excuses. First of all, he said, "Sir, I have no man, when the water is troubled, to put me into the pool." He could not walk, so when the pool was stirred by the angel, no one bothered to help him get into the pool. They were probably all too busy trying to get in themselves. They were probably too busy trying to get a blessing to help him receive a miracle from God. Many today are the same way.

Second, he said, "But while I am coming, another steppeth down before me." Not only did he lack friends who were concerned enough to help him get into the pool, but he was too slow as well. While he was struggling to drag his body into the water, someone else who was not invalid or lame would outrun him to the water. They would receive the blessing, and he would receive nothing! But, what he was actually doing was blaming others for his own condition.

So many people do the same thing today! They blame others for their crippled spiritual condition. They use others

131

as their excuse for not living for God. But laying the blame on someone else does not change the facts of the situation.

It was not that this man had lost his will to be healed, for he was still hanging around the pool, waiting. His problem was that he had not yet come to the right source of help! Man's most intense struggles can not save him from the crippling paralysis of sin! Jesus Christ was the only remedy for this man's situation, and He is the only remedy for this world's situation.

JESUS STILL DELIVERS THOSE WHO OBEY HIS COMMAND, JUST LIKE HE DELIVERED THIS MAN AT THE POOL OF BETHESDA.

Jesus brushed aside all of this man's excuses and issued a command which tested his faith: "Rise, take up thy bed, and walk."

No doubt, by this time, the attention of all around the pool of Bethesda was on Jesus and this poor man. Some probably laughed at this command. They probably thought, *If he only knew whom he was telling to get up and walk! Why, this man has been here longer than any of us, and he has never been healed.*

I do not believe it was by accident that Jesus chose this particular man out of all of the multitude around the pool. I believe He chose him because he was the most helpless case of all. Jesus specializes in the hopeless and the helpless!

The man could have made more excuses. He could have said, "Arise! That is exactly what I have been trying to do for 38 years! And, here you come along in one day and tell me to get up! Why, the water is not even stirred! Everyone knows that nothing is going to happen unless the water is stirred!"

But he did not make any more excuses. To the utter amazement of everyone else around the pool, he just stood, took up his bed, and walked away. Someone said, "He came with his back on his bed, but he left with his bed on his back."

Along with the command of Christ came the power to accomplish what He said! This man was not healed by his own power. All he did was obey. Christ supplied the power.

Though many respond to Christ's challenge today with excuses, Jesus brushes aside these excuses by revealing His victory over sin at Calvary. Then He issues a loving call, "Come unto me, all ye that labor and are heavy laden, and I will give you rest." If we obey His call, He will give us the power to overcome our circumstances.

THERE WILL ALWAYS BE THOSE WHO WILL TRY TO HINDER AND CRITICIZE ABSOLUTE FAITH IN CHRIST.

Almost immediately, the Jews began to criticize this man. They were not interested in the fact that he had been miraculously healed. They were not interested that he had found the Messiah. All they wanted was to criticize him. There will always be a Judas in the bunch who will want to criticize someone being ministered to by someone else.

CONCLUSION

After you receive salvation or healing from Christ, do not forget about those that are still waiting by the pool. Please do not fail to remember those who have also been crippled by the effects of sin. Do not forget those who are living on the verge of the miraculous—waiting for the stirring of the water. Point them to the Great Physician who can heal their broken hearts, regardless of the circumstances of life.

WALKING WITH GOD

J. Ralph Brewer

SCRIPTURE: Genesis 5:21-24

INTRODUCTION

According to medical authorities, walking is one of the most profitable forms of physical exercise. It stimulates the heart and lungs, strengthens the bones and muscles, increases the blood flow throughout the body, and reportedly contributes to the loss of excess weight. Because of its multiple values, Americans have been encouraged to leave their cars in the garage and participate more frequently in the exercise of walking.

A Television commercial sometime ago reminded us that "walking makes the good life better."

Did you know that the average pair of feet take 7000 to 8000 steps a day; about two and one-half million steps a year. It makes you tired, doesn't it? That means that in a lifetime, you will walk approximately 115,000 miles.

The first man to walk around the world was a man by the name of David Kunst of Waseca, Minnesota. He completed his historic walk on October 5, 1974, after walking 15,000 miles. The trip required four and one-half years, during which time

David went through 22 pairs of shoes and wore out two mules. At the completion of his historic journey, an auction was held with eager bidders paying $150 for his right shoe, $170 for his left shoe, and $140 for his remaining mule.

Most people find it neither appealing nor practical to be a David Kunst and accept the challenge to hike around the world. However, God wants us to understand that the Christian life is a walk—a journey which requires dedication, courage, and persistence. It calls for self-surrender, a fully yielded life, and an intense desire to please God rather than ourselves.

The spiritual walk of which the Bible speaks is a dynamic exercise of faith, and the successful completion of this walk is dependent not upon one's natural or physical resources but upon the strength, leadership, and controlling influence of the Holy Spirit.

Enoch is one of the most striking personalities of the Old Testament. He is one of but two men of whom it is said "he walked with God." He is one of but two men who lived on this earth and went to heaven without passing through the portals of death. He is the only one, except our blessed Lord, of whom it is written that "he pleased God." The reason for the remarkable qualities and successes of this man is recorded in Genesis 5:24: "He walked with God."

Let me suggest several things regarding this spiritual walk that I think are important:

FIRST, THIS IS A WALK WITH GOD.

Our text says, "Enoch walked with God." This is not an ordinary walk and you do not keep company with the ordinary. You are walking with God. However strange it may seem to our finite minds, it is possible, according to the Word of God, to live in the realm of the Spirit and walk in fellowship with the heavenly Father. Enoch's walk emphasizes an important relationship between humanity and divinity, between God and man, between that which is weak and limited, and that which is powerful and unlimited. Think of the high and holy privilege of walking with God. What an exciting thought that I can walk with God.

God—who clothes Himself with honor and majesty

135

God—who covers Himself with light as with a garment

God—who stretched out the heavens like a curtain

God—who laid the beams of His chambers in the waters

God—who makes the clouds His chariot

God—who walks upon the wings of the wind.

God—who makes His angels spirits and His ministers a flaming fire

God—who laid the foundation of the earth that it should not be removed forever

God—who sent the springs into the valleys

God—who gives the fowls of the heaven their habitation and causes them to sing among the branches

God—who waters the hills from His chambers

God—who causes the grass to grow for the the cattle and herb for the service of man that He may bring forth food out of the earth

God—who planted the cedars of Lebanon and provided the high hills as a refuge for the wild goats and the rocks for the conies

God—who appointed the moon its seasons and the sun its appointed time to go down (see Psalm 104).

You mean I can walk with a God like that? The answer is, Yes, you can. God said in Leviticus 26:3, "If you walk in my statutes and keep my commandments, and do them; I will walk among you and will be your God, and you shall be my people."

How can I, a mere mortal, a mere human being, walk with God?

We read 1 John 1:7, "If we walk in the light, as he is in the light, we have fellowship one with another, and the blood of Jesus Christ his Son cleanseth us from all sin." True fellowship with God and true fellowship with one another are made possible through and by Jesus Christ, God's Son.

The walk of which the Bible speaks means you have discovered the road of truth. The quest for truth is as old as the human race. Pilate was not the first man to ask, "What is truth?" Men of every generation have asked that question. The followers of Buddha have answered it by saying truth is following the teachings of Buddha. The disciples of Confucius have answered it by saying, truth is observing the teachings of Confucius. The devotees of the Prophet Mohammed have answered it by saying Allah is God and Mohammed is his prophet. But the voice of Jesus Christ speaks loud and clear above all others as he declares, "I am the Way, the Truth, and the Life. No man comes to God except by me."

Some people say, "Let's be broad-minded. All roads lead to heaven. You go your way and I'll go mine and we'll arrive at the same destination." But the truth reveals there is only one way to heaven. The Bible says it is a narrow way; it has a strait gate, and only a few will find it.

Others have said it doesn't really matter what you believe so long as you are sincere in believing it. But I beg to differ with such an opinion. Sincerity is commendable only so long as it is based on truth. I have no doubt that Adolph Hitler was a sincere man. He believed in what he was doing and sold a nation on it. Jim Jones with his cult in South America was sincere—but his sincerity could not be commended when he coaxed or forced nearly 1000 people to commit suicide in the name of religion. It does matter what you believe. Our faith must be based upon truth.

The psalmist says, "Teach me thy way, O Lord, I will walk in thy truth: unite my heart to fear thy name" (86:11).

SECOND, THIS WALK IS A WALK OF FAITH

The Bible says that Enoch had this testimony that "he pleased God" (Hebrews 11:5). How was Enoch able to please God? The writer of Hebrews tells us that "without faith it is impossible to please [God]" (11:6). Enoch could walk with God because he was a man of faith and placed his trust in God. God is a big God. He is the God of the maximum and not the minimum; the God of might and miracle. He is the God of unlimited power and He will reveal Himself to us if we will believe and trust Him. He will shake heaven and earth in order to reveal His glory and power to His people.

In 2 Corinthians 3:5 Paul says, "Not that we are sufficient of ourselves to think anything as of ourselves; but our sufficiency is of God." Paul never glories in the flesh, but ascribes the winning of life's battles to "Him that loved us."

1. Walking in faith means walking in power for God is power. His power is at work in us and through us and for us. This being true, our lives do not have to be sick and anemic, but we can be men and women of faith keenly aware of the adequacy of divine grace for every need. In Ephesians 1:19 Paul states, ". . . according to the working of his mighty power." Other phrases in his letters such as "the effectual working of his power" (Ephesians 3:7) and again "to Him that is of power to stablish you" (Romans 16:25)—these and fifty other passages give us authority to echo Paul's words, "Be strong in the Lord and in the power of his might."

2. Walking by faith also means growing in Christ. In Colossians 2:6, 7 we read, "As ye have therefore received Christ Jesus the Lord, so walk ye in him, Rooted and built up in him and stablished in the faith, as ye have been taught, abounding therein with thanksgiving."

In this one passage Paul talks about four elements of the Christian experience. Walking—Growing—Building—and Abounding.

Walking expresses Life.

Growing expresses an inner power.

Building up shows progress of character until God perfects His work in us.

And *abounding* reflects abundance of joy and proper attitude for the marvelous benefits that God gives to us along the way.

If you walk with God, you will grow in Christ. You will walk—grow—build, and abound.

The reason some people have so little joy in their Christian experience is that they are not following these four steps. As one preacher put it, some people sit, soak, and sour. But true life, the Christ-life, is a growing life. Our life must first be built downward, "rooted in Christ." Next we must build upward, "built up in him and established in the faith." Then abounding joy and thanksgiving are the results of this dynamic growth experience in our Lord Jesus Christ.

3. When we walk with God by faith, we will also experience intimate fellowship with Him. "What a fellowship, what a joy divine, Leaning on the everlasting arms . . . I have blessed peace, with my Lord so near, Leaning on the everlasting arms." We have discovered, as did Enoch, that walking and

living in the presence of God is an experience of blessed fellowship and sweet communion.

It is always a pleasant experience to walk with someone you love. Two young people who feel they have discovered the wonderful world of love stroll hand in hand together. A beautiful sight is an elderly couple who have been married for 40 or 50 years walking along hand in hand. God's love for us and our love for God is a relationship of beauty and blessedness.

There are some wonderful things that God, our walking companion, does for us as we put our trust in Him. I want to mention three. He guides us, He comforts us, and He protects us as we walk together.

First, He is our Guide. The psalmist wrote, "For this God is our God for ever and ever: he will be our guide even unto death" (48:14). That's a wonderful promise. Life can be a frustrating journey. It has many uncertain turns. I, for one, need a trusty guide and friend to show me the way. When you take a journey with a capable and trusted guide, you can leave your worries behind. He arranges the details of the journey. He knows the destination because he has been there before; all you have to do is go with him, listen to him, and follow his instructions.

Martin Luther once said, "I know not the way God leads me, but well do I know my Guide." He can always be trusted. Thank God our traveling companion is trustworthy—He knows the way, He knows the pitfalls, and He erases worry from our minds when we put the details of the journey in His hands.

Second, our walking companion also gives us comfort and and strength for each traveling day. The Bible says in Deuteronomy 33:25, "As thy days, so shall thy strength be." These words were part of a blessing Moses pronounced upon the tribe of Asher, but they stand as a testimony of God's faithfulness to all His people. We sometimes wonder if the demands of life will be too heavy for the circuits? Will we make it? But the answer of the Word of God is, "As your days may demand, so shall your strength be." God has promised that when you walk, you will never walk alone. He is with you. He reminds us, "They that wait upon the Lord shall renew their strength; they shall mount up with wings as eagles;

they shall run and not be weary; and they shall walk, and not faint" (Isaiah 40:31).

Third, our walking companion also protects us on our journey. The psalmist declares, "The Lord is my rock, and my fortress, and my deliverer; my God, my strength, in whom I will trust; my buckler, and the horn of my salvation, and my high tower. I will call upon the Lord, who is worthy to be praised: so shall I be saved from mine enemies" (Psalm 18:2-3).

When we hear these words, we recognize God as the defender and protector of His people—an ever-present help in the time of trouble. David says God is like a great fortress whose walls cannot be penetrated by the enemy. He also says God is my coat of armor and shield against the arrows that come my way. He is the strength of my life. When I would be faint and weary, He refreshes and restores me.

How many times have we thought we would perish on our journey? How many times have we thought we would die in the heat of the battle? But God raised up a standard against our enemy. When the enemy came in like a flood, God raised up His army against him. God protects His people from the enemy and surrounds them with His loving care. Thank God for His watchful, caring, loving protection, along the journey of life.

THIRD, THIS WALK LEADS HOME.

We read in Hebrews 11:5, "By faith Enoch was translated that he should not see death."

The word *translated* is an old Latin word, which simply means "carried over" or "carried across."

God carried Enoch across to the other side. Someone described it by saying, "One day Enoch and God were walking along and God said to Enoch, 'Enoch, why don't you just come on home with Me today. You've been down here now 365 years. Just go home with Me.' So Enoch said, 'Yes, God, I have been walking with You all these years; anyway, I think I would like to come on up to Your house.' So God, whether by a fiery chariot or a jet-propelled cloud, whisked Enoch away and took him on home." God carried him across—carried him across death. Death is that force that divides this world from the world to come. God somehow picked up Enoch and carried him across to the other shore. One moment, walking with God in time,; the next, in eternity. One moment, communing with God by faith; the next, by sight. Enoch's life of faith was at last crowned by an abundant entrance into the life of perfect fellowship.

CONCLUSION

From the last book in the Bible—the Book of Revelation —comes a pointed promise, "Thou hast a few names . . . which have not defiled their garments; and they shall walk with me in white: for they are worthy. He that overcometh, the same shall be clothed in white raiment, and I will not blot out his name out of the book of life, but I will confess his name before my Father, and before his angels" (Revelation 3:4-5).

What a wonderful promise! We shall walk with Him in white. White garments in heaven signify purity, perfection, and holiness. It doesn't matter whether it is a white robe or a three-piece white suit or a totally new design from heaven's wardrobe, the important thing is that we shall walk with God in everlasting perfection.

Now we walk by faith, but then our eyes shall be open to the fullness of all His eternal wonders. Now we walk with limited understanding, but then life's most baffling mysteries will be resolved in the light of His eternal wisdom.

Yes, this walk with God leads home. Let's be sure that we daily "walk worthy of God, who hath called you unto his kingdom and glory" (1 Thessalonians 2:12).

MY POSITION AS A BELIEVER

A. A. Ledford

SCRIPTURE: John 15:7

INTRODUCTION

Being a child of God is more than a guarantee to go to heaven. There are present benefits to Christian living. God is as concerned with our daily life as He is with our future life. The entire Godhead is involved with our present secure position in the Lord. This must be realized in order to enjoy the blessings of being a Christian.

God's attitude is expressed in Luke 12:32: "Fear not, little flock; for it is your father's good pleasure to give you the kingdom." I emphasize the word *good* to note His pleasure. Just to say it was His pleasure would have been sufficient, but He added the word *good* to accent His will to us.

GOD'S PART

"If God be for us, who can be against us?" (Romans 8:31).

As a child of God, I am assured God is for me! God stated in Genesis 1:26, "Let us make man . . . and let [him] have dominion. It amazed the psalmist that man should have dominion over all the works of His hands (Psalm 8:4-6).

142

This statement was not to reduce man to puppet status in God's hands, nor was man to be a toy for the devil. Man was made to be victorious. Some men have tried to give man more credit than is due. He is not master of his own fate, but a possession of his divine Creator. We must never seek to rise above that level.

At the same time we must remember we rank as children of God through Jesus Christ our Lord. Our first relationship to God is through creation, and our second is through re-creation in Jesus Christ and His offering at Calvary.

God has no stepchildren, in-laws, or half-breeds for children. If we are children of God, we are equal. There are no degrees of sonship. God is no respecter of persons. We are made in His image to glorify Him and not ourselves.

If one uses Scripture to bolster any idea of personal or material gain and looks at another as being inferior, he loses sight of the real meaning of Scripture and is likely to become carnal. This must not be!

It would also be carnal to censure a person who has achieved much of this world's goods through rightful attitude and adherence to the Scripture. A rich person is not to censured just because he is rich. I have no more right to condemn him for his wealth than he does to condemn me if I am not wealthy. It is carnal to judge spirituality by the size of a bank account.

Jesus did not die to make us possessors of this world's goods without a life dedicated to the things of God.

The dilemma raised by Jesus which caused His disciples to ask, "How hardly can a rich man enter the kingdom?" and is a question we have a right to ask. But wealth was not the sin; attitude was the sin.

Jesus gave us the example of Lazarus laid at the rich man's gate. The rich man lifted up his eyes in hell, while Lazarus was taken by the angels to Father Abraham's bosom. Scripture does not say you have to be a Lazarus to go to heaven, but it says being a Lazarus will not prevent you.

In this world of sin, while confronted with the devil, I have assurance I am a child of God. His Spirit bears witness with my spirit that I am the son of God. Paul reminds me, "And if children, then heirs, heirs of God, and joint-heirs with

Christ" (Romans 8:17). As a joint heir of Jesus Christ, I have the highest rank possible.

Sometimes in my travels I see people who are defeated. Provided our goals are what they should be, there is no room for defeat in God. Our victory is not in our own achievements but by accepting the provisions God has made for us as His children. We are not our own. We are possessed by him.

To be what God intends us to be, it is an absolute must that we know our proper relationship to the Creator.

These are not the words of a preacher expecting to elevate the level of his reader's hopes by hitching to a star of positive thinking. We are not gods. We are not ever going to evolve into gods. We will not be reincarnated into another spirit being, but we will always remain a subject of God's divine grace through His Son Jesus Christ.

I am an overcomer, not of a falling stock market, but of this world and the devil.

I am an overcomer, however, only through Christ by whose grace Paul said, "If God be for us, who can be against us!" (Romans 8:31).

JESUS' PART

Jesus said, "All power is given unto me in heaven and in earth," (Matthew 28:18). And again He said, "The glory which thou gavest me I have given them" (John 17:22). All power was given to Him and He now gives it to us!

Another noteworthy statement comes from Matthew 28:28: "Lo I am with you alway, even unto the end of the world."

So we see God is for us and Jesus is with us. He of whom it is said, "All things were made by him" (John 1:3) is now involved with each of us who are believers. Paul wrote, "Christ came who is over all," (Romans 9:5); and John put it in these words, "He that cometh from above is above all" (John 3:31), thus giving Him undisputed claim to the position of Son of God.

For this creator of all things to say to me as a believer in Him, "I will be with you always, even to the end of the world," is reason for me to rejoice.

I have no problem accepting the salvation He provides for me. I have accepted eternal life in Him.

But my blessing does not stop there!

I have God for me!

I have Jesus with me!

In Him I live and move and have my being!

"Wherefore God also hath highly exalted him, and given him a name which is above every name: That at the name of Jesus every knee should bow" (Philippians 2:9, 10). If every atheist is to bow, if every unbeliever will be required to bow, how much more important is it that I should bow before Him now!

It thrills me when I think of all those people who have tried to remove His name from our vocabulary and realize they too will have to bow. The ones who have declared Him no more than any other man—they too will have to bow. Pilate, Voltaire —both will have to bow and honor Christ.

We are so blessed to know He is with us always.

THE HOLY SPIRIT'S PART

"Greater is he that is in you, than he that is in the world" (1 John 4:4).

"Even the Spirit of truth; whom the world cannot receive . . . for he dwelleth with you and shall be in you" (John 14:17).

". . . according to the power that worketh in us" (Ephesians 3:20).

God is for me!

Jesus is with me!

The Holy Spirit is in me!

The language of the Scripture is very clear concerning the experience of receiving the Holy Spirit. Numerous and sundry scriptures accent the Old Testament saints as having the Holy Spirit to move "upon" them but only three where the Spirit is spoken of as being "in" the individual. Daniel is said to be a man in whom the Spirit is. God instructs Moses to choose Joshua, a man in whom the Spirit is. John the Baptist is said to be filled with the Holy Spirit from his mother's womb. Paul stated in 1 Corinthians 3:16, 17 and in 6:19, we are the temple or the dwelling place, of the Holy Spirit. That accounts for the importance of living a holy life. The Holy Spirit does not dwell in an unclean temple.

145

All the references in the Book of Acts make it clear the Holy Spirit came "in" the candidate. On the Day of Pentecost they were "filled." We are also instructed in Ephesians 5:18, 'Be not drunk with wine, wherein is excess; but be filled with the Spirit." If we are "filled," he is "in" us to be sure. In fact, Paul makes it as great a sin not to be filled with the Spirit as he does to be drunk with wine. It is not an instruction which is to be taken lightly.

I have God for me!

I have Jesus with me!

I have the Holy Spirit in me!

THE ANGEL'S PART

"The angel of the Lord encampeth round about them *that* fear him, and delivereth them" (Psalms 34:7).

We do not really know how many angels there are but we know that, if one third of them fell with Lucifer (Revelation 12:4), God still has two thirds of them left.

"Are they not all ministering spirits, sent forth to minister for them who shall be heirs of salvation?" (Hebrews 1:14). So God has two angels available to Him for every one demon which fell with Lucifer.

We certainly must not pay more attention to the one demon sent by the devil to tantalize us while overlooking the many angels sent to minister to us.

God is for me!

Jesus is with me!

The Holy spirit is in me!

And angels are all around me!

How can I fail?

The fact remains, though, that it is possible to have all these provisions and still not realize it. When the servant of the prophet fretted about the queen's army arranging to take their lives, the calmness of the prophet astounded the troubled servant. He reminded the prophet their lives were being sought. Then came the words, "Lord open, the young man's eyes." Then came the announcement, "They that are with us are more than they that are against us!"

146

CONCLUSION

We are serving the same God!

I am overwhelmed when I think of what we have available and how little we appropriate those blessings. Luke showed us God's love when He recorded Jesus' words, "Fear not, little flock; for it is your Father's good pleasure to give you the kingdom" (Luke 12:32).

God is for us, Jesus is with us, the Holy Spirit is in us, and angels are all around us.

How can we fail? We are more than conquerors (Romans 8:37).

DOING RIGHT THE WRONG WAY

William A. Reid

SCRIPTURE: 2 Samuel 6

INTRODUCTION

David decided to bring the ark to Jerusalem. The Philistines had captured it during the last sad days of Eli. It caused them so much trouble they put it on a cart and returned it, and for awhile it stayed at the house of Abinadab (1 Samuel 7:1).

David undertook to bring the ark to Jerusalem. His motive was good, but his method was wrong. He was right in his intentions, but wrong in the implementation. God had ordered that the ark should be carried only on the shoulders of the Levites. David loaded it on a new cart to be drawn by oxen. He probably got the idea from the Philistines, so it was an expedient borrowed from the enemies of Israel. On the way the oxen stumbled; Uzzah put forth his hand to steady the ark, and God struck him dead (2 Samuel 6:2-8). This strange tragedy has some serious lessons for us.

BORROWING FROM THE ENEMY

David borrowed his idea from the Philistines. The Philistines were not familiar with God's instructions for handling the ark. God did not punish them for transporting the ark on a cart. God was merciful to them because of their ignorance.

To the Philistines the ark of the covenant was only part of the bounty they had captured. They had no cherished memories of the ark. To them the ark meant very little. They had defeated the Israelites and captured their god.

The church today has borrowed from the world the vehicles of her ministry. We study the techniques of this age—the gadgetry of the business, social, and entertainment world—looking for new carts on which to carry the ark of our testimony. Instead of asking, "How does God do it?" we ask, "How does the world do it?" Vance Havner says, "We are religious copycats; we mimic the manikins of this 'Punch and Judy' show we call progress. We have called Hollywood to our aid as though the gospel were a form of entertainment. Our worship is streamlined, our preaching slanted to tickle the ears of a generation that cannot endure sound doctrine."

David's whole procedure was wrong. He had heard of the new cart made by the Philistines. They had experienced no difficulty. They had moved the ark successfully. Now David presumes to move the ark, adopting the methods of the Philistines. Many in the church today want to adopt the methods and standards of the world to do the work of God. It simply will not work.

BECOMING TOO FAMILIAR WITH THE THINGS OF GOD

Too many people today are like Uzzah. Uzzah had no regard for the sanctity of the ark. He was the son of Abinadab and had seen the ark all his life. The ark was a familiar piece of furniture and had become to him just a box. Some in the church have grown so familiar with the gospel, with the worship, and with the ordinances of the church they have lost their reverence and respect for the things of God.

Uzzah had lost his regard for the sacredness of the ark as the symbol of God's presence among His people. Matthew Henry says, "Perhaps he had affected to show before this great assembly how bold he could make with the ark, having been so long acquainted with it. Familiarity, even with that which is most awful, is apt to breed contempt."

149

There are those who have grown up in Pentecostalism as Uzzah grew up around the ark. Somehow these folks have become too familiar with the moving of the Spirit. They just assume everything will continue as they have always known, but they do very little to ensure the abiding presence of God. Others have become so familiar that they ignore the moving of the Spirit. They can be in a service where the Holy Spirit is moving and ministering in a dynamic manner but still be unaffected. Yet others resist the Spirit's move as unnecessary or unrefined.

BEARING THE ARK

God had instructed that bearing the ark of the covenant would be a personal thing. The Philistines had devised the plan to put the ark on the cart. Carrying it on the shoulders of the priests represented a personal commitment and a sharing of responsibility.

One of the greatest needs of the church today is personal commitment—a commitment to pray, to fast, and to get involved in the work of God. Our modern society lacks commitment. You can see this lack of commitment in the home —between husbands and wives, with parents and children; in companies—between employer and employee; and even in the church—between brothers and sisters.

There was much fanfare for David's new cart. The Bible says, "The thing was right in the eyes of all the people" (1 Chronicles 13:4). This was the voice of the people, not of God.

Just because the people approved the plan did not mean that the plan was acceptable to God. On the contrary, as evidence of His disapproval God struck Uzzah dead when he touched the ark of God. Even so today, just because the masses give their approval does not mean it is God's plan. Much of what is done today in the church meets man's approval, but is not being found acceptable to God. You can determine that, because the anointing of God is not being experienced as it was in the days of the early church. What the church must do today is find God's plan and do things God's way.

The work of the church is also personal. David finally came to his senses. After his initial indignation at God for striking Uzzah dead, David began to pray and seek God's direction. As he studied the Law, he discovered how God wanted the ark transported. He learned a valuable lesson in being obedient to the word of God.

The first thing we need to do in church today is to discover that God's work must be done by God's people, God's way. Under the Old Testament Law, only the Levites were qualified to carry the ark. Even for the Levites to carry the ark there were very strict instructions for their personal purification and preparation.

If the work of God is going to be successful today, the people of God must be willing to get personally involved. They must be willing to be dedicated to the work of God. Only separated and dedicated people can do the work of the church and be found pleasing to the Lord.

There are three questions to be asked if we want to do things God's way. First, am I one of God's people? Have I come into that personal relationship where Jesus Christ is really the Lord of my life? Am I willing and ready to surrender all of the areas of my life to the lordship of Jesus Christ?

We should ask ourselves, "Am I doing God's work?" As you begin to look at your life, are you really doing God's work? There is no doubt that there is much to be done. Everywhere you look people are hurting, people are in need. Every believer should be involved in the work of God: preaching, teaching, witnessing, praying, fasting, caring, sharing, and so forth. If you are not involved, now is the time to get involved.

We should also ask, "Am I doing God's work God's way?" Those that have been in the church for a long period of time must guard against doing God's work their way. If a person is not careful his desires and motives can be superimposed over God's desires. Jesus told His disciples that the first and greatest commandment is this, "Thou shalt love the Lord thy God with all thy heart, and with all thy soul, and with all thy mind. This is the first and great commandment" (Matthew 22:37,38).

God has a work for His people to do. The fields are ripe unto harvest. Let's get back into the word of God to see how God desires for His work to be accomplished. Let's not find ourselves as David, trying to carry on the work of God using the new cart of the world.

WITHOUT A VISION

T. David Sustar

SCRIPTURE: Proverbs 29:18

INTRODUCTION

This is an old revival theme. I have heard numerous sermons from this text; however, I believe the wrong emphasis is often placed on the message. Sermons from Proverbs 29:18 usually tell me about the terrible sinners of this world who are going to perish because they have no vision of God.

It is true that sinners do need to catch a revelation of God. But this verse was not written to sinners; rather, it was written to God's people. The word *perish* in the original means, first of all, "to make naked." In other words, garments or ornaments are taken away and the person is exposed to shame, or armor is removed and he is open to danger.

Next, *perish* means people will become idle. When there is no revelation, no call to God, no challenge to godliness, the people sit idly by.

Further, *perish* means the people will be scattered abroad. Jesus saw the people as sheep having no shepherd. When there is no focal point, there is no rallying point.

The word *perish* also carries the meaning of Hosea 4:6, "My people are destroyed for lack of knowledge." Proverbs 29:18 is a message for the church, a message for you and me. It is simply this: Without a constant revelation of God's power and glory in and through us, we shall perish AND the world with us! God is simply reaffirming a basic tenet of faith—before anything great can ever be done, somebody has to catch a vision of it.

God says that any way other than His is futile. In Ezekiel 7:15, He says that without God you'll only find a famine within and a sword without. Unless we see as God sees and understand as He would have us, we will perish. I would like to point out three times in the Bible when there was no vision or revelation from God.

THREE PICTURES OF PEOPLE PERISHING WITHOUT A VISION

And the word of the Lord was precious in those days; there was no open vision (I Samuel 3:1).

The scene surrounding this verse is pitiful. Eli, the aged priest in the house of the Lord, is old and going blind—physically and spiritually. His two sons, Hophni and Phinehas, who serve also as priests in the temple, are so low that they commit sexual acts with the women coming to offer sacrifices. The Bible calls them "sons of Belial."

God sent a man to tell Eli about his sons and what the future held as his house would be cut off, but Eli had no influence over the boys.

The Philistines came to fight against the people of God, and when it looked as if they would overtake the land, Hophni and Phinehas remembered how the ark of the covenant seemed to always insure victory for God's people. They took it to the field of battle; however, God was not with them because of their sins. Although the Israelites shouted when they saw the ark, they soon learned that spiritual things in the wrong hands are of no avail.

The Philistines conquered Israel that day. Thirty thousand Israelites were killed that day, including Hophni and Phinehas. The ark of the covenant was taken by the Philistines. A man ran from the battle back to Shiloh to tell Eli the sad news. With torn garments and dirt upon his head, the man sorrowfully related the deaths of Hophni and Phinehas. Then he reported that the ark had been taken. When he mentioned the ark, Eli fell backwards from a wall, broke his neck, and died.

The messenger then went to Phinehas's house, where Phinehas's wife was about to deliver a child. When he told her the sad news, she went into labor. A boy was born and the mother died, but before she died, she proclaimed, "Name the child Ichabod, saying, The glory is departed from Israel."

Talk about terrible conditions! Without a vision, there is nothing but desolation, destruction, and death.

"Behold, the days come, saith the Lord God, that I will send a famine in the land, not a famine of bread, nor a thirst for water, but of hearing the words of the Lord: And they shall wander from sea to sea, and from the north even to the east, they shall run to and fro to seek the word of the Lord, and shall not find it. In that day shall the fair virgins and young men faint for thirst . . . . even they shall fall, and never rise up again" (Amos 8:11-14).

God continued to declare that there would be no escape for them. If they climbed up to heaven, He would bring them down. On top of Mt. Carmel or in the depths of the sea, they would not escape His wrath. Whether they were in captivity or free, the sword would slay them. His stern rebuke was, "All the sinners of my people shall die by the sword, which say, The evil shall not overtake nor prevent us" (Amos 9:10).

Notice that He said, "All the sinners of my people." Tragic, isn't it? God's people without a revelation of God become laws within themselves and are destroyed.

The third time in the Bible where there is no vision of God is in the period between the Old and New Testaments. There were over 400 years without a word from God. During those years Jerusalem was invaded 27 times by alien armies. As soon as they rebuilt the walls, an enemy would tore them down again. They tried to restore the Temple and it was burned.

The Maccabees and others tried to point people toward God but they had little or no success. Everything moved toward that awful day when Antiochus Epiphanes came into Jerusalem and killed 40,000 Jews in one day. He then went into the

154

house of God and killed a swine, a sow, on the altar of God, thereby desecrating the house of God.

But the saddest thing that came out of this time of spiritual darkness was a religious organization that was so far from God that they could not recognize His Son when He came. It produced the people who crucified the Son of God.

For too long we have seen prodigal sons wandering away, coins lost in the dust, sheep going astray, and other lost men and have chosen to call this a vision. But this is not the vision the church needs. You can tell the sinner he's living in torment, but it will not set him free. You can tell men they are bound, but that will do them no good. They already know they are held in sin's strong sway.

The revelation we need today, if we're going to minister to the needs of the world, is a revelation of a God who has the answer to the world's ills!

THREE PICTURES OF THE GOD WHO HAS THE ANSWER

God is a deliverer. When Eli strayed so far from God and Israel was under attack by the Philistines, a little lady began to pray. Her name was Hannah, and I think she said something like this to God: "O God, there's no one here who listens to You. If You'll give me a boy, although I am past the years of having a child, I will give him back to You so You'll have a servant to listen to You all his days." Her burden was so heavy and her concern so great that she staggered like a drunk woman.

But God heard that cry from her heart and gave her a son. She called his name Samuel and later took him to the house of God. She told Eli that Samuel was the answer to the prayer she prayed years before when he thought she was drunk. She left Samuel at the house of God as she had promised.

You can almost see Samuel walking around his new home as if looking for something or someone. Under his breath, you can hear him saying, "I know You're here. Mom told me to search diligently for You. I'm here to hear from You, I was born for that purpose. Speak to me, O God."

Then it happened! One night after he had gone to bed, Samuel heard someone calling his name. He rushed to Eli to see why he had called. Eli said he had not called and sent the boy back to bed. Twice more the voice came and he ran to Eli. Suddenly, it struck the old priest. He was so far from God that he had not recognized what was happening. But now he senses that God is about to reveal Himself. He instructs Samuel to answer the next time, "Speak Lord, for thy servant heareth thee." Samuel did as he was told, and God revealed Himself and told him of the end of Eli's family.

When the ark was taken to Philistia, these enemies of Jehovah experienced God's judgment.

The ark was sent to Gath where the results were the same. Death and sickness come upon the land. The citizens of Gath said, "Take it away to Ekron." But the men of Ekron were ready to send it home: "They have sent the ark of the God of Israel to us, to slay us and our people," they said.

When the ark was finally returned to Israel, Samuel had been raised up as a prophet and judge. He called the people together and said, "If ye do return unto the Lord with all your hearts, then put away the strange gods and Ashtaroth from among you, and prepare your hearts unto the Lord, and serve him only: and he will deliver you out of the hand of the Philistines." (1 Samuel 7:3).

The people responded and served the Lord only. They gathered to Mizpeh for prayer. While they were there, the Philistines came against them again. But Israel was different now. They were praying, they were open to God, they were serving Him. God thundered with a great thunder against the Philistines and they were smitten before the Israelites.

Samuel set a stone between Mizpeh and Shen and called it Ebenezer, saying, "Hitherto hath the Lord helped us." We are told in Verse 13 that the Philistines were subdued and came no more. There was peace in the land, according to verse 14.

The vision the church needs is of our great God's ability to deliver out of every circumstance of life. *He is the Deliverer!*

God is a restorer. Let's return to Amos. The people were scattered, running to and fro, thirsting, dying, being destroyed by the sword because of their sins. But God was not finished. He was not about to desert His people. He would not allow the prophet to stop without declaring the restoration He would bring to Israel.

Amos proclaimed that God would raise up the tabernacle of David and close up the breaches thereof. He would raise up the ruins and build them as of old. The people of God would possess the land and the blessing would begin to flow. The reaper would be overtaken by the plowman. The treader of grapes would overtake the sower of seeds. The mountains would drop sweet wine and all the hills would melt.

God would bring again from captivity His people Israel, and they would return to their land. The wasted cities would be rebuilt and inhabited. The people would plant vineyards and make gardens and eat the fruit of them. They would be planted upon their land and be pulled up out of it no more.

I've watched that happen in my lifetime. On May 14, 1948, Israel came into existence under the leadership of David Ben-Gurion. A nation was born in a day. The official census showed a population of 872,678 in 1948. In 1971, Israel reported 2,991,000 people. The restoration is underway. God is bringing His people home and we don't need to worry about them ever being plucked up again!

In the same manner, He is able to restore all things to the way He desires them to be. *He is a deliverer and a restorer*!

Our God is a Savior. The inter-testament period, as the spiritual dark ages, was a dismal time for the world. Humanity needed help; men needed a Savior! One night on the Judean hillside, a bright light penetrated the darkness. A multitude of the heavenly host began to sing of a Savior. They spoke of good tidings of great joy, which would be to all people.

The message revealed the birth of Christ the Lord. Jesus, the One who came to take away the sins of the world, had arrived. Those who sat in spiritual darkness saw a great light. He came to bring light and life through the gospel. He came to be the Light of the World.

An old man at Jerusalem, Simeon, was just and devout. He waited on the consolation of Israel. He had been told by the Holy Spirit that he would not see death before he had seen the Christ Child. I believe the Spirit woke him one morning, saying, "Rush to the temple. This is the day you've been waiting for!" I can imagine him getting dressed and shuffling along to the Temple. It was the day that Mary and Joseph brought Jesus to the Temple to follow the custom of the Law.

When Simeon saw the child, he took Him in his arms and blessed God. He said, "Lord, now lettest thou thy servant depart in peace, according to thy word: For mine eyes have seen thy salvation, Which thou hast prepared before the face of all people; A light to lighten the Gentiles, and the glory of thy people Israel" (Luke 2:29-32).

Simeon did not want to die before he embraced the Savior! What a vision of the answer needed by this world! *He not only is a deliverer and restorer, he is our only Saviour!*

CONCLUSION

Oh, what a Savior! John saw in Him the answer to the searching heart. "For God so loved the world, that he gave his only begotten Son, that whosoever believeth in him should not perish, but have everlasting life" (John 3:16).

This is the answer we need today! Oh, my friend, if you think a vision is catching a glimpse of all the terrible things of this world, you are wrong! That's not vision. The vision God wants us to have is one that makes us stand with solid assurance and faith to declare: "I know the God who is able to deliver out of every circumstance. I know the God who is able to restore. I know the God who is able to save unto the uttermost those that come to Him by Christ Jesus."

Paul saw it and was never disobedient to the heavenly vision. There is a loss, an eternal loss, that comes with the failure to keep your eye upon Him. The arm of the flesh will fail you. The world will overtake you.

Setting your affection on things above will save you. Having a clear vision of the God who is able to deliver, restore, and save will keep you. Through your life, the needs of others will be met and Jesus Christ will be glorified!

THE SEARCH FOR SIGNIFICANCE

R. B. Thomas

SCRIPTURE: Matthew 20:20-28

INTRODUCTION

Wherever groups of people are gathered you can observe behaviors revealing a universal "search for significance." The group may be political, commercial, social or even religious, but the signs will be there. The drive for significance seems to be a part of our genetic strain. The struggle of Jacob and Esau at birth tends to confirm this. Even Cain and Able, in their competition for acceptance, lend credence to this possibility.

Many believers view the quest as being totally carnal. It can be, and often is, a "fleshly-motivated" behavior, but it need not be. It is not always a carnal manifestation. Jesus did not rebuke nor condemn the disciples for having ambition nor for expressing their desire to be significant. The reason why we want to be great and the way we go about achieving it are the issues to be concerned about.

Try to imagine where Christianity would be today if the surrender of ambition were a prerequisite to being a disciple of Jesus. Jesus motivated His followers by assuring them they were the salt of the earth and the light of the world. He told them to let their light shine before men. The purpose, however, was "that men may see your good works and glorify the Father who is in heaven."

Jesus gives us clear direction. He taught appropriate ways to achieve significance. When we learn the basic biblical spiritual principles and apply them, we may be assured of His blessing and smile of approval. I am certain that God wants His people to be achievers. It is the "why" and the "how" that we must pay close attention to. We will identify and examine three of these spiritual principles.

YOU MUST HAVE AN ALL-CONSUMING AIM

No one will be happy, productive, or fulfilled until he has an all-consuming purpose. This aim must become an obsession. The lives of successful people reveal this. Most significant people have an identifiable objective that borders on being an obsession. Often these people are thought of as having a "one-track" mind. While much good may be said about being a balanced and multi-talented person, it is possible to be such a generalist that we become good at almost nothing in particular.

Students in college make poor grades, become discipline problems in some cases, and later dropouts because they lack an aim. Without a purpose, they cannot see how studies relate to anything, because they do not know where they are headed. People are in and out of different jobs, churches, social groups and communities because they feel no ties to anyone or anything.

Jesus is the best model of an all-consuming aim. When He was 12 years of age, He was found in the Temple talking man-to-man with the rabbis and scholars. Confronted by His parents after three days of frantic searching, He responded, "Did you not know that I must be about my Father's business?" At such an early age Jesus knew who He was, that He was here on a mission, and He understood what that mission was (Luke 2:49).

In John, Jesus explained to His disciples the necessity of passing through Samaria (John 4:4). The classic one-on-one encounter with the woman at the well and the revival that followed reveal how this fit with His aim and purpose. Luke records the conversion of a publican named Zacchaeus in the city of Jericho. The conclusion of this story finds Jesus saying, "The Son of man is come to seek and to save that which was lost" (Luke 19:10).

Speaking years before Jesus' birth, Isaiah, the prophet, said of Him that His face was set like a flint (Isaiah 50:7). Jesus looked neither to the right nor to the left, but straight ahead to His call and mission. Never has any one person accomplished so much in such a short time as Jesus. With Him there was no lost energy or motion. He wasted no time trying to unravel the mystery of His mission to this world. *All* of His efforts were focused upon the supreme objective of the Cross and His subsequent resurrection.

Jesus vividly displayed an unrelenting commitment to His all-consuming aim in the garden of Gethsemane. He struggled with the ordeal of the Cross and the weight of the sins of the world upon Him. If there was a way the aim could be fulfilled short of the bitter cup, Jesus would welcome it. If not, He was subject to the will of the Father. The test of commitment to an all-consuming aim will repeat itself over and over again. In the case of Jesus, and sometimes with others, it comes down to a choice between compromise or commitment. An all-consuming aim is our best assurance against compromise.

Paul is another prime example of the principle of an all-consuming aim. In his testimony to King Agrippa he said, "Whereupon, O King Agrippa, I was not disobedient unto the heavenly vision" (Acts 26:19). Paul graphically pinpoints this concept in his letter to the Corinthians. "I run . . . not with uncertainty . . . I fight, not as one who beats the air. I discipline my body and bring it into subjection, lest, when I have preached to others, I myself should become disqualified" (1 Corinthians 9:26-27, *New King James Version*). To the Philippian believers Paul reveals his obsession regarding his single purpose in life. He used the phrase, "This *one* thing I do" (Philippians 3:13). He emphasized his point by using the definite article when referring to the goal and the prize. He did not speak of *a* goal or prize, it was always the goal or prize.

One of the most-quoted statements from the pen of Paul comes from the remarkable upbeat letter to the Philippians.

He wrote, "For me to live is Christ, and to die is gain" (1:21). He had completely neutralized himself on the issue of life or death. He had a preference, but whatever would best serve his Lord and contribute to his all-consuming aim would be the deciding factor. Who am I? What am I doing here? What is my mission? These and other introspective questions need to be asked and answered. The puzzle of life will never be solved for us until we come to grips with the issue of "an all-consuming aim."

YOU MUST BE WILLING TO BE A SERVANT

The second principle for a Christian in the search for significance is a willingness to be a servant. This principle runs counter to the philosophy and practices of the world. In this world the status of a person is measured by the number of people who serve him, rather than the number he serves. A really great person by this world's standards will never need to do anything for himself, not to mention doing something for someone else.

For a model of this principle, look again at Jesus. "Whoever desires to be first among you, let him be your slave—just as the Son of Man did not come to be served, but to serve, and to give His life as a ransom for many" (Matthew 20:27-28, *NKJV*). Jesus did not insist on a principle for His followers that He himself would not observe. The servant principle is epitomized in the incarnation of Christ. "Being in the form of God, [Jesus] did not consider it robbery to be equal with God, but made Himself of no reputation, *taking the form of a servant*, and coming in the likeness of men. And being found in appearance as a man, He humbled Himself and became obedient to the point of death, even the death of the cross. Therefore God also has highly exalted Him" (Philippians 2:6-9, *NKJV*). Jesus, who was God, became man, the servant. No height of greatness nor depth of servanthood will ever match, or even come close, to the model of the Master.

The Master becoming a servant was illustrated in the last Passover Feast Jesus shared with His disciples. Jesus drank from the common cup with them and washed their feet. "[Jesus] rose from supper and laid aside His garments, took a towel and girded Himself. After that, He poured water into a basin and began to wash the disciples' feet, and to wipe them with the towel with which He was girded. . . . If I then, your Lord and Teacher, have washed your feet, you also ought to wash one another's feet" (John 13:4, 5, 14; *NKJV*). The true leader, the genuinely significant person, must become willing to serve. The world cannot comprehend the validity of this principle. A Master washing the feet of a slave is unthinkable; yet this is exactly what Jesus teaches us to do.

In Luke 22:27 Jesus announced, "I am among you as he that serveth." If you want to be significant, you must do the hard, dirty work of serving your fellowman. Why is there a shortage of truly significant people in the world today? The answer is simple: It costs too much! As long as we cling to the standards of the world, we will be no better than mediocre.

In West Germany I visited a king's castle near Ludwigsburg. This castle had 474 rooms. It was easy to see the line that was drawn between royalty and servants. Even a distinction between the king and the queen was made. The king had three steps to his throne while the queen had only two. According to law, the queen could never sit higher than the king. What a contrast with King Jesus, who was God, yet, for our sake became a servant! In the search for significance we must conform to the principle of voluntary servanthood.

YOU MUST BE FAITHFUL IN SMALL THINGS

The third principle in the search for significance is *faithfulness in small things*. Perhaps you have been wondering why your life is at a standstill? Why is it that so many people your age, some who are not as bright or skillful as you appear to be, are passing you by? Obviously, there can be many answers to these painful questions. A great danger is that in our search for a face-saving rationale we ignore the real answer. In many situations faithfulness is a higher virtue than skill or talent. In fact, a highly skilled person who has not learned to be faithful can be a detriment to any cause. An outstanding military general who deserts his post is worse than no general at all. A skillful employee who shows up for work only when he or she feels like it is a liability instead of an asset. No matter how good a person is, if he cannot be depended on, he becomes the enemy—a foe, not a friend!

Jesus teaches the principle of *faithfulness in small things* in the parable of the talents. "Because you were faithful over a few things, I will make you ruler over many things" (Matthew 25:21, 23, *NKJV*).

No one wants to think that he is not *trustworthy*. But honesty leads us to the reality of what Jesus teaches. He makes it clear that we will be rewarded if we are faithful in small things. "Blessed is that [faithful] servant whom his master, when he comes, will find so doing" (Matthew 24:46, *NKJV*). When the Master comes He will make the faithful servant ruler over all His goods.

It is required of a steward that he be faithful (1 Corinthians 4:2). If we are faithful unto death we shall receive the crown of life (Revelation 2:10). Jesus became a faithful and merciful high priest (Hebrews 2:17). Paul admonished Timothy to commit the Gospel unto faithful men (2 Timothy 2:2). The one-talent servant blamed his negligence on fear of his master, but the real reason for his failure was wickedness and laziness (Matthew 25:24-26). "For to everyone who has, more will be given, and he will have abundance; but from him who does not have, even what he has will be taken away" (Matthew 25:29, *NKJV*).

The principle of faithfulness was taught with word and example by Jesus, and embraced by the Apostle Paul. "Let us not grow weary while doing good, for in due season we shall reap if we do not lose heart. Therefore, as we have opportunity, let us do good to all, especially to those who are of the household of faith" (Galatians 6:9, 10, *NKJV*). In 2 Thessalonians 3:13 Paul repeats this principle. Some of the Thessalonians were walking disorderly. Some were doing no work at all. Some were busybodies. All of these negative influences can take the very heart out of the constructive work for the Kingdom. Paul puts it all in perspective by saying, "But as for you, brethren, do not grow weary in doing good."

CONCLUSION

Jesus knew that men and women everywhere want to be significant. He understands human nature better than anyone. "[He] had no need that anyone should testify of man, for He knew what was in man" (John 2:25, *NKJV*). He is the world's greatest psychologist. Tennyson called Him "the greatest of the great." He knew that deep within us is the ambition to be outstanding, to be distinguished. We all want to amount to something. Nobody wants to be remembered as a "nobody." Jesus encourages us to excellence. The difference is in the how and the why!

The world says, "Whoever wants to be great among you, let him assert himself; man can do anything he wants to do if he wants it strong enough." Some Christians would say, "Whoever wants to be great is carnal; the desire is sinful and must be put out of the heart immediately." But Jesus disagrees with both views.

Whoever wants to be significant, Jesus says, let him find an all-consuming aim, let him become a willing servant of others, and let him learn to be faithful in the small things. He will be made ruler over all things.

TIME IS RUNNING OUT

John E. Hedgepeth

SCRIPTURE: Romans 13:11, 12

INTRODUCTION

Paul declared many years ago, "Time is running out." Looking back over history, there are some startling signs that point to the end of this age. Look at the following sequence of events:

—From the sailboat to the steamboat-5,000 years

—From the steamboat to the airplane-100 years

—From the airplane to the satellite-52 years

—From the satellite to Star Wars-25 years

—From Star Wars to ? ? ?

Could this valuable thing called *time* be running out for Planet Earth? Are we reaching the culmination of all things? Are we close to the time (1) when we hear the whole creation groaning and travailing in pain until now (Romans 8:22), (2) when "the Lord himself shall descend from heaven with a shout" (1 Thessalonians 4:16), (3) when we shall hear the heavens pass away with a great noise and the elements melting with the fervent heat (2 Peter 3:10), (4) when we hear the sounds of Armageddon (Revelation 16:16), and (5) when the

Lord shall stand in that day upon the mount of Olives, which is before Jerusalem on the east; and the mount of Olives shall be split in two from east to west by a very wide valley, so that one half of the mount shall withdraw northward and the other half southward (see Zechariah 14:4).

There are some things that are happening now that give us a real feeling that time is running out and the blessed hope will appear.

THE INCREASE OF VIOLENCE AND LAWLESSNESS

There is a bombardment of violence and lawlessness that the earth has never witnessed. The disciples asked Jesus, "What shall be the signs of Thy coming?" Jesus said, "There will be signs in the sun, moon and stars. On the earth, nations will be in anguish and perplexity at the roaring and tossing of the sea (Luke 21:25, *New International Version*). Paul said there would be worldwide lawlessness: "There will be terrible times in the last days. People will be lovers of themselves, lovers of money, boastful, proud, abusive, disobedient to their parents, ungrateful, unholy, without love, unforgiving, slanderous, without self-control, brutal, not lovers of the good, treacherous, rash, conceited, lovers of pleasure rather than lovers of God—having a form of godliness but denying its power. Have nothing to do with them" (2 Timothy 3:1-5, *NIV*).

In the United States, there are 35 million victims of crime annually; 20 percent of all murders are family-related—crimes of passion. Violent crimes are on the increase. One out of 12 women will be assaulted or have attempts made against them; five out of six children will be assaulted during their lifetime. One third of all female homicides are committed by husbands or partners.

Not long ago a woman in our area murdered several of her husbands. She cleverly fed poison into their system. Finally, after several husbands had died, autopsies revealed the poison. Her motive was unknown. She later repented, but she went to her death in the state prison in Raleigh, North Carolina.

In another incident, a quiet, retired couple was murdered in the privacy of their home. Two young military men slipped into their home through an open window, caught the couple by surprise, and cut their throats. After the murderers were arrested, they showed no remorse. They simply said they were following Satan's orders. The father of one of the boys later said his son was greatly influenced by a game called Dungeons and Dragons.

A young man in the high school my daughter attends shot another student while walking in the hallway. On another occasion, a carload of young people pulled up beside another car, opened fire with a shotgun and struck the driver in the head. A 17-year-old high school senior was instantly killed. Paul said, "abusive . . . disobedient . . . without love . . . without self-control . . . brutal."

Crimes against children is another indicator of the final times in which we're living. Reported cases of child abuse doubled between 1976 and 1981 and, according to Pat Robertson, had gone up 400 percent by 1984. The treatment of little children is appalling! Children are being taken and sold into slavery. Authorities have discovered that some of these children are victims of demonic worship. Phil Donahue interviewed children who told of being taken captive by people who sexually abused them during Satan worship. The children were threatened and were afraid to mention it for fear of their lives and their parents' lives.

Bizarre tales are told by children who have been made to drink the blood of animals or have been forced to watch other children being beaten, sexually molested, and even dismembered. The *Buffalo News*, Buffalo, New York, told of a telephone number one can dial to listen to a bizarre pornographic message. Parents were warned by the newspaper, "Check your children's calls." Is it any wonder we are reaping a whirlwind of psychologically impaired children?

Violence is not just local—it's worldwide! Not only are violence and lawlessness in the family, in the schools and on the campuses, but among nations. Lack of respect for law and order plagues the international community. Tourism to the Middle East and European countries has been altered by hijacking and holding hostages. Terrorists do not hesitate to kidnap citizens of another country and hold them for ransom. Innocent people are terrorized by lawless groups throughout the world. Fear strikes the hearts of people every time they travel to another country. They wonder, "Am I safe?" "Will I be terrorized?" "Is there a grenade, a bomb, a lawless person on this plane?" We screen, we check, we run radar tests; we're in search of the lawless, the brutal, those who have no respect for the rights of other people. These things indicate that we are coming to the end.

THE INVOLVEMENT OF THE SOVIET UNION

The Bible is very clear about Soviet intervention in the Middle East prior to the end of the age. The Old Testament prophet Ezekiel describes the full-scale attack by the Soviets on Israel. His prophecy reveals an attack on Israel that will be international in scope. Israel's enemies will come, not from the surrounding areas and immediate neighbors, but from much farther away. He says they will come from the north. The Bible gives this warning: "I am against you, O Gog, chief prince of Meshech and Tubal. I will turn you around and drag you along. I will bring you from the far north and send you against the mountains of Israel. On the mountains of Israel you will fall, you and all your troops and the nations with you" (Ezekiel 39:1,2,4 *NIV*).

Hal Lindsey, well-known writer on prophecy, says, "Every time the north is referred to in Scripture it is to the north of Jerusalem." If you draw a line straight from Jerusalem to the north, that line will go to the Soviet Union. Ezekiel mentioned even the chief city Meshech from which Moscow gets its name.

We already see the Soviet bear turning south. Afghanistan is a good example of Soviet intervention. The Soviets installed their Marxist government and claimed to be friends of the people, but when this government was in danger of being toppled, they moved in with a brutal, warlike spirit, with tanks and ammunition to subdue the people. Could it also be possible that they invaded Afghanistan because of its proximity to the Persian Gulf? We know that many nations would like access to the Persian Gulf, a major world trade route. Can you see prophecy being fulfilled?

Mike Evans, in his book *The Return*, quotes columnist Jack Anderson as saying that seven Soviet MIGs were shot down over northern Israel in 1972. The bodies of seven Soviet pilots were shipped from Jerusalem to Moscow in caskets according to one of the top ministers of the Israeli Government, Yaacov Meridor. Anderson also stated that the Soviet Union has 26 divisions stationed on its border with Iran.

Damascus, Syria, is a stronghold of the Soviets. According to Anderson, the Soviets control virtually the entire military operation in Syria. They don't run the Syrian army, but Soviet advisers are very evident. The Syrians have positioned themselves in the Bekaa Valley in Lebanon. The Israelis continually make strikes against these forces. Their actions are criticized by the media, but it is apparent that the Israelis have motives for their military action. It is to strike the Soviet surface-to-air missiles which are present in the Bekaa Valley.

Let me tell you what was told us recently by an Israeli guide. In 1973, during the Yom Kippur War, the Syrians, with hundreds of tanks and thousands of men, made their way into the Golan Heights. It was Yom Kippur, the Jewish Day of Atonement. Most of the people were observing this holy day, but Captain Devi Zievka went to the Golan Heights, where there were only 120 Israeli border guards and 20 *unmanned* Israeli tanks. He saw tanks coming and thought, *I must stop the Syrians!* Upon taking another look, he saw that they were not Syrian tanks, but Soviet tanks. He began to maneuver his tank; only his driver was with him. For 24 hours he went from one side of the mountain to the next, one side of the pass to the next, blowing up tank after tank. The Soviet tankers began to wonder, *How many Israeli tanks are there?* Through some type of supernatural intervention, Captain Zievka worked by himself, knocking out one tank after another, keeping the Soviet force from coming any farther on the Golan Heights, until finally the reservists came. The army stopped the Soviet tanks and blew them up, causing about 100 Soviet tankers to jump from their tanks and run for their lives. This reminds me of Joshua as he captured the kings in the cave and hanged them on trees (Joshua 10:5-27).

During a recent visit to northern Galilee, I saw the remains of the Syrian bunkers. There is a monument there, the tail of an Israeli jet. It's a monument to those men who fought and destroyed the Syrian stronghold. The Syrians had set up a fortification over northern Galilee. They were going to completely demolish northern Galilee and take that part of Israel for themselves. But Elie Cohn, an Israeli spy in Damascus, had convinced the Syrians to plant eucalyptus trees around those bunkers to offer shade from the sun. He sent word back to the Israelis, "Everywhere you see a eucalyptus tree, bomb it." They did this and recaptured the area.

Today when you talk to an Israeli about Soviet involvement, he will tell you very quickly, "We know we're not fighting against the Arabs alone. It's not just the Syrians or the Libyans. It is the Russians!" They sense their presence. They know they're there. They know they're fighting against somebody big, so they have to keep on guard all the time. We are living in the last days. The end is about to come. Time is running out.

NEW LIFE IN DEAD PLACES

There is a beautiful picture in Ezekiel 47 that shows us some signs that time is running out. Just a few weeks ago as I stood at En Gedi near the Dead Sea, I was excited to hear words that fulfill the prophesy of Ezekiel 47:8: "This water flows toward the eastern region and goes down into the Arabah, where it enters the Sea. When it enters the Sea, the water there becomes fresh" (*NIV*). Ezekiel said that the Dead Sea shall live and that creatures will live in it—great numbers of fish. Fishermen will stand on the banks of the Dead Sea and will pull in great catches of fish.

One of the best guides in Israel related some sobering news to me. He said, "Did you know, John, that the Israelis have started a channel flowing out from Jerusalem toward the Dead Sea? Over a year ago we began to construct it, but it was stopped just a few months ago." When I asked why, he said, "Because of a lack of funds." But we know that everything is on God's calendar. It will not be one day early or one day late.

The passage in Isaiah 35:1 (*NIV*) came into focus: "The desert and the parched land will be glad." The Bible says the wilderness and desert shall actually be glad and rejoice with joy and singing. This is a sign of the end. The Valley of Armageddon has been nothing but swampland for thousands of years. Now this land is some of the most fertile, crop-yielding land in the whole world. Trees, flowers, and food abound. Israel has blossomed into a leading exporter of flowers, fruits, and vegetables. It is the third largest exporter of roses and the world's leading exporter of Jaffa oranges.

Israel reported an overabundance of rainfall during the month of January. Even they are astonished to see the dry, barren hills come alive with green grass. It is plentiful! When you look over the green hills and see the poppies and multicolored flowers blooming, you can almost hear the hills and valleys singing and rejoicing. I believe it is a fulfillment of prophecy.

THE LACK OF EXPECTANCY

Last, but not least, Jesus said that the time would come when men would *not* expect the coming of the Son of Man. "So you also must be ready, because the Son of Man will come at an hour when you do not expect him" (Matthew 24:44, NIV). The Lord also said: "Be careful, or your hearts will be weighed down with dissipation, drunkenness and the anxieties of life, and that day will close on you unexpectedly like a trap. For it will come upon all those who live on the face of the whole earth. Be always on the watch, and pray that you may be able to escape all that is about to happen, and that you may be able to stand before the Son of Man" (Luke 21:34-36, NIV).

We read this warning in the Book of Revelation: "Behold, I come as a thief. Blessed is he that watcheth, and keepeth his garments, lest he walk naked, and they see his shame. And he gathered them together into a place called in the Hebrew tongue Armageddon" (16:15). The Lord would have us know that just prior to the coming of the end, just before time runs out, men and women all over the earth will not expect the coming of the Son of Man. But you may say, "Oh, that's not possible!"

An appalling thing is now happening. Ministers who once fervently preached about the coming of the Lord, are not preaching about it. And some theologians, pastors, and preachers are beginning to talk about the rapture as a mere theory, not as a promised fact. We play into the hands of Satan when evil thoughts keep us from watching for Christ's return.

172

At Jesus ascension, the angels said, "Men of Galilee, why do you stand looking into the sky? This Jesus, who has been taken up from you into heaven, will come in just the same way as you have watched Him go into heaven" (Acts 1:11, *New American Standard Bible*).

Billy Graham says he believes the world is coming to an end, sociologically, technologically, and physiologically. I believe it this, not just from what Billy Graham said, but from what Jesus said—time is running out.

Can you feel a tug on your heart, or have you gotten cold and indifferent to the coming of the Lord? Do you ask in a tone of unbelief, "Where is the promise of His coming? for since the fathers fell asleep, all things continue as they were from the beginning of the creation" (2 Peter 3:4). Have you gotten to a point where you think, *Well, He didn't come yesterday, and I guess He won't come today.* Have you grown cold in your witness to the Lord? Do you think, *I've got plenty of time*! If you have come to such a place, I ask you not to lose hope. Keep your eyes upon the sky. "And when these things begin to come to pass, then look up, and lift up your heads; for your redemption draweth nigh" (Luke 21:28). Time is running out. Let's be ready!

THE FIRE THAT COULD NOT BURN

Ted Gray

SCRIPTURE: Daniel 3:27

INTRODUCTION

The first part of a little child's prayer goes something like this, "God is great, God is good." Do you find that easy to believe? Is God great and good? In every situation?

You know, and I know, we all encounter the testing of our faith in God's goodness and greatness. Especially does it happen when we experience some threatening problem or tragedy in our lives.

Bad things—and I mean terrible things—can happen to believers just as they happen to unbelievers. If you do not believe that, just read again the first two chapters of Job in the Old Testament. The tragedy he experienced was almost too bad to believe.

To remind us how severe his personal tragedy was, his wife asked him to curse God and die. Job rejected her advice and continued to put his trust in God. It wasn't easy for him. In fact, it was a real struggle, but in the end things turned around for his good and God gave him twice what he had before. Job is a role model for us today when we are experiencing a terrible problem and life-threatening tragedy.

You see, Satan brings all kinds of things against us to get us to doubt and deny God. He does not want us to put any trust in Him. Satan would have us to believe that he is going to defeat and ultimately destroy us. That is what he is up to when he puts problems and tragedies in our way. Jesus tells us the devil will come around and try to steal, kill, and destroy (John 10:10). We must do as Job and respond out of faith and complete trust in God, rather than fear and doubt.

Regardless of what the enemy might bring against us in the areas of finances, marriage, family, sickness, or job security, God is good, God is great, and God can turn it around. Paul said, "And we know that all things work together for good to them that love God, to them who are the called according to his purpose" (Romans 8:28).

In Daniel 3:27 we have a text that speaks about God turning a bad situation around. The story is about three men whom the devil set out to literally destroy. They were Shadrach, Meshach and Abed-nego. What looked like total defeat ended up being something harmless.

It is an old story we all know about, but we need to take a new and deeper look at all the factors involved in light of present world conditions.

My text reads,

"And the princes, governors, and captains, and the king's counselors, being gathered together, saw these men, upon whose bodies the fire had no power, nor was an hair of their head singed, neither were their coats changed, nor the smell of fire had passed on them."

God took the power out of the fire. It was the fire that could not burn!

A HEATHENISH PROPOSITION

First of all, let us consider that Shadrach, Meshach and Abed-nego were confronted with a heathenish proposition. It is clearly stated:

"Now if ye be ready that at what time ye hear the sound of the cornet, flute, harp, sackbut, psaltery,

175

and dulcimer, and all kinds of music ye fall down and worship the image which I have made; well: but if ye worship not, ye shall be cast the same hour into the midst of a burning fiery furnace; and who is that God that shall deliver you out of my hands?" (Daniel 3:15).

Who were Shadrach, Meshach and Abed-nego? They were the three young men (along with Daniel) from Jerusalem who were taken captive to Babylon by the army of King Nebuchadnezzar. Upon arriving in Babylon, they were hand-picked to enter into a very special three-year educational program sponsored by the office of the king.

They were young and handsome. They were single and had a good education under their belt. They were away from home out from under parental care. They were holding prestigious positions in the government. They were on their way up the "corporate ladder."

Then came an unexpected proposition. You might think at first that it sounded harmless, that it wouldn't hurt anything. But since we know the first three commandments, we know that this proposal is totally and completely offensive to God. They tell us in no uncertain terms that there are to be no other gods, no graven images, and no one is to bow down and worship any image. God has made this commandment absolutely clear!

It seems there are heathenish propositions all around us today. Proponents tell us they are for our good . . . they will enhance society in general and the quality of our life in particular. There is the pro-abortion proposition, the sexual orientation proposition, the situation ethics proposition, and the permissive proposition. They may sound good at first, but they are in conflict with God's word. What we believe and practice should be based on Scripture and not mere human reason.

The Scriptures tell us something unexpected happened causing everything to look bad for Shadrach, Meshach and Abed-nego. The king had an image of himself made that was 90 feet high and 9 feet wide. The next thing he did was to require everyone to worship the image when they heard the music. For sure, those working for the government would have to do it. But Shadrach, Meshach and Abed-nego did not.

The king was told of their refusal to worship the image, and he became angry and called them into his "oval office." He told them what he expected them to do and that if they complied things would go well with them. Then, with anger in his voice, he told them what would happen if they didn't.

The king did not tell them to stop their worship of Jehovah. He just wanted them to include his "image" in the picture. But the Bible teaches that you cannot serve two masters. God will not share His glory with another.

The men were told that if they did not go along with the plan, they would lose their jobs and their lives. God help us to have people who will not give in to the evil request of an unethical or immoral boss. If the boss wants you to tell a lie for any reason, may you have the courage to say no. If the boss wants you to join with him in some sinful pleasure, may you have the strength to say no—even if it costs you your job. If the company wants you to always work on Sunday and keep you from worship with your family, may God give you the courage to say no, even when you know that you might get fired or have to find another job. We must not let the threats of evil kings determine the level of commitment we maintain with God.

A HEAVENLY PERSUASION

Shadrach, Meshach and Abed-nego already had their minds made up before the king actually confronted them. Their righteous upbringing caused them to have a stable and sincere commitment to God. It is reflected in Daniel 3:16, "Shadrach, Meshach, and Abed-nego, answered and said to the king, O Nebuchadnezzar, we are not careful [worried] to answer thee in this matter."

They didn't even need time for personal consultations. They thought more about their God than they did about their jobs! A persuasion from heaven was greater to them than a proposition from a king.

Let me say a good word for parents who bring up their children in the ways of the Lord! When Shadrach was born, he was given by his parents the name Hananiah, which means "God is gracious." When Meshach was born, they named him

Mishael, which means, "Who is what God is?" And when Abed-nego was born, his parents named him Azariah, which means "whom God helps." This certainly tells us something about parental influence. Although they were away from home, they did not get away from their upbringing. What a lesson for today!

Those three guys stood together. They were united. It is so good to see friends sticking together when trials come. The same is true for families. There is such courage and strength in unity and oneness.

We must also notice the three men were willing to suffer the full consequences of their firm decision for God. They were willing, even if God did not come to their aid.

> If it be so, our God whom we serve is able to deliver us from the burning fiery furnace, and he will deliver us out of thine hand, O king. But if not, be it known unto thee, O king, that we will not serve thy gods, nor worship the golden image which thou hast set up (Daniel 3:17, 18).

There were no special deals to be made with God or with the king. You don't need a deal with God when you have a solid and growing relationship with Him. Walking with God is all you need.

A HORRIBLE PUNISHMENT

The Bible tells us what happened to Shadrach, Meshach and Abed-nego. It was a horrible act of human cruelty.

> And he commanded the most mighty men that were in his army to bind Shadrach, Meshach and Abed-nego, and to cast them into the burning fiery furnace. . . . And these three men, Shadrach, Meshach and Abed-nego fell down bound into the midst of of the burning fiery furnace (Daniel 2:20,21).

Because they stood up to the king for what they knew was right, they were attacked. How committed are we to what is right? How do we know what is right? I believe the answer can be found in the Bible. It is there! We can discover it by the help of the Holy Spirit, and then we must be willing to risk our lives for it. Is that what this story tells us?

178

Look how severe was the attack. They were cast into the furnace of fire. The soldiers physically threw them into the fire. We are told they were cast down into the fire. That is what the devil wants to do to us. He wants us down. But even when we are physically down, we can be standing up on the inside. Notice this diabolic treatment—they were bound before they were cast down into the fire. It does happen. The devil can physically, mentally and emotionally harm us. Sickness is a very common way.

In my early years as a Christian, I thought that the closer you got to God, the fewer problems and attacks you would encounter. But that is not true. It seems to me that the closer you get to God in your walk with Him, your worship of Him, and your work for Him, the greater Satan tries to oppose you and attack you in unbelievable ways.

We must understand that the enemy is out to destroy our faith in God.

A HOLY PRESENCE

It is true that Shadrach, Meshach and Abed-nego were cast into a seven-times-hotter fiery furnace because they would not go along with the king's ungodly proposition and compromise their relationship with God. But let me tell you there is more to this testimony.

The king asked a troubling question. He asked, "Did not we cast three men bound into the midst of the fire?" (v. 24).

The king then made a glorious but unplanned confession. "Lo, I see four men loose, walking in the midst of the fire, and they have no hurt; and the form of the fourth is like the Son of God" (v. 25). I believe the very moment Shadrach, Meshach and Abed-nego entered the furnace, the Fourth Man was there to protect them.

The king extended a very welcome invitation. He said, "Shadrach, Meshach and Abed-nego, ye servants of the most high God, come forth, and come hither" (v. 26). And they came walking out on their own with no harm done to them.

CONCLUSION

We know what changed the king's mind. It was what he

saw. There had to be the painful obedience on the part of Shadrach, Meshach and Abed-nego before there was the mighty miracle on the part of God.

There was the fire. It was real. But it did not destroy the three that chose to trust in God. The fire had lost its power. It could not burn. What a miracle! They came out without any hurt.

By the way, the three young men who were told they would lose their jobs and their lives if they did not compromise got promoted. God turned their problem into a miracle. We serve the same God today, and He can do the same thing for us.

God still keeps the fire from burning!

IF THERE WERE NO FIRE IN HELL

Richard Dillingham

SCRIPTURE: Revelation 20:15

INTRODUCTION

Four Bible words are translated *hell*: the Old Testament Hebrew word *sheol*, also meaning "grave" and three New Testament Greek words—*hades*, meaning "grave" (Revelation 1:18); *tartarus*, meaning "place of punishment" (2 Peter 2:4); and *gehenna*, also meaning "place of punishment" (Revelation 19:20; 20:10, 14,15; and 21:8).

In the Book of Revelation, hell is called the lake of fire.

Gehenna comes from a term meaning "Valley of Hinnom," which lies just outside the City of Jerusalem. During the time of Christ, Gehenna was used as a trash dump and it was here that the bodies of criminals were thrown and burned. It was a place of terrible odor, continually smoldering and burning. When Christ described the place of punishment, chosen by those who refuse to accept Him as Lord, He likened it unto the fiery Valley of Hinnom.

The word *hell* has become an overused byword by many people of our world. Its frequent use may cause one to lose sight of the terrible place implicated by the Word.

181

Jesus said hell was a place so terrible it would be better to be deformed and blind than to go there (Matthew 18:8-9).

Hell, or the lake of fire, was not originally made for man. It was prepared for the devil and his angels (Matthew 25:41). Some have said, "How can a just, loving God send anyone to hell?" The answer is simple. God gave man a choice to do right or wrong, live good or bad, go to heaven or hell. The choice and decision is man's. God gets no pleasure from people being lost eternally and He sends no one to hell.

In fact, people who go to hell must make a desperate effort to get there. They must walk over the caring death of the Lord Jesus Christ, push aside the love of Almighty God, and be insensitive to the constant call of the Holy Spirit. They must push past the prayers of the righteous, count as nothing the preaching of God's ministers, and shut their eyes to the open doors of churches everywhere. All good must be bypassed, and all creation which loudly shouts of a great, loving God must be ignored.

No, God does not want any person to go to hell.

The Bible is plain in its declaration that hell is eternal and a place of punishment by fire (Matthew 25:41; Mark 9:43-44). Yet, there are some who declare there is no hell. For these there remains a rude awakening at death or the day of judgment.

Still others declare that, even though there is a hell, it is not a place of fire. This is contrary to the Scriptures. I want it perfectly understood that I personally believe in a literal, everlasting, burning hell; but it is not the fire alone which makes hell a reality of judgment.

HELL IS A PLACE BEYOND DESCRIPTION.

If there were no fire in hell, it would still be beyond description. Hell is a place of putrefying flesh. Sin in the beginning brought about disease. Nowhere in the Bible does it say that disease will be done away with in hell. Those who choose hell will live with the diseases of this life. There will be the terrible stench of the decaying flesh of the lepers, the open running cancerous sores, and the bloody spittle of those with diseased lungs. Every disease with which sin has plagued men will be present there. All fever, pain, torture, and suffering

182

will be present forever—no death to eliminate, no hospitals for treatment, no doctors to cure. Screams of the anguished will be a permanent part of hell's society.

Hell is a place of weeping. How sad to see someone cry! Here we are able to get away from the sorrowful and see bright faces, but not in hell. Everyone there will be weeping, night and day. Sorrow will prevail. There will be no one to comfort or give a kind word or brush away the tears.

When you remember the greatest time of sorrow in your life—the death of a loved one, news of global disaster, sickness of one dear to you, the mistreatment of an innocent child, the dissolvement of a marriage—you have not yet experienced, even in the smallest degree, the sorrow of hell.

Hell is a place of memories. The mind of man will still function in hell (Luke 16). The people in hell will forever remember. They will hear the prayers of the saintly mother, the counsel of a caring father. They will hear the pleas of a Christian husband or wife. They will remember times of conviction when the Holy Spirit dealt with their heart, times when they almost decided to accept Christ. Forever and forever, they will remember.

Hell is a place of no rest. Here, even the most weary can find some rest. If the body cannot provide it, the mind will become unconscious and rest will come. Not so in eternal hell. In hell there will never be rest from physical, mental or spiritual turmoil. Exhaustion is eternal.

Hell is a place of profanity. It will be like the condition described in Revelation 16:11, "They blasphemed the God of heaven because of their pains and their sores" (Revelation 16:11).

No song will ever be sung in hell. The music of hell will be the moaning and screaming of the lost. No kind words will ever be spoken.

Hell is a place of ever-present evil. These terrible demons described in the New Testament and countless thousands more like them will be the neighbors of those who go to hell. Time will never remove the sinister, chilling fear of the devil's presence. He will be the next door neighbor of the person in hell, forever.

HELL IS A PLACE WITHOUT THE PRESENCE OF GOD.

Since the earth was formed, God's presence has been known (Genesis 1:2). It is almost inconceivable that there is a place not touched by the refreshing presence of God. Yet hell is such a place.

Because God's presence is absent from hell, there is no love in hell (1 John 4:8). In times of hurt, pain, or suffering, what a source of strength just to know someone loves. It will never be so in hell.

Hell is a place of darkness, a place of weakness, a place of lies, of utter confusion. Hell is a place of corruption, of turmoil, of eternal death, of unbridled passions. The desires and passions which literally drove and possessed men in this life will continue to do so with never any relief from their rages.

In hell the greedy will want more and more and have nothing. Jealousy and envy will drive men to madness, but it will never abate. Hatred and anger will be rampant. Fear will reign thick as darkness.

HELL IS A PLACE OF ETERNAL SEPARATION.

Hell destroys all hope of togetherness. There will not be any looking forward to a friend's visit or a child's returning home. There will be no time for being alone with one's companion. Neither will there be any more tears of joy, hugs and kisses, hearts leaping with excitement. Hell separates, not for a day, not for a short while, but forever. Lovers will be separated. Brothers and sisters will be parted. Dad will never again look upon his son. Friends will never again know the joy of good times.

Hell will never know the greenness of spring, the brightness of summer sun, the colors of autumn, the whiteness of newly fallen snow. Hell will never know the smile on a friendly face or the dancing eyes of hopeful expectancy.

Hell will never know joy, but residents can see the joyful reunion of the redeemed and know that one step not taken, one confession never uttered, has forever separated them from God.

The roll call of hell's residents will be long and infamous. Some of them are listed in Revelation 21:8. The cowardly will be there, the faithless and unbelieving, the corrupt, vile and polluted; the dredges of earth's society; murderers; the pornographer and smut peddlers; those who traffic in sex; those who worshiped idols; all liars; gamblers; and all whose names are not found in the Book of Life (Revelation 20:15).

The church attender who never got serious with God, the church member who once was saved but turned back to the things of the world, the good moral person, the one who was a good neighbor but never accepted Christ as Lord, the one who felt that too many good times would be missed if he served God, the person who was planning to get saved next weekend, the person whose intentions were good—they will all be there. The roll call goes on.

CONCLUSION

But not for the saints, those who believed and through faith accepted Christ as Lord of their lives.

"I heard a loud voice from the throne saying, 'Now the dwelling of God is with men, and he will live with them. They will be his people, and God himself will be with them and be their God. He will wipe every tear from their eyes. There will be no more death or mourning, or crying or pain, for the old order of things has passed away'" (Revelation 21:3-4, *New International Version*).

This sermon is not a mythical story, but factual truth based on God's Eternal Word. All of it will soon be a reality. Every one of us will answer to a roll call.

Which one will you answer?

God does not send nor does He want anyone to go to Hell. The choice is yours.

THE PRESENT INHERITANCE OF THE CHURCH

H. Lynn Stone

SCRIPTURE: Ephesians 1:1-22

INTRODUCTION

Let your mind be a time machine.

Travel backwards a little more than 19 centuries to the imperial city of Rome. About 35 years have passed since Jesus died, arose and ascended into the heavens.

Paul, the great missionary of the church, is a prisoner, "an ambassador in bonds" (Ephesians 6:20). It's uncertain whether this is the time when he "dwelt two whole years in his own hired house" with a soldier who kept him (Acts 28:30) or the time he was secluded with only Luke, his physician, in a damp cell, longing for Timothy to bring to him a cloke and some parchments (2 Timothy 4:11-13).

Times are troublesome.

Paul is soon to be beheaded.

Within the decade Rome will sack the city of Jerusalem, murdering thousands of innocents, not leaving a stone of the city.

The church is known as a troublesome sect, composed mostly of ignorant and unlearned men and women. It meets mainly in the homes of its persecuted members. There are no church buildings, no parsonages, no Bible schools, no headquarter buildings, no publishing houses, no earthly possessions.

IN CHRIST, THE CHURCH BLESSES GOD (Verses 3-6).

Hear Paul. "Blessed be the God and Father of our Lord Jesus Christ, who hath blessed us with all spiritual blessings in heavenly places in Christ" (v. 3).

How is Paul enabled to so bless God? Because God has "chosen us in him before the foundation of the world" (v. 4), "predestinated us unto the adoption of children by Jesus Christ" (v. 5), and "made us accepted in the beloved" (v. 6).

Paul is no common prisoner.

In the damp darkness of a prison cell his eyes of faith see the dawning of a new day. It is a day of settlement, a day of inheritance. Paul is of royal lineage, an heir to the throne. So he gives praise to God, to the "glory of his grace."

Even in prison, Paul enjoys his inheritance. He carries the down payment of the riches of heaven in his own bosom. It is sealed in his heart by the Holy Spirit of promise. He is the adopted son of the King of all kings.

How is this possible? Only through redemption!

IN CHRIST, THE CHURCH IS REDEEMED (Verses 7, 8).

To redeem is to buy a slave's freedom with a price. Paul's imprisonment was insignificant when he remembered his greatest bondage. He recalled the harshness and total depravity of his servitude to sin. He had been a slave of slaves persecuting the Church of God and kicking his heel against the pricks.

Now he rejoices in redemption. Notice as he reviews its scope. The price was the Lord's blood, and in giving His blood, the Lord gave His life.

The blood of God's only begotten Son was effective. It purchased redemption and the forgiveness of sins, according to the riches of God's grace. And His grace abounded, bringing forth wisdom that the world cannot know. God gives His saints a new understanding that only spiritual royalty can comprehend.

IN CHRIST, THE CHURCH RECEIVES A NEW REVELATION (Verses 9-12).

Paul had received the revelation of a mystery, hidden in all previous ages.

Now, in prison, he rejoices over the revelation of that mystery. Even today, in a world with damp, dark cells of troublesome times, we rejoice.

We joy not because of pain and heartache, or a hospital ward, or the loneliness of a broken home, or the sorrow of a funeral parlor. But like Paul, we rejoice as redeemed sons and daughters of the King who have received the revelation of a royal mystery.

God has shown to us the goal of redemption. "That in the dispensation of the fullness of times he might gather together in one all things in Christ both which are in heaven, and which are on earth" (v. 10).

Through Christ we have obtained an inheritance. This is certain beyond all circumstances. It is predestinated, according to "the counsel of [God's] own will" (v. 11) if we have "trusted in Christ" (v. 12). This is "to the praise of his glory" (v. 12).

Further, our inheritance is sealed. The Holy Spirit within us is the earnest, or down payment, of our inheritance. Joy, ecstasy, and fulfillment abound within us when the Spirit of God moves within our hearts and gives utterance to our lips, enabling us to cry, "Abba, Father." And that Spirit within is our own personal guarantee, written on the tables of our hearts, that our inheritance is sure for all eternity.

CONCLUSION

Therefore, we pray as Paul that "the God of our Lord Jesus Christ, the Father of glory" may grant to us the fullness of our present redemption.

May God grant to us, in a world of turmoil and confusion, *the Spirit of wisdom.* May we be given not the knowledge of this world, nor the encyclopedias of man's understanding, nor a computer mind of mere facts, but the knowledge of God's dear Son.

May we know *the hope of his calling.* When life is hopeless and dark as midnight, when cancer eats ruthlessly within our frail, bent frame, when our children look at us with longing eyes for a word of hope, may we know the hope of His calling.

May we know the *riches of the glory of His inheritance in the saints.* When the money has been spent and the home has been sold and the food has been eaten and the clothes have worn thin, may we know the riches of glory.

May we know *the exceeding greatness of His power to us-ward who believe.* When temptation causes our knees to tremble, may we know His power. When Satan comes to us in the wilderness, may we know His power. When long hours of travailing prayer for a wayward child brings no results and there is no news from a far country and there is no prodigal on the horizon, may we know His power.

When Satan wraps his cruel tentacles around our loved one and possesses their very being with his demonic hold and intoxicates them with wine and drugs their mind, may we know His power.

Yes, Lord, let us know the exceeding greatness of Your power. It is the power wrought in Christ when He was raised from the dead. It is resurrection power!

When evil engulfs us like a troubled sea, and the cold, icy waters freeze our faith, may the Easter Son shine on the sepulcher of our souls. Let the earth shake at Thy presence. Let the imperial guards of this world stand back. Let the stone roll away. Let the angelic messengers fold the shroud of the dead, and let us be raised like Him by resurrection power!

Let us know the power of His ascension. When the weight of this world would hold us down and our feet are tired of its muddy paths, when the clouds have broken forth with hail and rain and darkness frightens our souls, lift us up, O Lord. Let us ascend with Thee. Let us hide above the cold rain and walk on top of silvery clouds in the warm presence of heavenly places.

May we know the power of His exaltation. When principalities and powers and might and dominions exalt themselves, He lifts us up in Him. He exalts above every name—the rich, the mighty, the famous. He exalts us above the name of every governor, ruler, prince, princess, premier, president, sheik, king, and queen. For we are exalted in His name—a name above all that is in this world and in the world to come.

Brothers and sisters in Christ, God has put all things under His feet.

When Joshua fought against the Amorites, he prayed that the sun would stand still upon Gibeon and the moon would halt over the valley of Ajalon. The five kings of the enemy nations hid themselves in the cave of Makkedah.

At the end of the battle Joshua opened the cave and had the five cruel rulers brought out. Joshua then called for the captains. "Come near, put your feet upon the necks of these kings. And they came near, and put their feet upon the necks of them" (Joshua 10:24).

Oh, frightened child, running from the enemy, hidden deep in the caves of your own soul, hear the word of our Commander. Let Him bring forth all your enemies and speak this word in glorious assurance:

"He hath put all things under his feet."

This is the present inheritance of the saints.

TRUE WORSHIP

Orville Hagan

SCRIPTURE: *John, Chapter 4*

INTRODUCTION

Jesus had just met a woman of Samaria—an immoral woman, a sinful woman, but a *sad* woman.

He could have heaped judgment upon her, but He didn't. She already had enough judgment.

She needed help.

She needed kindness.

She needed love.

They talked about water and then He drew her to the subject of religion. "The woman saith unto Him, Sir, I perceive that thou art a prophet" (v. 19). She classified Him as a prophet because He revealed her sin to her. In her opinion only a prophet could do that.

WHAT TRUE WORSHIP IS AND WHY IT IS IMPORTANT

"Our fathers worshipped in this mountain; and ye say, that in Jerusalem is the place where men ought to worship. Jesus saith unto her, Woman, believe me, the hour cometh, when ye shall neither in this mountain, nor yet at Jerusalem, worship the Father. Ye worship ye know not what: we know what we worship: for salvation is of the Jews. But the hour cometh, and now is, when the true worshipers shall worship the Father in spirit and in truth: for the Father seeketh such to worship him. God is a Spirit: and they that worship him must worship him in spirit and in truth" (John 4:20-24).

Please underline the word *must.*

We read in Luke 19:10, "The Son of Man is come to seek and to save that which was lost."

Here where our Lord is "seeking" sinners, we have the same word. The Father is seeking worshipers, just as the Savior is seeking sinners. You know He sought for you with love, persistence and concern. The Savior hounded you. He did not let you go. He came seeking—seeking to save you.

Jesus said, "The Father is seeking worshipers." People say, "Jesus, You are my Savior." That is beautiful, but He is also seeking people who will worship.

Worship means adoration. Worship means the lifting of the heart. Jeremiah writes in Lamentations 3:41, "Let us lift up our heart with our hands unto the God in the heavens." Isn't that some picture! True worship is lifting up your heart with hands to the Lord. This is worship. Worship can be praise or paying homage. Worship must have a basis. You just do not worship in thin air.

True worship is based on an acquaintance with God, a knowledge of God, an appreciation for God. The heathen worship with fear, with terror and superstition. Your worship should be based on a wide, expanded knowledge of Jesus as our adorable Savior. He is the best friend we have ever had —one who will never leave us or forsake us; one who goes with us whether it is on the mountain or in the valley, whether the days be dark or bright. He is One who has taken upon Himself our sorrows and our sicknesses and He is still performing miracles of healing today.

He has baptized us with His blessed Holy Spirit into a new relationship with Himself and into a new place of worship and power. A part of the ministry of the Spirit is to teach us to worship. This is why we must be filled with the Spirit so we will know how to worship the Lord.

"Now unto the King eternal, immortal, invisible, the only wise God, be honor and glory for ever and ever. Amen" (1 Timothy 1:17).

"That thou keep this commandment without spot, unrebukeable until the appearing of our Lord Jesus Christ; Which in his times he shall shew, who is the blessed and only Potentate, the King of kings, and Lord of lords; Who only hath immortality, dwelling in the light which no man can approach unto; whom no man hath seen, nor can see; to whom be *honor and power everlasting.* Amen" (1 Timothy 6:14).

That is grounds for worship! Let's also note some words from John in Revelation:

"The four and twenty elders fall down before him that sat on the throne, and worship him that liveth for ever and ever, and cast their crowns before the throne, saying, *Thou art worthy, O Lord,* to receive glory and honor and power: for thou hast created all things, and for thy pleasure they are and were created" (Revelation 4:10, 11).

This is worship:

"And when He had taken the book, the four beasts and the four and twenty elders fell down before the Lamb, having every one of them harps, and golden vials full of odours, which are the prayers of saints."

"And they sung a new song, saying, Thou art worthy to take the book, and to open the seals thereof: for thou wast slain, and hast redeemed us to God by thy blood out of every kindred, and tongue, and people, and nation; And hast made us unto our God kings and priests: and we shall reign on the earth."

"And I beheld, and I heard the voice of many angels round about the throne and the beasts and the elders: and the number of them was ten thousand times ten thousand, and thousands of thousands; Saying with a loud voice, Worthy is the Lamb that was slain to receive power, and riches, and wisdom, and strength, and honor, and glory, and blessing."

They got excited about praising the Lord.

"And every creature which is in heaven, and on the earth, and under the earth, and such as are in the sea, and all that are in them, heard I saying, Blessing, and honor, and glory, and power, be unto him that sitteth upon the throne, and unto the Lamb for ever and ever."

"And the four beasts said, Amen. And the four and twenty elders fell down and worshiped him that liveth for ever and ever" (Revelation 5:8-14).

THE MEASURE OF TRUE WORSHIP AND WHAT HAPPENS

"And there was given me a reed like unto a rod: and the angel stood, saying, Rise, and measure the temple of God, and the altar, and them that worship therein" (Revelation 11:1).

We are going to measure the worshipers. He said measure those who worship. Measure their sincerity, wholeheartedness, love, dedication, consecration, holiness, and sanctification. Measure the total man. This is an order. "There was given to me a reed" and the angel said to start measuring now.

In Luke 17:11-19, we read the story of Jesus' healing the 10 lepers who were crying to Him. He spoke to them to go show themselves to the priests. Verse 14 says, "As they went, they were cleansed." They went in faith.

They didn't wait to be healed. As they went they were healed. Healing doesn't stop if you are not healed at the altar. The healing wants to go with you. Do not leave the altar and say I did not receive anything. The Lord is not through with you yet! He may meet you on the way home. He may meet you after you get home. He may meet you a week later. The reason so many people are not healed is they leave everything they come for. And when they do not get it at the altar, they ask, "What's the use?"

These men were healed as they went, and one of them came back and began to praise the Lord. And Jesus said, "Were there not ten? but where are the nine?" Only this stranger came back to glorify God. He came back to worship. He returned to give praise.

I'll tell you why some healings do not last. People are healed and forget to worship. People are healed and forget to give God thanks.

The other nine got what they wanted and said goodbye. This stranger, this poor man—touched by the grace of God, touched by the love of God—returns and worships.

In 2 Timothy 3:5, Paul speaks of men who, "[have] a form of godliness, but [deny] the power thereof." He tells us to turn away from such. This is a thankless day. Thanklessness is a curse.

EXAMPLES OF TRUE WORSHIP AND THE RESULTS

"Now Abraham was old, advanced in age; and the Lord had blessed Abraham in every way. And Abraham said to his servant, the oldest of his household, who had charge of all that he owned, `Please place your hand under my thigh, and I will make you swear by the Lord, the God of heaven and the God of earth, that you shall not take a wife for my son from the daughters of the Canaanites, among whom I live, but you shall go to my country and to my relatives, and take a wife for my son Isaac" (Genesis 24:1-4, *New American Standard Bible*).

Here Abraham's oldest servant is requested to find a bride for Isaac. Notice in verse 12 that the servant begins this task with prayer. He asks the Lord to let it come to pass that the daughter whom God would chose would invite him to let her draw water for him and his camels.

What credentials for a bride! Notice she was asked to draw water for his camels, not horses. Have you ever watched a camel drink? Gallons and Gallons! Then notice what he does. He worships as a result of God answering his prayer (v. 48).

Let us look at Exodus 4:30, 31: "And Aaron spoke all the words which the Lord had spoken to Moses. He then performed the signs in the sight of the people. So the people believed; and and when they heard that the Lord was concerned about the sons of Israel and that He had seen their affliction, they bowed low and worshiped" (*NASB*).

They were still in bondage. They were still making brick. They were still being whipped and beaten, but they heard a message, believed and worshiped. Deliverance had not come;

195

but it was promised. Oh, if we could get people to worship God in faith for healing, in faith for baptism in the Holy Ghost, and in faith for needs.

Israel only heard there was a chance of being redeemed and delivered and started to worship.

In faith, believe the promises and start worshiping!

Later Moses had installed Joshua as the commander in chief. Joshua became leader of Israel in Moses place. "Now it came about when Joshua was by Jericho, that he lifted up his eyes and looked, and behold, a man was standing opposite him with his sword drawn in his hand, and Joshua went to him and said to him, 'Are you for us or for our adversaries?'" (Joshua 5:13, *NASB*).

I do not know what he was going to do if he was for adversaries. This took courage!

"And the captain of the Lord's host said unto Joshua, Loose thy shoe from off thy foot; for the place whereon thou standeth is holy. And Joshua did so" (Joshua 5:15).

This was Joshua, the five-star general, Joshua, the top man—ordained by God, blessed by Moses. Here comes an unannounced, unnamed man. "I am taking charge." Joshua salutes him and worships. He is demoted, yet he worships. He is moved from the top, yet he worships. How many problems could be solved if people could be demoted and worship.

In 2 Samuel 12, we find that King David's son was sick unto death. Here the man of God had fasted and prayed seven days for God to answer his prayer and to heal his son. I can imagine that David's servant said, "If King David is this upset about the boy's sickness, what will he do when he finds the boy is already dead?"

Finally a servant of David informed him that his son was dead. God had not answered David's prayer. Notice 2 Samuel 12:20, "So David arose from the ground, washed, anointed himself, and changed his clothes; and he came into the house of the Lord and worshiped" (*NASB*).

He didn't get offended at God. It was during this time David spoke the remarkable words that have been quoted so often at funerals, "I shall go to him, but he shall not return to me."

196

The important point here is that no matter what happens to us, if we will worship, God will bring us out victoriously!

The last example of true worship is found in Job 1. Verse 1 states that Job was upright, feared God, despised evil. He was also the richest man of the East. He had 10 sons and daughters.

How much can one man take in one day. When the sun came up that day, Job was wealthy, happy, and the father of 10 children. When evening came, he had lost all his wealth and his children.

Notice in verses 14 and 15 that a messenger told Job that his oxen and asses were stolen by the Sabeans and his servants slain. Verse 16 states that while he was yet speaking another messenger said that fire burned up the sheep. While he was yet speaking another messenger announced that the Chaldeans fell upon the camels and carried them away. While he was yet speaking another messenger stated a great wind hit the four corners of the house and all his children were dead.

What can you do when you lose everything in one day? "Then Job arose, and rent his mantle, and fell down upon the ground and worshiped" (v. 20).

CONCLUSION

Never allow anything in life to stop your worship. Notice the last chapter of Job, verse 12: "So the Lord blessed the latter end of Job more than his beginning."

TRIVIA OR TREASURE

E. M. Abbott

SCRIPTURE: Exodus 4:2-4

INTRODUCTION

It has been said that one man's junk is another's treasure. There was a time when we took our discards to the junk heap, or put them out for the garbage man to pick up. Now we have yard sales!

We have discovered that possessions we view as trivia are, at times, important. Often, those items stashed away in our closets or attics, unused and gathering dust, are important and have value to someone else.

This is especially true in our relationship with God and in our interpersonal relationships with each other. There are several points to consider.

FIRST, EVENTS THAT SEEM INSIGNIFICANT ARE OFTEN VERY IMPORTANT.

Actions that appear to be trivial and unimportant at the moment, later become very meaningful and far-reaching in life.

A classic example is the Battle of Gettysburg. Recognized by most historians as the turning point in the Civil War, it was actually a chance encounter. Some Confederate soldiers were sent to Gettysburg to get a supply of shoes! The rest is history. In just three days of fighting, 53,000 men lost their lives, and Lee's army was in full retreat.

A trivial assignment on an insignificant day in November became history. It has been etched forever in the hearts and minds of Americans everywhere.

SECOND, GOD OFTEN CHOOSES TRIFLES TO BRING ABOUT TRIUMPH.

In Exodus 4:3 we read the story of Moses tending the sheep of Jethro, his father-in-law, on a certain day. This day to Moses was like any other. He walked the same path, through the same dusty, desert trail, to the backside of the same mountain—Mt. Horeb.

In his hand he carried a rod—as did all shepherds. Perhaps had carried this rod hundreds of times before. It was only a crooked sapling, curved at one end, three to six feet in length, to help him in the base task of tending sheep.

Little did Moses realize that this trifling rod would soon become an instrument of great triumph and would help him care for an entire nation. The common, insignificant twig would become a symbol of victory. There were thousands just like it in that country. A sharp knife could cut it. Carelessness could lose it. Human strength could break it. Fire could devour it. There was nothing in it to distinguish it from any other rod except for one thing. Moses allowed it to become God's instrument.

THIRD, GOD OFTEN DOES HIS MIGHTIEST WORKS BY THE MOST LOWLY MEANS.

"What is that in thine hand?" God asked Moses (v.2). And Moses answered, "A rod." God continued, "Cast it on the ground." Moses cast it on the ground and it became a serpent.

Now there was no other shepherd's stick like it in all the world. Junk became treasure—for it was now God's chosen instrument. The rod of God! The ordinary, lowly sign and instrument of Moses' menial occupation, cast down and taken up through obedience, became the power of God. The lowly became mighty.

199

God is continually putting us to the test of obedience. "What is that in your hand?" He is asking. A rod, a shepherd's stick, a cake of barley meal, an earthen pitcher, five loaves and two fishes, a mite, a grain of mustard seed—the list can go on and on.

And He is saying to us, "Give it to Me. Cast it at My feet in obedience, in humble dedication; and then take it up again to use for My Glory." He reminds us that He has chosen the foolish things of the world to shame the wise and the weak things of the world to shame the strong. He uses "the lowly things of this world and the despised things—to nullify the things that are" (1 Corinthians 1:28, *New International Version*).

FOURTH, SMALL MOMENTS OFTEN BECOME GREAT EVENTS.

A battlefield at Gettysburg, Pennsylvania, was to be consecrated as a National Cemetery. The date set was November 19, 1863. Edward Everett, one of the greatest orators of all time, was selected to give the keynote address of dedication. Possessed of an extraordinary memory, a melodious voice, and brilliance of style and delivery, this statesman, who graduated from Harvard at the age of 17, delivered a two-hour oration. In the days that followed, his address was front-page news with unqualified praise.

A tall, thin, scraggly-bearded man was also invited to speak —primarily out of courtesy because he was President of the United States. His speech was only two minutes in length and was relegated to the inner pages of the newspapers. Lincoln himself said in that two-minute address, "The world will little note nor long remember what we say here." How wrong he was!

That short speech, brought about by a chance battle and made because of a courtesy invitation, is now recognized, 125 years later, as one of the greatest, most moving, classic utterances of all time "The Gettysburg Address."

A small tent was erected on a tiny island in the Atlantic Ocean just off the coast of Virginia. A relatively known pioneer preacher was the "new-field" evangelist. With no financial assistance—with just sheer, simple faith—he was endeavoring to plant a Church of God on Chincoteague Island. I was a lad of 10, singing duets with my sister, Elizabeth. The pioneer preacher was my father, C. J. Abbott.

Small wonder anyone came to hear! But they did. By the hundreds. Among those who came was a teenager, curious like the others about "tongues" people. And God touched him. And he became one of us—a Pentecostal.

I remember the first time I heard him preach. He, too, was asked to speak out of courtesy. To help him get started in the ministry. He was a good preacher. But little did I dream that I was listening to the future general overseer of the Church of God —Raymond Crowley. A small moment became a great event.

It has been so throughout church history. God says to man, "What is that in your hand?"

"A sling," says David. "That's all I need, go slay the giant," says God.

"A sword," says Jonathan. "That's sufficient; go defeat the Philistines."

"A piece of parchment," says Martin Luther. "It's enough. Write on it and nail your theses to the door of the University of Wittenburg."

"A weakness of speech, and an unattractive physique," says Paul. "Go in the demonstration of the power of God. Use that stylus in your hand to write My Epistles."

CONCLUSION

I can't help but believe God is saying to us today, "What do you have in your hand?" I believe He is urging us to take our trivia, gathering dust, locked in our hearts and minds, and to cast it at His feet—so it too can become His treasure.

We have a choice. We can take what we have, and strain and strive all our lives. Or, we can say, "Lord, here's what I have. I give it to you." Then the ordinary will become extraordinary.

On Fifth Avenue in New York City at the entrance to the RCA Building, is a gigantic statue of Atlas, the Greek god of mythology, holding the world upon his powerful shoulders. His beautifully proportioned physique depicts every muscle in his body straining under the tremendous burden.

201

Just across the street inside St. Patrick's Cathedral is a statue of the boy Jesus. With no effort, and no show of strain, He is holding the world in one hand!

Once we give Him what we have, it becomes His. He performs the supernatural, the miraculous, for us with ease. We just make ourselves available servants—to become His treasure.

WHEN IT DOESN'T MAKE SENSE

H. B. Thompson, Jr.

SCRIPTURE: 2 Corinthians 4:8, 9

INTRODUCTION

She was 10 years old and a beautiful child. Looking up through tears she said to the pastor, "Why did my mommy have to die?"

It just didn't make sense!

It was about 5:30 a.m. when the doctor walked from the Intensive Care Unit and said to the grandmother of a 17 year old, "I'm sorry, we did all we could, but it wasn't enough."

It just didn't make sense!

In the casket was the body of a 13-month-old baby. Before the casket stood bewildered and brokenhearted parents. With voices hardly able to speak, they said to me, "Pastor, we don't understand. He was the joy of our life! What will we do now?"

It just didn't make sense!

The headlines flashed around the globe, "Missionaries brutally slain by natives." Immediately the questions flood the minds of believer and non-believer alike: "Why?" "How can this be?" "Would God permit such an atrocity?"

It just doesn't make sense!

Suffering, sorrow, separation, and sadness have all become such a part of life that we are almost shocked when some good news crosses the headlines. There are so many unexplainable problems plaguing our society today that even psychologists need each other for counseling.

Furthermore, the frustrations are magnified by the fact that no one really seems to have any answers that make sense. There are many explanations offered, but very few real answers today.

Homes are being destroyed at record levels. Children are hurting from dissension and divorce. Families are fractured by the anxieties of this society. Suicide has almost become an epidemic. And over and over again I hear it verbalized and see it in expressions, "It just doesn't make sense!"

How then do we as Christians in this topsy-turvy world make any sense out of what makes no sense? That's a dilemma we face. Beyond that, how do we cope with those things in our lives that just don't make sense!

It seems to me the Word of God speaks to us in these times with four steps to take when it doesn't make sense!

STEP ONE, RECOGNIZE OUR FRUSTRATION.

By this we simply mean that we do not deny frustration exists, nor do we ignore it in the vain hope that it will disappear. We certainly do not give up to the frustration, but we acknowledge what it is and that it does exist.

Now, along with this recognition, we must know that just because some things fail to make sense presently does not mean they will never make sense. Many times hindsight clears our understanding.

Many things God does or allows we do not presently understand. We may understand better later, but right now it may not make sense. We must allow for the fact that the "foolishness of God is wiser than man's wisdom" (1 Corinthians 1:25, *New International Version*).

To help us to deal with these frustrations, a simple illustration may help. We do not eat flour alone. Nor do we make a meal of only sour milk or salt or soda by themselves. But when grandma puts these ingredients together in the right proportion and bakes them awhile, we love to feast on those great southern biscuits. So it is that at times there are events in our lives which are extremely disturbing when we try to digest them by themselves.

God has a way of putting them into a recipe of life and when they come out of His oven, in the light of eternity, we see them as a part of "all things working together for good to them that love Him." Troubles triumph and frustrations multiply when we try to isolate certain experiences or to understand them torn from the context of life.

We cannot become like the proverbial ostrich with our heads in the sand, nor can we allow the frustrations to frazzle our emotions to an uncontrolled state; but we must recognize our frustration. This is not a lack of faith or a negative confession; it is simply coming to grips with reality, which is often a catalyst for our faith.

Notice particularly two sections of Scripture from the Phillips' translation of the New Testament:

"We are handicapped on all sides, but we are never frustrated; we are puzzled but never in despair. We are persecuted, but we never have to stand it alone: we may be knocked down but we are never knocked out!" (2 Corinthians 4:8-10).

"Don't worry over anything whatever; tell God every detail of your needs in earnest and thankful prayer, and the peace of God, which transcends human understanding, will keep constant guard over your hearts and minds as they rest in Christ Jesus" (Philippians 4:6, 7).

What encouragement this gives us. It helps us know we can deal with our frustrations for what they are. Further, it tells us we do not always have to understand in order to trust God in Whom there is perfect understanding.

The account of Martha's frustration over the death of her brother—a death she felt would not have happened if Jesus had been present (John 11:21-24)—is a classic example of an individual not understanding and yet implicitly believing that the Lord was the answer.

STEP TWO, REALIZE OUR LIMITATIONS.

So often this is the cause, or at least the complication, of our frustrations—we fail to recognize our own limitations. Just because it doesn't make sense to me does not mean it does not make sense at all. Casting an empty net into a sea where he had fished all night and caught nothing (Luke 5) made no sense at all to Simon Peter. But at the instruction of Jesus, he did just that and caught more fish than he could handle.

We are not omniscient. Our understanding is incomplete. That's just part of being human. We are limited creatures in ability and understanding. In fact, God sometimes allows things that defy our understanding as a reminder to us that His ways are above ours and His thoughts superior to ours.

Again, the story of Lazarus comes to mind—(John 11:1-44). It made no sense for Jesus to know Lazarus was sick and yet let him die. That just didn't add up at all in terms of the disciples. It did not make sense to them, but that did not mean it made no sense at all.

Realize that when you face frustrations, you may not understand because you are human and as such have limitations. That fact does not make us good or bad; it only helps us diffuse some of the anxiety our frustration can create.

STEP THREE, REALIGN OUR REVELATION.

Get things in focus with scripture (1 Peter 1:24, 25). Sometimes things that make no sense to our ordinary reasoning can make sense to our spiritual reasoning when we get the proper alignment with the Word of God.

David had to do this (Psalm 73:1-17), and so did Job (Job 42:1-6). This is what Jesus did for Mary and Martha in John 11:25, 26. These people simply got their lives aligned with God's Word. A new focus occurred and new understanding came.

The highest lesson we can ever learn is to trust God regardless (Philippians 2:13). If everything made sense to our understanding, we would need no faith. Carry that thought to its logical conclusion and we would ultimately need no God.

Now, when these senseless times come, we can react in any of several ways. We can grow bitter and resentful, grumbling and murmuring about God. We can become stoic, grit our teeth, and bear it. We can develop a martyr's complex and just endure the inevitable. Or we can search for faith to see God working for our good. That is what Joseph did in the Old Testament, and the realignment of his revelation helped him understand that what was intended for his harm, God ultimately used for good (Genesis 45:1-8).

You do not hear Paul, the apostle, saying, "I know why I believe," but rather "I know whom I have believed" (2 Timothy 1:12). His alignment of revelation from the Lord taught him there was an evacuation route from every temptation (1 Corinthians 10:13).

It could not have made sense to the servants at Cana to fill water pots with water when wine was what they needed. Nor could they fully comprehend why they should then take the water and carry it to the guests. But they realigned their revelation, and between the well and the tables, the water was turned into wine.

I once read of a man in the sunset years of his life who was so enthusiastic and positive that those who knew him marveled at his exuberance. One day someone asked him, "What is the secret of your joyous lifestyle? How is it that you have such a positive attitude about the future?"

With no hesitation the man replied, "It's really very simple. The answer is found in the Bible." The inquirer responded, "You found it in the Bible? Where is it in the Bible?" Again, without the slightest hitch, the senior gentleman said, "Well, the Bible says over and again 'It came to pass.' Nowhere does it say that it came to stay."

His interpretation may be exegetically shaky, but he had his revelation aligned right.

STEP FOUR, REMEMBER OUR DESTINATION.

This is not an escape from reality; it is rather an anticipation of reality. This is the concept that kept Paul going: "For I reckon that the sufferings of this present time are not worthy to be compared with the glory which shall be revealed in us" (Romans 8:18).

Phillips puts it in these words: "In my opinion whatever we may have to go through now is less than nothing compared with the magnificent future God has planned for us."

This life is but for a moment and then real living begins. We are simply pilgrims and strangers passing through. Our time is only transitory according to Philippians 3:20.

And when you compare our present paranoia with the future parousia (rapture), the present looks different. When we live each day with eternity in mind, it changes our outlook.

This is what Jesus did when He told us, "Whosoever liveth and believeth in me shall never die" (John 11:26).

We must live every day "looking for that blessed hope and the glorious appearing of the great God and our Savior Jesus Christ" (Titus 2:13).

CONCLUSION

This life is filled with times that just don't make sense. There are days filled with dilemmas for which there seems no deliverance. There will be nights plagued with nausea for which there seems no relief. There are times we feel trapped with no means of escape. There will be circumstances that go in unending circles for which we can find no control. But in these times if we can (1) recognize our frustration, (2) realize our limitations, (3) realign our revelation, and (4) remember our destination, we'll be able to cope with the crises until the Christ of every crisis comes with comfort or cure.

ONE GOSPEL—ONE TASK

Jim O. McClain, Sr.

SCRIPTURE: Acts 1:8

INTRODUCTION

When Christ commissioned the Church, it is interesting to note that His specific instructions concerned what to do, what to say, and where to go.

WHAT TO DO

Regardless of the position one holds, whether in the local church or the church in general, the basic fact and primary concern should be to testify and tell what the gospel of redemption has done for us. Our own personal testimony will verify with all others that the effects of the gospel are the same, and it has power to save.

Our own personal testimony will be just as effective as that of Paul the Apostle. The vision that changed his life will change the lives of others also; and as true disciples we will not be disobedient but will ask of the Lord, "What wilt Thou have me to do?"

Paul wrote, "Which is come unto you, as it is in all the world; and bringeth forth fruit, as it doth also in you, since the day ye heard of it, and knew the grace of God in truth" (Colossians 1:6). A contemporary translation of this particular verse would be, "The same good news that came to you is going out over all the world and is changing lives everywhere as it is changing yours."

The same transforming experience in our lives as that of the Apostle Paul on the dusty road entering into Damascus will cause us to testify of what Christ has done for us. After his conversion, everywhere we see Paul the Apostle, whether in the marketplace or before the Sanhedrin, he referred to this experience and boldly declared, "I was not disobedient unto the heavenly vision" (Acts 26:19).

What are we to do? We too must testify to the gospel of Jesus Christ and witness to others that what He has done for us, He will do for them. Our testimony can be just as effective as the testimony of the Apostle Paul.

WHAT TO SAY

We are to tell everyone, "If thou shalt confess with thy mouth the Lord Jesus, and shalt believe in thine heart that God hath raised him from the dead, thou shalt be saved" (Romans 10:9). The gospel of redemption is to tell of the Resurrection of Jesus Christ, that He is alive. The Book of Acts bridges the message and the mission.

In order to witness as Christ has commanded, we must be empowered. The whole Book of Acts revolves around this key verse: "But ye shall receive power, after that the Holy Ghost is come upon you: and ye shall be witnesses unto me both in Jerusalem, and in all Judaea, and in Samaria, and unto the uttermost part of the earth" (Acts 1:8).

Many translations render this passage, "you shall receive power when the Holy Ghost comes upon you." You become a whole man or woman, so it is the whole gospel for the whole man for the whole world.

When those early believers came down from the Upper Room, they were filled with the Spirit. They all had the same testimony, the testimony of the Resurrection. From the Upper Room to Jerusalem, Judaea, Samaria and unto the uttermost part of the earth, their message was, "He's alive! He's alive!

He's alive! Come, see the place where the Lord lay. He is not here: for He is risen, as He said."

They went everywhere, the Lord working with them, confirming the Word with signs following. In the name of Jesus they cast out devils. They laid hands on the sick and they recovered. "Therefore they that were scattered abroad went every where preaching the word" (Acts 8:4). The command was not *maybe*, but *must*. They received power as a driving force. They received an experience that motivated their lives and mastered them by vibrant fire. They had power to back up their claims, to verify their Christian witness; and they had miracles and healings to substantiate their claims.

I was a delegate to the World Pentecostal Fellowship in Jerusalem in 1961. I did not have to go to the empty tomb to realize that Jesus is alive. The fact that the Comforter is come is evidence of the Resurrection. Jesus said, "If I go not away, the Comforter will not come unto you; but if I depart, I will send him unto you" (John 16:7).

We know Jesus came out of the empty tomb because He said, "If I go not away, the Comforter will not come unto you." The Comforter has come, as He said, and it is evidence that Jesus now sits at the right hand of the Father. He is alive and the promise has come.

To be filled with the Spirit is to have the power to do what Christ said to do and to say what Christ told us to say. Some scriptural admonitions and examples are "go ye; go near; go thy way; they went away; they went down; I must needs go by; salute no man (that is, do not tarry); occupy till I come again."

Not only does the Spirit tell us what to do and what to say, but it gives us the boldness to stand up and defend our faith. As you know, Peter denied the Lord. He even swore when the little lady said, "I know you are a Galilean." But this was Peter before Pentecost.

After Pentecost, Peter was the preacher. The believers were accused of being full of new wine. "But Peter, standing up with the eleven, lifted up his voice, and said unto them, Ye men of Judaea, and all ye that dwell at Jerusalem, be this known unto you, and hearken to my words" (Acts 2:14).

Peter was then able to stand before them without embarrassment, without running as he did before, without blushing, without question. He simply looked them in the face. Let it be understood! Let it be known! Let there be no doubts in your mind! "These are not drunken, as ye suppose, seeing it is but the third hour of the day" (Acts 2:15).

So we are to preach the gospel, give personal testimony of our faith, and be filled with the Spirit as our driving force. Then we will automatically do and say what Christ commissioned the Church to do.

WHERE TO GO

The gospel is for the world. It is universal in scope. Missions is God's business and the first order of the day. It supersedes and precedes all other business. The commission to preach the gospel everywhere is the basis for world evangelism. Go into all the world and preach the gospel to every creature. Preach and teach the gospel everywhere. "Go ye therefore, and teach all nations" (Matthew 28:19). "The field is the world" (Matthew 13:38).

A universal curse needs a universal cure. The gospel is that cure. This glorious gospel is life and a cure for a universal curse. The gospel is for everybody, everywhere, in all positions of society:

> "I am debtor both to the Greeks, and to the Barbarians; both to the wise, and to the unwise. So, as much as in me is, I am ready to preach the gospel to you that are at Rome also. For I am not ashamed of the gospel of Christ: for it is the power of God unto salvation to every one that believeth; to the Jew first, and also to the Greek" (Romans 1:14-16).

Regardless of their academic background and scholastic achievements, we are indebted to the educated and the illiterate. We are indebted to the rich and poor, black and white, male and female. We are debtors, regardless of who they are and where they are.

If the gospel isn't worth sharing with the world, it is ridiculous to try to share it with anyone here at home. We are to evangelize the world. God will never ask or expect us

212

to do an impossible task. We are promised, "They that sow in tears shall reap in joy. He that goeth forth and weepeth, bearing precious seed, shall doubtless come again with rejoicing, bringing his sheaves with him" (Psalm 126:5, 6).

CONCLUSION

The "one gospel and the one task" is obedience to the commission, love for the work, doing God's perfect will, and total commitment.

Christ has outlined for us what to do, what to say, and where to go. If we are obedient and true followers of Jesus Christ, we will not disobey or slacken our pace. We will recognize, realize, have a revelation of Jesus Christ, know our position as a member of the body of Christ and our relationship to the body, and will communicate the gospel of Jesus Christ to the world, especially since it is outlined to us so clearly.

He has told us what to do and what we are to say and where we are to go.

PRAYING UNDER PRESSURE

Larry G. Hess

SCRIPTURE: 1 Peter 4:7; Romans 12:21, New International Version

INTRODUCTION

We hear a great deal today about pressure, stress, and anxiety. Many people speak with an authority that says, "I have the answers." However, when you look at some of their theories, they appear to be abstract concepts that never get down to where all of us live.

Some speakers give harshly simplistic solutions to complex problems. They seem to lack a compassionate sensitivity to the very real struggles rumbling inside people who may even look happy and content.

Each one of us is facing the pressures of our life-style, our work, and our world. The pressure is on! Sometimes there is little we can do to avoid the pressures we face. At other times we face pressures because we are driven to extreme feelings and behavior. We are driven by our needs, our emotions, and our undisciplined life-styles. At times we feel that we must achieve or that we must win or that we must be in control.

Learning how to pray even when under extreme pressures is a vital part of living out our commitment to Christ. In this message, when I say we are to PRAY, I am saying that we are to do these things:

1. Praise the Lord and proclaim His greatness.

2. Remember and rejoice with thanksgiving because of who God is and because of what He has done.

3. Acknowledge our sins and ask His forgiveness.

4. Yield to God's guidance and faithfully obey His Word. Christ said, "Without me ye can do nothing" (John 15:5). Since we can do nothing for God in ourselves, we must be willing to sacrifice self-glory. We must be willing to give up our plans in order to obey God, for God works through people who offer themselves totally to Him.

Praying under pressure requires we be "clear minded and self-controlled" (1 Peter 4:7, *NIV*), so that we may overcome the problems and pressures that would control us.

WHAT DOES PRESSURE DO TO US?

Pressure has a way of depressing us. It causes us to feel out of control. All too many of us can identify with the feelings of Matilda Nordtvedt, the wife of a pastor and missionary. In her book, *Living Beyond Depression*, she writes, "For years I lived part-time in the tunnel of depression. Nine years ago I became a permanent resident there. For six months I stared at the walls, cried into my pillow, found life meaningless, and wished to die."

Matilda's problem began with the pressures of being an overachiever. She felt she had to prove her worth by trying to excel in everything. When she felt so out of control that she could not function she went to a doctor. He told her she was suffering from "nervous exhaustion" and sent her away for a six-month rest.

The rest and tranquilizers brought a measure of relief, but she had lost her zeal to live. While in a psychiatric hospital for one month she received shock treatments, drug therapy, and counseling. They released her labeled "cured" even though she was severely depressed and still on a heavy dosage of tranquilizers.

Her passionless, empty life changed one night when God spoke to her heart as she read a book. God told her, "Your problem is that you cannot see Me in everything that happens to you." She says in her book that, "Hope began to stir within me as I began to see meaning in my existence." She realized that self-pity would have to go, along with unbelief, pessimism, grumbling and fear.

God told her to focus on gratitude, faith, hope, and optimism. It wasn't easy for her to let go of these perverted sources of security. It was a struggle to pray under the pressure of depression. It was not easy for her to see God in everything in her life. She tended more toward self-pity than to praising God.

Her deliverance from depression did not happen overnight. At first there was just a glimmer of light in her dark tunnel, but as she obeyed God and prayed in faith, the light grew brighter. Just three weeks later she was praising God and shouting that she was out of that tunnel of depression.

The devil would like to put all of us in that black cave where we are miserable and ineffective as Christians. At times many of us, under the pressures of life, begin to indulge in self-pity. We give up too soon under the pressures and we stop praying. We fail to see God in everything that happens!

E. M. Bounds said, "Only God can move mountains, but faith and prayer move God!"

We put too much of our faith in ourselves and our ability to achieve. We might feel like Florence Littauer, in her book, *Blow Away the Black Clouds*. After she heard her second son had the same brain-damaged condition which had taken the life of her first son, she wrote, "I was no longer interested in my social status, my big house, my fur coats, or my money. It could not restore my sons and I was sure that I could never be happy without having my sons alive and healthy." She also said, "I had achieved everything in life I set out to get, but I was left miserable and empty."

WHY IS IT HARD TO PRAY UNDER PRESSURE?

The pressures of life cause us to believe in our own helplessness. They cause us to doubt God's love and concern. We become anxious and fearful of what is going to happen. At

216

times it seems as if we live under a dark cloud that just will not go away.

Dr. Gerald L. Klerman, professor of psychiatry at the Harvard Medical School, says that as a nation we are suffering "an epidemic of melancholia (depression)." Research at Yale University shows that most Americans could report one or more of the symptoms of depression every day.

So many Christians pray so little. No wonder so many churches are spiritually dry. We have lost our joy! Our victory is gone because we really don't expect to see the power of God at work in our lives. It has been said that "you cannot make yourself happy, but you can make yourself rejoice." We are encouraged to "add up your joys and never count your sorrows."

Hebrews 12:15 says, "See to it that no one misses the grace of God" (NIV). God renews His grace to us day by day as we need it. There is a song that says:

"He giveth more grace when the burdens grow greater;
He sendeth more strength when the labors increase;
To added affliction He addeth His mercy, to
multiplied trials, His multiplied peace.

His love has no limit, His grace has no measure, His
power has no boundary known unto man;
For out of His infinite riches in Jesus, He giveth, and
giveth, and giveth again."

Let us fix our eyes on Jesus! Let us begin to see God in everything that happens to us. Not that everything that happens is best for us, but if God allows it to happen, we know that we have His promise that He is with us when it happens and that He will work it out for good in some way!

"Therefore my beloved brethren, be steadfast, immovable, always abounding in the work of the Lord, knowing that your toil is not in vain in the Lord" (1 Cor. 15:58, New American Standard Bible).

It is not easy to make yourself see God in all of life. When life is so terrible and painful that it hurts to remember the past, we wonder where God was when we needed Him.

217

HOW DO WE HANDLE THE MEMORIES OF OUR BROKEN PAST?

The pressures of life often cause us to relive memories of our broken past. We are at times tormented with the pain of our personal rejection. We wonder why we were so bad that no one really loved us.

Carolyn Koons, in her book, *Beyond Betrayal,* tells a true story of her struggle for survival within an abusive family. She was the object of her father's hate and anger all his life. Through prayer she learned how to allow God to heal the pain as she turned it over to Christ and felt His arms of love around her. There is incredible healing power available when we learn to pray under pressure until we are set free from the stress and fear that burdens us down.

Did you ever wish God had transformed you into a mature Christian instantaneously? It sure would have been easier than all the pain and suffering that is so often a part of our personal growth. Some people keep looking at the Promised Land but never seem to get over there. It is time for us to make it and to turn our lives around.

That sounds great, you may say, but how? Let us activate our faith, motivate ourselves to pray, dedicate ourselves to God no matter what. Also we should anticipate the mercy of God to bring us to victory!

WHY SHOULD WE PRAY TO GOD WHEN UNDER LIFE'S PRESSURES?

No matter what the pressures you should keep on praying because of these things:

1. God is King of the universe. "Who is this King of glory? The Lord strong and mighty, the Lord mighty in battle. He is the King of glory" (Psalm 24:8, 10). This means that all circumstances are ultimately in His hand.

2. God is righteous (Psalm 119:137). This tells us that God cannot sin against us. God never lets us down.

3. God is love (1 John 4:8). He wants to help us get the most out of life.

4. God is all-knowing (2 Chronicles 16:9). He knows all about me and my situation and how to work it out for good.

5. God is everywhere (Psalm 139:7-10). There is no place I can go that He will not take care of me.

6. God is all-powerful (Job 42:2). There is nothing He can't do on my behalf.

7. God is faithful and unchangeable (Malachi 3:6; Romans 15:5). I can depend on Him to do what He has promised.

We can pray and praise God even under the pressures of life because we know who we are in Christ! Our eyes have been enlightened so that we can see the hope of His calling, the riches of His inheritance, and the surpassing greatness of His power toward us who believe (Ephesians 1:18,19). The pressures and the problems of life do not change who we are in Christ. If you are a believer, then you can say the following about yourself:

—I am God's child.

—I am shielded by You, Lord, and encouraged so I can hold up my head.

—I will not be afraid.

—I am at peace.

—My heart is glad.

—I rejoice and shout for joy.

—I will praise You, Lord, with my whole heart.

—I will be glad and rejoice in Thee.

—You are my refuge in time of trouble.

—I shall not be moved.

—I shall not want.

—I will fear no evil.

—I know You are with me.

—I will dwell in the house of the Lord forever!

Josh McDowell said, "Being able to remember who God is and who you are in His sight is important as you meet the traumas and stresses of life." Our most basic need is the need to be loved and to sense that we belong. Because God loves us, He does more than change circumstances in our lives, He changes us. We know that some pattern of life's pressures will always be coming and going! If we allow our thoughts and inner feelings to be controlled by these troubles we will always be slipping in and out of depression. Our joy and our peace will be repressed to the point that we stop praying in the Spirit.

Don't focus on the problems. Look to God who is bigger than any problem. Don't give in to negative feelings! Give praise and thanks to God every day.

Learn to see God in everything and in every situation. He is there all the time! We must never give up and never stop praying. With God we are always on the brink of a miracle. So let's never give up.

PRAY YOUR WAY OUT FROM UNDER PRESSURE.

Here are some simple steps to follow that will cause the Spirit to blow away the dark clouds and lift the pressures you are under:

1. Believe that Christ came to save you and then present your body a living sacrifice to God.

2. Realize no problem or pressure that has overtaken you is unique to you alone. You are not the only one who has faced this problem. God is faithful and He will not allow you to be pressured beyond the point that you are able to bear.

3. You must be willing to get out of your depression or despair. Some people are happy with their depression and would be unhappy to get out of it. You must want to get on top and not stay under the burden.

4. Be willing to confess your faults and take responsible action. "If we confess our sins, he is faithful and just and will forgive us our sins and purify us" (1 John 1:9, NIV). Who has to go first? We do. If we . . . then He. We must take that first step by confessing our sins.

5. Ask God to give you joy. God does not want us to be miserable, mournful, and gloomy. He wants our faces to shine and sparkle with His glory and peace.

An old-timer once said, "Some folk bring joy wherever they go, and some bring joy when they go."

Ask God for joy! Without joy we are in anguish and "anguish lives where hope is dying."

6. Forget the past. Stop digging it up and just let go of it and press on in faith.

7. Keep your eyes on Jesus. God's way is to have your eyes fixed on Jesus. Take your eyes off yourself and get them

on Jesus. "Thou wilt keep him in perfect peace whose mind is stayed on thee: because he trusteth in thee" (Isaiah 26:3).

We pray our way out from under pressure, and we see ourselves standing on the mountain top with the clear wind of freedom and joy blowing in our faces. Then before long other pressures arise, and we feel ourselves tumbling off our mountain top. But that doesn't mean that we have to stay down!

We will keep our minds clear and control our attitudes by keeping our eyes on Jesus. We will overcome evil! The prophet Micah says, "Rejoice not against me, O mine enemy: when I fall, I shall arise; when I sit in darkness, the Lord shall be a light unto me" (7:8).

"The Lord shall preserve thy going out and thy coming in from this time forth, and even for evermore" (Psalm 121:8).

LATCH ONTO GOD'S LOVE

Fred G. Swank

SCRIPTURE: Ephesians 3:14-19; John 3:16

INTRODUCTION

Some years ago I was introduced to a book entitled: *Love, Acceptance and Forgiveness.* I have had this book in my library for over 10 years now, but I still haven't taken the time to read it. Although I have read and studied a good number of books over the years for some reason I have not read this book. However, I did latch onto the title and it has revolutionized my life and ministry. For more than 10 years now we have been emphasizing the three words of its title and have pledged ourselves to the following: that we will love everyone who comes through our doors with Jesus' love; we will accept everyone who comes through our doors regardless of their appearance; and we will forgive everyone who comes through our doors, regardless of their past, realizing that only God can forgive them of their sins.

On another occasion I latched on to the title of a little booklet entitled: *Keep Your Romance Alive.* Again, I did not read the booklet, but I put the title into practice, and my wife and I have kept our romance alive for over 29 years now.

I am sure all of us have latched on to different things in the course of our life that has helped us greatly, but the day we latched on to God's love was the greatest of them all. In the past 30 years of my ministry, there is one thing that means more to me than anything else: I have come to know God as a God of love.

The master story teller, Bennett Cerf, told a story about a little 8-year-old girl who was living in an orphanage. She was extremely shy and very unattractive. The other children would not play with her and she was left alone. She was a problem to the teachers, and the management of the institution sought to get rid of her. She had already been transferred twice. In this particular home there was an iron-clad rule that any outside communication had to be censured by the director or the associate. Late one afternoon this little girl climbed a tree whose branches overhung the main wall and placed an envelope on a limb as far as she could reach. She had been watched by the director; and when the girl had returned to her room, the director in a most undignified fashion climbed the tree and retrieved the mysterious message. After she had read it, without a word, she passed it on to her associate. The letter read: From Susan to anybody who reads this, I love you.

Long ago on a tree, outside the city walls of Jerusalem, a man died. His word to all the world from that Cross was this: For any who pass this way, I love you, I love you. God loves you and me more than we have ever recognized, more than we can ever know. To emphasize this wonderful truth of God's love to you and me, I want us to bring together two great texts of the New Testament, one from Ephesians 3 and the other, John 3:16. Let us look at John 3:16 through Ephesians 3:17-19.

Notice that this kind of love, God's love, surpasses human knowledge or recognition. We cannot comprehend it. We can only receive it. In John 3:16 we find the dimensions of love illustrated in a rather profound way. It's a familiar verse, easy to learn and hard to forget. It's the gospel in miniature, in a nutshell. We must not let its familiarity rob us of its profound meaning. John 3:16 illustrates in graphic form the meaning of the dimensions of God's love; its breadth, length, depth, and height. "For God so loved the world, that he gave his only begotten Son, that whosoever believeth in him should not perish, but have everlasting life."

THE BREADTH OF THE LOVE OF GOD.

"God so loved the world." God so loved the *world*! Can you imagine all that this means? God not only loves the world but He loves all the people in the world.

Today we don't know if there is life on other planets. If there is, how would this affect the way we view our world and the way we relate to one another? It would make a profound difference. *But please note*: If there is life out there somewhere, God's love in Jesus Christ on the Cross is big enough to include all of that life. "For God so loved the world." If there is not intelligent life out there and we are the only ones for whom Jesus died on this planet, then how wonderful and great the love of God is!

God knows every breath we breathe, every heartbeat within our breast, every movement we make, every thought we think, every emotion we have—God is aware of it all. He deals with us as individuals. Augustine, the church father said, "He loves us as though there was only one of us to love." That is the breadth of God's love.

THE LENGTH OF THE LOVE OF GOD

"He gave His only begotten son." God help us to never forget this!

Martin Luther was translating his Scripture of the New Testament into German. As he was working with it and notes and slips of paper were falling to the floor, his little daughter picked up a page which said, "For God so loved the world, that he gave." The notation stopped there. She became very excited and happy. When her mother questioned her about her excitement, she showed her mother the piece of paper with, "For God so loved the world, that he gave." and Luther's wife, wanting to prompt their little daughter about what it all meant, asked the little one what did it mean, what did God give us? The child replied, "I don't know what He gave us, but if He loves us enough to give us anything, then we don't have to be afraid of Him anymore." We can complete the sentence: "For God so loved the world, that he gave His only begotten Son."

This is the real test of love: To what length will it go? Some people who say they love us are never willing to go to any great length for us. So much of life is shallow. It's about like the rhymes you can buy in the card shops—something to fit almost any occasion. Paul says in I Corinthians 13:4, "Love suffers long" (*New King James Version*). Yes, my friends, God's love is as long as the longest day, it is as long as the longest night, it is as long as the longest life, it is as long as eternity. God's word says, "I have loved you with an *everlasting* love" (Jeremiah 31:3, *NKJV*). "I will never leave you nor forsake you" (Hebrews 13:5). "Love *never* fails" (1 Corinthians 13:8, *NKJV*).

God gave His son. He gave Him to Calvary. Please stand with me for a moment before Calvary, for it is only as we get a glimpse of Calvary that we can try to comprehend the lengths of the love of God!

Dr. Bill Tanner tells about the Chickapia Indians in southern New Mexico who do not have a word in their language for love. They translate John 3:16 in this way: "For God so hurt in His heart, that He gave His only Son." Could it be that God does hurt, that He feels? That God so hurt in His heart that He gave His Son for you and me. *That is the length of God's love.* A little boy was standing before his daddy and asked if his daddy loved him "this much" as he held out his hands about six inches. "Yes, son," the father replied, whereupon the boy extended his hands about two feet. "Yes, son that much too," his dad replied. Reaching his arms out as far as he could stretch them, his body forming a cross, he asked his dad if he loved him that much. "Yes," the father said, "I love you that much!" There is One who loved us that much and was willing to die for us, Jesus Christ our Savior and Lord. *There again is the length of God's love.*

THE DEPTH OF THE LOVE OF GOD

"That whosoever believeth in him should not perish." We cannot corner God.

We cannot put Him in a box. We cannot declare whom He will relate to and whom He will not consider. The Bible says,

225

"Whosoever shall call upon the name of the Lord shall be saved" (Rom. 10:13). That "whosoever" covers a lot of ground. It included me. One day I came to an understanding that I needed Jesus Christ in my life. So I turned myself over to Him, and He saved me. It includes people from all walks of live.

I once heard of an elderly grandfather who was working in his cornfield early one morning. As he was hoeing the corn, he saw a piece of paper about the size of a silver dollar. He was not as privileged as many are today, and he was unable to read what was on the paper. He had a deep feeling that he wanted to know what was on that piece of paper. So he stuck it in his shirt pocket. Sometime later his grandson, who was a bright young fellow, came hopping through the field on his way to school; and the grandfather said, "Grandson, I have something I want you to read to me." And the grandson read, "For God so loved the world, that he gave His only begotten Son, that whosoever believeth in him should not perish, but have everlasting life." He gave the paper back to his grandfather and went skipping on his way to school. Just as he was crossing the old rail fence the grandfather called, "Grandson, what does that big word 'whosoever' mean?" As the grandson straddled the fence, he cupped his hands and called back to his grandfather, "Granddaddy, that means you or me and everybody else in the whole world."

There is no "whosoever" with many of us. But with God . . . there is love, acceptance and forgiveness for all. But you say, "Pastor what about the misfits, the losers, those who are out of step in our world? What about those who have made a mess of their lives and seemingly are on a roller coaster ride toward destruction? What about them?" The depth of the love of God indicates they are included in the "whosoever." Whosoever believeth in Him shall not perish. God's love is so graphically portrayed in the Old Testament prophecy of Hosea. God had told the prophet to marry Gomer Bath Diblaim. Can you imagine a woman named Gomer Bath Diblaim? Bath means "daughter of" and Diblaim was the name of her father, so her name was Gomer Bath Diblaim. Hosea loved this woman. Born to their union was a child named Jezreel, meaning "gift of God, God sows." It was a happy home, but then the storm clouds began to gather. Word got out that Gomer was being unfaithful to her husband. A second child was born, Loruha-man meaning "not pitied."

Hosea began to suspect the unfaithfulness of his wife. Then a third child was born, Loami. Hosea named this little child "no kin of mine" or "not my own," and it was evident something was going on in that parsonage. One day Hosea came home from doing God's work and discovered three hungry children; Gomer was gone. He set about the task, as many single parents have to do today, of raising those children. The word of the Lord came again to Hosea and said, "Hosea, your wife is being sold on the auction block. I want you to take your money and what grain you can put together, and I want you to go down into the marketplace and buy her back. Bring her home, love her and accept her." Hosea did it. The Book of Hosea is a parallelism for you can set parallel alongside the love Hosea had for this fallen woman the kind of love God has toward people who have committed sin. Then you have *the depth of God's love.*

THE HEIGHT OF THE LOVE OF GOD

"But have everlasting life."

All of us know about and long for everlasting life. However, there is another word in John 3:16 we need to look at. There is no escaping the word *perish.* It's in the Book! We'd like to overlook it, but it's there. We know what it means for the body or the mind to perish. We know what it means for the body to be destroyed, but what does it mean for the soul to be destroyed, to perish?

Your personality, that part of you responding to these words, your ability to think, all of this makes up who you are as a living soul, someone meant for fellowship with God, intimacy with Him. The thought of the soul perishing refers to a kind of final condition. The meaning here is of an ultimate, irrevocable, separation from God. That is what it means for the soul to perish. The soul's perishing means eternal, conscious existence and separation from God. We must avoid two extremes, which are popular but not at all biblical. One is Universalism, which says God will ultimately save everyone, no matter what. That makes a mockery of the Cross. There would have been no need for Jesus to die, no purpose for

His death on the Cross if this theory is accepted. I don't believe Universalism is taught in Scripture. Nor is the other extreme of annihilationism, which teaches that ultimately, following judgment, God will simply annihilate or wipe people out. But the Scripture says that believers "shall not perish but have everlasting life." Yes, we are going to live eternally in a place that Jesus called heaven or a place that Jesus, the most tender voice that ever spoke, called hell. Today God wants to change that word *perish* to an everlasting *cherish* and give unto you everlasting life. Eternal life comes to those who believe it. It is not just mental assent to propositions or truths. To believe means a life-changing relationship. It means turning your life over to Christ, who can make a difference right now. You don't have to wait until you die or until Christ returns. You have it the moment you believe. The royal blood that flows from Calvary flows through our veins, and we are adopted into the family of God. *That is the height of God's love.*

CONCLUSION

All of my life I have heard the expression: "Blood is thicker than water." Experience teaches us that this is true. Let me assure you the royal blood that flows through our veins is thicker than water. This is one truth we should never forget. Dwight L. Moody was holding a meeting in Boston. On the last night the hall was packed with people. Many were turned away. Even the governor was turned away. Then a plainly dressed man came to the ushers and said, "Tell Dwight that his brother George is here." A note was sent up to Mr. Moody and when he read it, he said to those on the platform, "Make room for my brother George." His brother was brought in and given an honored seat on the platform.

Friends, one day the great kings of earth will be turned away at the gate of heaven if they have no admission tickets. But the humblest Christian who has latched on to the love of God and is trusting Christ for salvation can go up and say, "Tell my elder brother Jesus that I am here." Then that Christian will be brought into heaven. There is plenty of room in heaven for you.

TRANSFORMING YOUR THINKING

Paul L. Walker

SCRIPTURE: Acts 27:20-36

INTRODUCTION

In Margaret Mitchell's novel, *Gone With The Wind*, Will Benteen delivers an oration at Mr. O'Hara's funeral which sets the context for present-day living. Will says, "Everybody's mainspring is different. And I want to say this—folks whose mainsprings are busted are better dead."

Because we live in a day of stretched, twisted, overworked, and broken mainsprings, we need strong inner resources that will provide us with resources for courageous living in Christ.

Thus, the purpose of this sermon is to chart a course from the experiences of the life of Apostle Paul in Scripture to enhance and enrich the development of these resources to their highest potentiality through transformed thinking.

TRANSFORMING YOUR THINKING

It was a long, fearful struggle with the tempest. The winds blew a gale; the waves ran wild and high; the rain poured down in torrents; the angry elements beat with ceaseless rage upon the torn sail, the shattered mast, and the reeling deck.

229

The groaning timbers parted and let in water as fast as a hundred hands could bail it out. Everybody on board was wet—through and through. There was no opportunity to take food or rest. There they were—276 passengers and crew members with a load of wheat and a prisoner-preacher. They had been driven by the storm 14 days and nights, helplessly, in a canalboat-like scow, which was bluntly rounded at both ends with no shape and sharpened lines to cut the water. One lumbering mast stood upright in the middle, and it scarcely could stand the battering of the terrific fall winds.

It became so bad that all hope was lost—apparently the ship would crash on the rocky seashore. Then the prisoner-preacher—the Apostle Paul, headed for Rome to face Emperor Nero on charges of blasphemy and heresy—took charge.

Everything was bedlam. The captain and crew were in a state of panic. With confident, authoritative words piercing through the howling winds, the apostle exclaimed, "And now I urge you to take heart, for there will be no loss of life among you, but only of the ship" (Acts 27:22, *New King James Version*).

Sounds encouraging! But how did Paul know? How did he speak with such confidence? How did he keep his balance in such circumstances? The apostle explained:

> "For there stood by me this night an angel of the God to whom I belong and whom I serve, saying, 'Do not be afraid, Paul; you must be brought before Caesar; and indeed God has granted you all those who sail with you'" (Acts 27:23,24, *NKJV*).

Sounds okay! However, it is a double message: *You will be saved, Paul, so you can die later at the hands of Nero.*

At first glance we may think that such a message doesn't make much sense. But then Paul exemplified that kind of inner attitude that transcends all of life's double messages and contradictions. He said, "Therefore take heart, men, for I believe God that it will be just as it was told me" (Acts 27:25, *NKJV*).

Somehow this man of God named Paul had a thinking process that enabled him to keep his balance in the toughest of situations. His faith saw him through to the end that "they all escaped safely to land" (Acts 27:44, *NKJV*).

A MATTER OF THE MIND

How can we, as twentieth-century people living in a tempestuous world, handle our personal storms with courage of heart and faith in God? Such an outlook is a matter of the mind *a pattern for transformed thinking.*

No wonder the Bible tells us that as a person thinks, so he is (Proverbs 23:7), and it is apparent that is why the apostle Paul called for a *spiritual* mind (Romans 8:6), a *renewed* mind (Ephesians 4:23), a *transformed* mind (Romans 12:2), a *Christ-like* mind (1 Corinthians 2:16) and a *sound* mind (2 Timothy 1:7). Paul knew that the only way to cope with the pressures of life is to live a life of transformed thinking.

A British grandmother applied this process of transformed thinking during World War II. At the very height of the London blitz, she refused to leave her downtown flat.

Practically every day, her son would urge her to move to his suburban home—located a much safer distance from the intensity of the bombing. Stubbornly, she refused. After all, she could not leave her work helping the wounded and the homeless. She was needed. Besides, she trusted the words of a plaque on her wall: DON'T WORRY! IT MAY NEVER HAPPEN! Constantly, she referred her son and family to the motto and reassured them that all would be well.

Then one day it happened—her apartment complex was hit. Two thirds of the building was demolished. The son's family rushed to her flat as soon as they heard the news. They found her rocking in her favorite chair and singing her favorite hymn. Debris was strewn all about her.

In exasperation the son shouted at her, "Now what about your motto? It didn't see you through!"

"Oh, my goodness," she exclaimed, "I forgot to turn it over." She turned from her chair and flipped the plaque to the opposite side. There in shining letters it said, DON'T WORRY! YOU CAN TAKE IT!

This is the message of transformed thinking. It is a double message: "Don't worry! It may never happen! Don't worry! You can take it!

A MOTIVATOR OF MEANING

In reality, the power of transformed thinking is found in the degree of meaning it brings to our lives. Thus, when Paul told us not to be conformed to this world but to be transformed by the renewing of our minds (Romans 12:2), he was saying that we are to fulfill the will of God. This is where the essential meaning of life is found—in the "good and acceptable and perfect will of God."

Consequently, when we talk about the will of God, it is not simply with regard to careers, vocations, relationships, and everyday decisions. The will of God is for us to be like Christ (Romans 8:28-30), to strive to live by the mind of Christ. As Paul told the Corinthians, "We have the mind of Christ" (1 Corinthians 2:16).

What this really tells us is that the mind of Christ is an attitude. We are what our attitudes make us, and by definition, attitudes involve our emotional, intellectual, and spiritual perceptions of life. Attitudes are formed by our tendencies to accept or reject certain individuals, groups, ideas, values, concepts, and social institutions. Attitudes literally involve the way we look at life in all of its complexity and variety.

Here is the message of meaning—*we live productively through attitudes that reflect the mind of Christ.* This is what happened in the life of one woman. As she read the name on the pastor's lapel tag at a convention, she immediately threw her arms around him in a bear hug.

In surprise he drew back and said, "What does that mean?"

With a rush of words and a glow on her face, she said:

"A couple of years ago I heard you speak at a rally. At that time I was suicidal. I was strung out on a combination of tranquilizers, barbiturates, and alcohol. I was literally killing myself through drug abuse and was nothing but a vegetable with no purpose, no hope, and no future.

"Coerced by a friend, I reluctantly came to the rally and heard you talk about the fact that I could have a new mind through Christ. I thought to myself, *Is that really possible?* I began to pray to God that somehow He would renew my mind and give me power over all the suffering and hurt which were at the very base of my drug problems.

"When the time came for you to share with people in prayer, I was the first to raise my hand. Something dynamic took place in my mind. Since that day I have made a successful comeback to meaningful living. I literally received the mind of Christ. Now I am delivered from drugs and set free from my depression. I have this good job, and I've always said to myself, 'If I ever see that pastor, I'm going to give him a big hug.' That is what I just did."

The mind of Christ is the resource of strength. Paul found this out in the storm. Without the mind of Christ, he never would have been sensitive to the revelation of the Lord through the angel. The voice of God would have meant nothing.

Here is Paul's formula for victorious living through transformed thinking:

Step One: Keep Your Head. Paul could have despaired. He could have said, "O, God, what kind of God are You to bring me to this point?" He could have said, "God, if this is the best You have for me, I don't want to serve." He could have said, "God, what great sin have I committed that You would bring this calamity on me?" He could have said, "God, you know I have not sinned, and I have done nothing but good works for You. Why am I suffering in this storm?"

Paul could have lost his head, but he didn't. He didn't blow his cool. He didn't lose his bearings. He kept his reason. Paul knew that there is no gold without the fire of a refinery, no steel without the heat of a blast furnace, no diamond without sharpness of a cutter's tool, no statue without the hammer and chisel of a sculptor, no faith without the fury of a storm.

How do we keep our heads? We internalize the Word! The psalmist says, "We have thought, O God, on Your lovingkindness, In the midst of Your temple" (48:9, *NKJV*). In Proverbs 12:5 we read, "The thoughts of the righteous are right, But the counsels of the wicked are deceitful" (*NKJV*). Paul says, "Whatever things are true, whatever things are noble, whatever things are just, whatever things are pure, whatever things are lovely, whatever things are of good report, if there is any virtue and if there is anything praiseworthy—meditate on these things" (Philippians 4:8, *NKJV*).

The Patterson family learned to keep their heads and dwell

on the positive. Their beautiful 17-year-old daughter went swimming and in the excitement of playing on the side of the pool with her friends, fell and hit her head. The result was paralysis from the neck down. The doctors told her parents, "We've done everything we can do. She will be paralyzed the rest of her life. Put her in an institution. She will be a vegetable. She will probably die within five years."

The mother refused such a negative prognosis. Her response was, "We're going to take her home and put her in her room where we will surround her with the mind of Christ. We are going to saturate her with the power of God, the love of Christ and the ministry of the Holy Spirit. We are going to give her the privilege of living out the rest of her life in the context of a Christian faith in a loving family."

And that is exactly what they did. At last accounting she was 22 and had just stood up before a minister to be married to the young man she loved dearly. She has been made perfectly whole with the exception of a slight impairment on one side. She still walks with a cane, but she is getting stronger every day.

The members of this family kept their heads, and this girl was surrounded with the mind of Christ.

Step Two: Keep Your Heart. Do not be afraid! Keep up your courage! Keep your heart! When we look at our world, keeping heart is not always easy. A giant cloud of gloom seems to hang over the entire planet, and anxiety appears to be the order of the day. In 1985 alone, over 55 million prescriptions were written for a tranquilizer drug called Valium. And Valium is only one among many such synthetics used to try to help us keep our hearts.

Presently, one out of every three hospital beds is occupied by a person who is suffering from an illness caused by alcohol or some other drug.

Every day we experience the threats of international disaster, the pressures of an urbanized, commuter life-style, the problems of maintaining economic stability, and the uncertainties of changing world governments. Sometimes we wonder if there is reliability anywhere. This is a menacing age, and we can easily lose heart.

234

It is as though the last-day prophecies of hearts failing from fear (Luke 21:26) and the elect's being deceived (Matthew 24:24) are rapidly closing in on us.

All of this combines to put an overload on the mind and an overstress on the body. Thus, we talk about a physical-chemical imbalance and an emotionally induced burnout. Our thinking is frustrated, our consciousness is confused, our memory is impaired, and our learning is inhibited.

It seems impossible for us to live up to the uniqueness that God has given us in the likeness of His own image. We talk about being made "a little lower than the angels" and being crowned with glory and honor (Psalm 8:5) and possessing dominion over all nature with all things under our feet (Psalm 8:6). However, many of us find that making that claim a reality poses a problem. We find it difficult to draw on our God-given resources. *We lose heart because we fail to generalize through the mind of Christ.*

Our uniqueness is such that we can learn a concept and store it in our memory for frequent recall. In this way we can generalize one experience into many different situations and circumstances. This can be good news or bad news. We can use what we have learned from past experiences to progress into confidence or regress into fear and anxiety. But we tend to generalize fear rather than faith, worry rather than assurance, depression rather than happiness, frustration rather than peace.

As a result, we overload with negative thinking and short-circuit ourselves into losing heart.

Thankfully, however, we have a choice. There is a different story to be told. There is a place in Christ where we can share the position of the Apostle Paul and keep heart. We can keep our joy by living in the mind of Christ with power to cope with whatever comes our way.

Perhaps it boils down to the witness of a dying 12-year-old girl. She had leukemia and all had been done that could be done. Her parents had to watch helplessly as she intermittently went in and out of consciousness.

One day her father and mother were standing at the hospital bed, and it was more than her mother could take. Suddenly, she broke into body-racking sobs. Grief, frustration, tension, confusion, and fatigue all seemed to rush to the surface at once.

By the disturbance the little girl was roused and sensed what her mother was experiencing. Out of a wisdom far beyond her years she said, "Don't worry, Mommy. God will take care of me."

Step Three: Keep Your Hope. The formula is clear: A cool head plus a clean heart equals a confident hope. Paul expressed that hope to his fellow passengers, and they were all encouraged.

By definition, *hope* is "the confident expectation of fulfillment." It is desire plus emotion.

Too often we give up. We get caught in temporal timetables of our own making, like a get-rich-quick, instant-prosperity scheme. Then when it all doesn't come our way, we are prone not only to throw the cargo overboard but to jump in after it and sink to the bottom of the sea.

Sometimes we try hard to bring God down to us instead of our going up to God through Christ. We find ourselves reducing God to fit our own selfish traps—and we miss His best for us.

We need the power of confessing faith. We need the confidence of claiming God's promises. But above all else, we need the personal commitment to Christ whereby hope becomes our motivator; faith, our activator; and assurance, our "ultimator." Commitment thereby enables not our ambition, but Christ's ambition in us; not our desire, but Christ's desire in us; not our goal, but Christ's goal in us; not our healing, but Christ's healing in us; not our miracle, but Christ's miracle in us.

This is the meaning of 2 Corinthians 2:14, "Now thanks be to God who always leads us in triumph in Christ, and through us diffuses the fragrance of His knowledge in every place" (*NKJV*). To triumph is to rise above. To triumph is to overcome. To triumph is to defeat. To triumph is to vanquish. To triumph is to keep joy through hope. This is the power of hope—to triumph in Christ.

In hope we *believe* (Romans 4:18); in hope we *receive* (Romans 8:24); in hope we *endure* (Romans 15:4); in hope we *survive* (1 Corinthians 13:13); in hope we *testify* (1 Peter 3:15); in hope we are *purified* (1 John 3:3).

In this context I have always been impressed with Helen Keller. Blind and deaf, she rose above her circumstances to make a mark on the world that will never be forgotten.

She became an eloquent speaker, yet never heard her own voice; she wrote nine books, yet never saw their bindings. She received an honorary doctorate from Glasgow University in Scotland and responded to an audience she could not see and a thundering applause she could not hear by saying, "Neither darkness nor silence can impede the progress of the human spirit."

She read her braille Bible so often that certain passages had been worn completely smooth. And when asked what she thought of Christ, she replied in confidence and assurance, "Jesus Christ in my life is triumphant love."

This is how we live the triumphant life: We transform our thinking by keeping our heads, our hearts, and our hope. Negative thoughts become a thing of the past as we adopt this way of thinking. Living the good life in Christ is a matter of the mind and a motivator of meaning.

CONCLUSION

Transformed thinking is the result of keeping our heads, our hearts, and our hope. Negative thought responses and behavior patterns are defeated and overcome as we program our thought life with the mind of Christ.

THE HOUR THAT CHANGES YOUR WORLD

Dan Beller

SCRIPTURE: Matthew 26:40-41

INTRODUCTION

Susan Wesley had 19 children, but she prayed for one hour each day. She had no place to pray in private, so she would cover her face with her apron and pray. The children were instructed not to bother her when her apron was over her head.

One hour of prayer each day can change one's world. Notice that one hour is less than one half of a tithe of one's time. Giving God one hour each day in prayer equals 365 hours per year, for a total of 45 eight-hour days. Imagine taking off six weeks from work and spending that time with God!

David Brainard stated, "Oh! One hour with God infinitely exceeds all the pleasures and delights of this lower world."

WHY PRAY?

Jesus commands us to pray: "After this manner therefore pray" (Matthew 6:9). He assumes we will pray when He states, "When [not if] thou prayest, enter into thy closet" (6:6). Jesus was also our example of prayer: "And in the morning, rising up a great while before day, he went out, and departed into a solitary place, and there prayed" (Mark 1:35).

Prayer changes one's life. "The effectual fervent prayer of a righteous man availeth much" (James 5:16). "And when they had prayed, the place was shaken" (Acts 4:31).

E. M. Bounds stated, "Prayer is the contact of the living soul with God. In prayer, God stood to kiss man, to bless man, and to aid in everything that God can devise or man can need."

Prayer gives eyes to our faith. In prayer we see beyond ourselves and focus our spiritual eyes on God's infinite power. Prayer is our ultimate indication of trust in the heavenly Father. Only in prayer do we surrender our problems completely to God and ask for divine intervention.

PRAY PATIENTLY.

Patience in prayer does not mean apathy, but waiting with confidence and boldness. Jesus said, "For every one that asketh receiveth; and he that seeketh findeth; and to him that knocketh it shall be opened" (Matthew 7:8). The psalmist stated that if we delight ourselves in the Lord—leading a life which glorifies His name—He will give us the "desires" of our hearts, or the "askings of our hearts." Jesus said, "If ye shall ask any thing in my name, I will do it" (John 14:14).

After we have prayed, we must wait on God's timing. We must have faith and patience in order to "inherit the promises" (Hebrews 6:12). A good translation of this word *patience* is "endurance."

Prayer not only demands patience; it also helps us to be patient and forgiving toward others. Jesus taught that if we have the "God kind" of faith, we can remove mountains and receive those things we desire. He then emphasized that when we pray, we should forgive (Mark 11:25, 26). We are inspired to forgive others when we realize how God has forgiven us. Jesus illustrated this truth by telling of a man who had been forgiven a debt of $10 million, but was then unable to forgive a small debt of $20 (Matthew 18:22-35).

PRAY SUBMISSIVELY.

Submission is a part of prayer. Prayer must not be based

239

on flesh or emotion, that is, praying only when we have extra time available or when our emotions draw us to pray. We pray because Jesus so commands us and because we believe God answers prayer. We display our submissiveness as we pray even when we do not "feel like it."

Honest, sincere prayer always involves a recommitment of oneself to God. E. Stanley Jones stated, "In prayer you align yourself to the purpose and power of God, and He is able to do things through you that He could not do otherwise. This is an open universe where some things are left open, contingent on our doing them. If we do not do them, they will never be done. God has left certain things open to prayer, things which will never be done except as we pray."

PRAY ALERTLY.

Jesus instructed the disciples to pray so they would not enter into temptation. He also told them to pray because the flesh is weak. Notice, as Jesus prayed in Gethsemane, the disciples slept because of sorrow (Luke 22:45). Because the disciples slept, they did not support Christ as He agonized; nor did they see the angel strengthen and anoint Him.

We also have the choice to be vigilant in prayer or to "sleep" and miss God's best. If we will commit ourselves to a daily hour of prayer, we can overcome the flesh and change our world. We can "walk in the Spirit, and . . . not fulfill the lust of the flesh" (Galatians 5:16).

PRAY THANKFULLY.

Prayer is a time of praise. We are able to recognize God's nature because we are in His presence. The prayer watch gives us a "holy alertness." "Continue in prayer, and watch in the same with thanksgiving" (Colossians 4:2). Waiting in prayer is like the "silent soul surrender." "Be still, and know that I am God: I will be exalted among the heathen, I will be exalted in the earth" (Psalms 46:10).

Prayer helps us to have an attitude of gratitude and to openly confess the blessings of God. "In every thing give thanks: for this is the will of God in Christ Jesus concerning you" (1 Thessalonians 5:18).

Prayer helps us to be in harmony and agreement with God, which is God's plan for man. Further, Jesus promises great results "if two of you shall agree" (Matthew 18:19).

PRAY EXPECTANTLY.

We must expect that God will respond to our prayers by opening doors according to His superior thoughts and ways (Isaiah 55:8); by giving us strength to go His perfect way (Proverbs 3:5); and by directing us by His Spirit (Ephesians 5:18).

As we pray, we must expect to gain victory over Satan. We must come against Satan in the powerful name of Jesus and with the "sword of the Spirit," which is the Word of God. "Submit yourselves therefore to God. Resist the devil, and he will flee from you" (James 4:7).

An officer in the British Army testified that he led a group of soldiers in front line combat for four years and did not lose one man. How could this happen? Every officer and soldier prayed daily, claiming Psalm 91. They testified that bullets were supernaturally deflected and none was lost.

PRAYER CHANGES US.

When the barren Hannah arrived at Shiloh, "she was in bitterness of soul, and prayed unto the Lord, and wept sore" (1 Samuel 1:10).

God answered by giving her a son, Samuel. This was not the lone result of Hannah's prayer, however; Hannah herself was also changed because of prayer.

We often look for the results of our prayers without considering how prayer has changed us. To change us is probably the most significant reason that God sometimes lets us seek desperately and earnestly for a period of time those things which we desire.

Let us live with an attitude of prayer and see our world change. God promises, "I will answer them before they even call to me. While they are still talking to me about their needs, I will go ahead and answer their prayers" (Isaiah 65: 24, *Living Bible*).

YADAH PRAISE—REACHING UP TO GOD

Mike Chapman

SCRIPTURE: Various Texts (Topical Message)

INTRODUCTION

The most prominent Hebrew word for praise is *hallal*. It carries the idea of the joyous celebration of the life and blessings of God. When combined with a shortened form of the word for Jehovah God (*Yaweh*), we have the premiere word for praise in the Bible—Hallelujah.

Following close behind in the frequency of use is the Hebrew word *yadah*. It appears 106 times in the Old Testament scriptures and is translated as "praise," "give thanks," "thank," and "confess."

In this message, we are going to take a look at this interesting "praise word." Our goal will be not only to understand what it means, but to take advantage of this powerful expression of worship that God commends to us.

THE ESSENCE OF "YADAH PRAISE"

Yadah literally means "to worship with extended hands, to throw out the hands, to give thanks to God." It is derived from the root word *yad* which is the Hebrew word for *hand*.

Raising our hands in worship is a powerful, visible expression of praise. Our hands are a part of almost every deep emotional reaction we feel. For instance

. . . an angry man will clinch his hand into a fist.

. . . a guilty man will try to hide his hands.

. . . a worried man will wring his hands.

. . . a desperate man will throw up his hands.

. . . an accusing man will point his finger.

In expressing strong feelings of praise, a believer will lift his hands in worship. This is the essence of "yadah praise."

EXPRESSIONS OF "YADAH PRAISE"

In addition to the actual occurrences of *yadah* in the Old Testament, there are specific admonitions to raise our hands in praise. The psalmist states, "I will praise you as long as I live, and in your name I will lift up my hands" (Psalm 63:4, *New International Version*). We are encouraged to "lift up [our] hands in the sanctuary and praise the Lord" (Psalm 134:2, *NIV*). Again the psalmist says, "May my prayer be set before you like incense; may the lifting up of my hands be like the evening sacrifice" (Psalm 141:2, *NIV*). From the New Testament come these words of Paul: "I want men everywhere to lift up holy hands in prayer" (1 Timothy 2:8, *NIV*).

There is no question that "yadah praise" is commended by God for His people. The obvious question is "why?" Why does God want us to raise our hands in worship? Of what value is it? Let me share four reasons for the appropriateness of lifted hands in worship:

1. *The raised hand is a salute to God.*

To salute someone is "to greet with an expression or sign of welcome, respect and honor. It is to honor in a prescribed way." To raise our hands in worship is to follow God's prescribed way of saluting His sovereignty and majesty. The Bible declares that God is worthy of such a greeting and of such honor: "You are worthy, our Lord and God, to receive glory and honor and power" (Revelation 4:11, *NIV*). "Worthy is the Lamb, who was slain, to receive power and wealth and wisdom and strength and honor and glory and praise!" (5:12, *NIV*).

"To him who sits on the throne and to the Lamb be praise and honor and glory and power for ever and ever" (5:13, *NIV*).

In the corporate worship of the church or in the private closet of prayer, the raised hand is to be viewed as a salute to God. It is a sign of reverence and respect and brings honor to God.

2. *The raised hand is the universal sign of surrender.* God still desires a surrendered people . . . a people whose hearts and wills are submissive to Him . . . a people who have yielded their lives to His service. While the surrendered life is an inward working, it is expressed outwardly, and one of the obvious ways of indicating this is by the raised hand. The visible display of open hands is a powerful sign of surrender. It indicates that nothing is held back, that nothing is hidden, that all has been released. The raised hand in worship symbolizes that we present our bodies as "a living sacrifice, holy, acceptable unto God" (Romans 12:1).

3. *The raised hand is a sign of intimacy with God.* Through the Cross, we are offered a whole new relationship with God. To the redeemed, God is not to be feared with a sense of dread or terror. Instead, He is our Father, and we approach Him as His children.

This truth is borne out clearly in two passages from Paul's epistles: "We have been given the Spirit of sonship whereby we cry 'Abba Father'" (see Romans 8:15). And "The Spirit in our hearts cries 'Abba Father'" (see Galatians 4:6).

Abba is a cry of intimacy. It is the Aramaic equivalent of *Daddy* or *Papa*. By using this word, Paul reveals to us the intimacy which we can share with our heavenly Father.

Any parent or grandparent knows what it means when a young child stands at your feet, looks up into your face and raises his hands. He is saying, "Hold me . . . pick me up . . . take me in your arms . . . let me sit on your lap." That's a child's way of showing his desire for closeness and intimacy. In like manner, we can lift our hands to our Father and enjoy intimacy with Him. We're also saying, "Hold me . . . pick me up . . . take me in your arms . . . let me sit on your lap."

4. *The raised hand is a sign of agreement and confession.* The word *yadah* is translated "confess" 16 times. When Ezra opened the Scriptures to read, the people stood and lifted

their hands and responded, "Amen! Amen!" (Nehemiah 8:6). This was a powerful sign of agreement.

We too must indicate our confession. One of the ways we can do this is by the raised hand in praise to God. In so doing we capture the spirit of the passage which says, "Let the redeemed of the Lord say so" (Psalm 107:2).

AN EXAMPLE OF "YADAH PRAISE"

In the passage in 2 Chronicles 20 is the dramatic story of Jehoshaphat's and Judah's victory over the Moabites and the Ammonites. After waiting upon the Lord, the people received a clear battle plan. They were to march into battle with an appointed choir in the front of the soldiers. As they marched toward the battle, the choir was given a special song, "Give thanks to the Lord, for his love endures forever" (v. 21, *NIV*).

It is interesting to notice the Hebrew word translated "give thanks." It is none other than the word *yadah*. They were to give thanks with their hands raised! Can you picture this? The entire army of Judah marched behind a host of singers into battle. The choir was not hiding behind shields. They were not wringing their hands in fear. They were marching with their hands lifted high in praise to God. What a sight it must have been!

What did their raised hands mean? It was a salute to their God whose battle plan they were following. It was a sign of their personal surrender to His will. It was a reaching up to God in an act of trust and confidence. It was a confession and an acknowledgment that they believed the revelation which they had received.

As a result, God gave them total victory. Their enemies turned on themselves and destroyed each other. Victory came on the wings of praise—"yadah praise."

CONCLUSION

Praise is a powerful force. It releases and expresses our faith which in turn releases God's power. Don't wait for the right mood to praise God. Praise Him as an act of your will. Choose to praise Him with the fruit of your lips. Choose to praise Him with your hands lifted up. March into your battle with the power of "yadah praise!"

A GUEST, A GUIDE, OR A STRANGER

J. David Stephens

SCRIPTURE: Acts 11:15-18

INTRODUCTION

In this text the Apostle Peter was explaining to the disciples in Jerusalem how he had been led by the Spirit to Caesarea and preached the gospel to Cornelius. Cornelius was not a Jew, and this was one of the first instances of a Gentile (the uncircumcised) receiving the gospel and being baptized.

Notice Peter's words in verse 17: "God gave them the like [same] gift as he did unto us."

God has a very unique gift for every Christian. It is not automatically given, but it is available to you if you request and desire it. I am talking about the gift of the Holy Ghost. Peter said in Acts 2:38, "Repent, and be baptized every one of you in the name of Jesus Christ for the remission of sins, and ye shall receive the gift of the Holy Ghost."

I want to point out some things about the Holy Ghost that will help us draw closer to Him.

THE HOLY SPIRIT CONVERSION

It is important to understand that we receive the Holy

246

Ghost (or Holy Spirit) into our hearts the very moment we are saved.

Jesus told Nicodemus in John 3:5, "Except a man be born . . . of the Spirit, he cannot enter into the kingdom of God." He told the woman at the well, "God is a Spirit; and they that worship him must worship him in Spirit" (4:24). The only way any of us can have fellowship with God is through the Holy Spirit.

One of our major problems in understanding this biblical truth is a problem we have with semantics. Our terminology often causes us misunderstanding. A very young evangelist observed that in the state where he ministered there was a major concern and even debate about using the term "Holy Spirit." Some evangelists refused to refer to the Holy Ghost with this term insisting that it was used by non-spiritual seminary (often they would say *cemetery*) graduates to "water down" the Word of God. They insisted that only preachers who were ashamed of the "Holy Ghost and fire" used the term "Holy Spirit."

The truth is that the Holy Spirit and the Holy Ghost are synonymous names for the third person in the Trinity . . . God the Father, God the Son, and God the Holy Ghost. The Scriptures use the term "Holy Spirit" and "Holy Ghost" interchangeably. Jesus used the terms "Comforter" and "Spirit of truth," but we know that there are not a group of various spirits, there is only one Spirit in the Godhead. Paul wrote in Ephesians 2:18, "For through him [speaking of Jesus] we . . . have access by one Spirit unto the Father." ONE SPIRIT! Regardless of what term we may use—"Holy Spirit," "Comforter," "Spirit of truth," or "Holy Ghost,"—we are speaking about the third person in the Trinity!

If you have been born again and know Jesus Christ as your personal Savior, the Holy Ghost is living in you! Jesus explained to His disciples in John 16:7, "It is expedient for you that I go away: for if I go not away, the Comforter will not come unto you." He knew He was limited by His human form and could only be in one place at a time but that the Holy Spirit was not limited and could work all over the world at the same time. Right now, across the seas in China and down in Brazil and all over this world the Holy Ghost is introducing men and women to a personal salvation in Jesus

Christ! His very purpose and ministry is to make known the saving grace of Jesus Christ. Jesus said, "Howbeit when he, the Spirit of truth, is come . . . he shall not speak of himself . . . he shall glorify me: for he shall receive of mine, and shall shew it unto you" (v. 13, 14). John proclaims in 1 John 4:13, "Hereby know we that we dwell in him, and he in us, because he hath given us of his Spirit."

THE HOLY SPIRIT AS A GUEST

When the Holy Ghost comes into your heart, He comes in as a guest.

His manner and demeanor are those of a guest. The Holy Ghost is always a gentleman and He is not abusive. He does not force Himself or His will on you, but His manner is the same as a guest would be in your home.

I have been the guest in many homes. A guest does not take over and make demands of his host. He does not rearrange the schedule or the furniture. He does not push the host and hostess around to make him comfortable. He is their guest not their landlord. This is the disposition of the Holy Spirit when He enters a willing vessel.

As a guest in many homes, I have been treated many ways. Some homes have extended a royal welcome and red-carpet treatment. They have made me feel wanted and important to them. I was not an intrusion nor an imposition, but a welcome addition to their home. Often the hostess asked me what kind of food I liked, and what time I preferred to eat my meals. This kindness always overwhelmed me. However, other places I've been the host was not so considerate and hospitable. The treatment was cold-tile instead of red-carpet, and I knew immediately that I was an imposition to the home. The only reason they invited me was that they were forced into the situation as the church pastor since I was the evangelist. Those visits were very uncomfortable and I always tried to be as little trouble as possible. Usually I spent most of my time in my room or in the church. When they asked, "Are you hungry?" I said, "No." But I stayed hungry the whole visit because I felt uncomfortable eating their food.

How have you been treating your unseen Guest? Have you extended the red carpet or has it been the cold tile? The way you treat the Holy Spirit determines what He will be able to accomplish in your life. He can be abused and offended. Paul exhorts us in Ephesians 4:30, "Grieve not the Holy Spirit of God." Again, he admonishes, "Quench not the Spirit" (1 Thessalonians 5:19).

THE HOLY SPIRIT AS A GUIDE

One of two things will happen in every Christian's experience: the Holy Ghost will be to you either a guest and a guide, or He will become a stranger.

It can be truthfully stated that to everyone seated in this sanctuary the Holy Ghost is either a guest and a guide or a stranger. What is He to you?

He wants to be your guide. His desire and goal is for you to make Him your general manager and supervisor. He does not want to be just a guest in your life, but He wants to also be your guide. The word *Comforter* means "one who goes along beside." "He will guide you into all truth . . . he will shew you things to come" (John 16:13).

"The Holy Ghost shall teach you" (Luke 12:12).

It was the Holy Spirit who led Peter to the house of Cornelius. It was the Holy Spirit who led the early church in every victory. It was the Holy Spirit who gave us the Word of God through the yielded vessels of men. It is the Holy Spirit who wants to be your guide and lead you into all spiritual truth. Paul wrote, "For as many as are led by the Spirit of God, they are the sons of God" (Romans 8:14).

Even though the Holy Spirit's driving thrust is to be your guide, He will not and does not force His will on you. It is always your choice. Wouldn't it be great if God would clone us to automatically serve Him? I have often prayed that He would make me do "right." He simply does not force us to follow Him. If you want Him to be your guide you must take the initiative and invite Him to. Not everyone wants His guidance. Many want Him only as a guest. They do not invite Him to take part in their decisions. They do not ask Him to show them what His will is for their life. They say, "OK God, You are here, and I don't want You to leave me, but I'll run things the way I want to . . . You just stay in the guest room." He really is an unseen guest and, in fact, an unheard

249

guest in their home. He does His best to hang around and He doesn't look for excuses to leave. Quite often He tries to get involved in their conversation. He points out the Word of God to them and He whispers, "Let me talk with you; won't you spend some time with me today?" He keeps trying, but He knows that He is just a guest. He knows that His host doesn't want Him to be his guide. He remains only as a guest in many hearts today.

In some cases the treatment is so abusive and offensive that He becomes silent. The Holy Ghost has been relegated to the back room and told, "You are going to have to understand that other guests visit this house also . . . You are not the only person that I enjoy having around." He is so mistreated that He simply cannot speak. He lingers on and doesn't want to leave His host, but there are some things that will force Him out. There is a point when He is forced to become a stranger. It happened to Samson who was filled with the Holy Ghost from his mother's womb, and it still happens today. The Holy Spirit will not cohabit with Satan! He will not dwell in an unclean temple. Jesus said: "No man can serve two masters . . . Ye cannot serve God and mammon" (Matthew 6:24). In James 1:7, we are told about a person who wants to hang on to the world with one hand and on to God with the other: "Let not that man think that he shall receive anything of the Lord." I believe many church members are in serious spiritual trouble, and I encourage you to heed the words of 2 Corinthians 13:5, "Examine yourselves, whether ye be in the faith; prove your own selves. Know ye not your own selves, how that Jesus Christ is in you, except ye be reprobates?" A reprobate has lost his fellowship with the Holy Spirit. To them He has become a stranger. Do not force Him to be a stranger in your life!

THE HOLY SPIRIT AS A GIFT

Is anyone here looking for a guide? If so, God has a gift for you . . . the gift of the Holy Spirit!

If you are looking for help and direction, if you are tired of missing the mark, if you want God to fill you with His Spirit; if you want to serve Him above everything else in your life; then He will baptize you with the Holy Ghost and fire. He will endue you with power from on high! He will give you the same gift Peter was talking about in the text. He will give you the same gift that He gave to the 120 believers in the Upper Room. His rushing mighty wind will blow into your heart and you will speak with other tongues as the Spirit gives you the utterance. The gift is for you . . . if you want the guide!

The believers in the Upper Room were not waiting for a guest, they were waiting for a guide. Cornelius wasn't praying for a guest, he was praying for a guide. I knew Jesus Christ as my personal Savior for several years before I received the gift of the Holy Ghost. I received the gift when I told God I wanted to be filled with His Spirit. When I wanted to please Him more than myself or my friends, He gave me the gift of the Holy Ghost. When I became so hungry for Him that the things of this world lost their attraction for me, then is when I received the baptism in the Holy Spirit. I'll never forget the excitement and the joy that flooded my soul. It was joy unspeakable and full of glory. He made me drunk on His new wine the night I was filled with the Holy Ghost. As the old song says, "It's real, it's real, Oh, I know it's real; Praise God! the doubts are settled, for I know, I know it's real!"

CONCLUSION

What is your relationship with the Holy Spirit? Is He just a guest in your life or have you permitted Him to become your guide? Has it been a while since you've fellowshipped with Him? Do you desire to rebuild your relationship? Would you like to be filled with the very Spirit of God? If so, you've already taken the first step. Jesus said, "Blessed are they which do hunger and thirst after righteousness: for they shall be filled" (Matthew 5:6). Now I'm going to encourage you to take the next step. Jesus said, "Ask, and ye shall receive" (John 16:24). As you come to God with your sincere desire it is important that you seek Him, and not merely an experience. He wants to bless you more than you want to be blessed; He wants to be your guide. You can leave this service singing . . . He Abides!

251

THE HONEY PATCH

Danny L. May

SCRIPTURE: Psalm 19:7-10

INTRODUCTION

Sunday morning a man and his wife, seated in the church balcony, worshipped God. His face seemed to glow, and the pastor's attention was continually drawn to him as he ministered through the Word of God. The next night the man died as a result of a brain aneurysm, and the pastor knew why God had so blessed him in worship. He had prepared him for his homegoing.

Early Tuesday morning the pastor drove to the man's house, knelt by his wife's chair, and they prayed. As the Holy Spirit moved her, she began to talk about her husband, the blessings of the Lord, and the fact they had no regrets. The first difficulty with the aneurysm had happened three years before. Knowing their time could be limited, they took leave from work and spent time together. She knew her husband was with the Lord and she was comforted; however, she said something that stirred me. She said to me, "Do you know why he loved to attend the church you pastor? He loved to be around people who had found the honey patch."

THE SPIRITUAL HONEY PATCH

Now, I don't know what the Honey Patch represents to you today. I suppose in a physical sense it would present to us a picture of a forest, a picture of trees with an old tree hollowed out where honeybees could enter making a cone and depositing their honey. Close-by there would be a meadow with flowers blooming and producing nectar. The honeybees would light on the flowers and draw the nectar from them. With the unique ability God gave the honeybee, the bee would carry the nectar back to the cone and produce that wonderful, sweet honey. Then someone would find that tree and would rob the honeycomb. They would pack it into quart jars, half-gallon tins, and buckets and take it home. Then, each morning they would get a saucer, pour some honey on it, put a large piece of butter in the middle of the honey, take a knife or fork and whip it up, and then put it on big buttered biscuits. They would say what a marvelous thing it is that the honeybee can make honey.

What she was talking about was a spiritual Honey Patch. What that really means is this: "A pleasant place or state of being, being successful, prosperous, or blessed—a sweet experience, position or taste." She meant that her husband loved to be around people who had found a pleasant place or state of being in God. In a very real sense there is a spiritual Honey Patch. We could call it "God's Honey Patch," for God has a place for every person to dwell where life can be blessed, heart can be full, and joy can be complete.

Some people when asked, "How are you doing?" or "Has the Lord been good to you?" say, "Well, you know I'm still in the valley. I've been in the valley so long. I just don't know when I'm going to come out." Or they say, "Oh, I've been going through a dry place. It is so dry I just don't know if I'm going to make it." It is true that we may go through the valley, but God never expects or wants us to stay in the valley. Start climbing out. He wants us to climb to the mountain top. He's got a Honey Patch, if we'll climb out of our valley. Search for that place in God that is full, good, rich, and wonderful.

GOD WANTS US IN THE HONEY PATCH

The Bible records 17 times where God said to the nation of Israel, "I want you to leave the Egyptian slave camp and come out from under Pharaoh. I want you to go to a land that is flowing with milk and honey." God is saying 17 times, "Get up. Get out of there. Go over to the land flowing with milk and honey. There is something better for you." There is something better than the valley, the old dry place, or the barren desert of spiritual laziness and complacency. There is a place of fruitfulness. There is a place of oasis. There is a place of fullness. There is a place of joy. We can find it. God wants us to find the Honey Patch.

Some people answer, "Oh, I'm barely hanging on preacher. I'm barely hanging on. I had to reach up to touch bottom this week. I'm barely holding on. In fact, I almost didn't make it to church today." Well, the good news is this. God wants you to do more than to barely hang on. The blood of Jesus Christ provides more than this for you. The power of Jesus' name provides more than this for you. The Lord says to us today that a Honey Patch has been provided. We don't have to have an occasional taste of spiritual sweetness. We can have a double handful if we will determine to follow the Lord and stand in the fullness of His promises. He does not want us to be down. He does not want us to be out. He does not want us barely holding on. He does not want us to be nearly backslidden every week.

He wants us to be strong, established, and victorious. In the Book of Exodus, chapter 16, the Bible says Israel began complaining that God had brought them into the wilderness to die—to starve to death. Well, this was not true. God brought them out out of Egypt to lead them to a land flowing with milk and honey. But there was a Honey Patch in the midst of their journey. They were starving, and God sent manna falling from the sky. Every day it came, and it doubled the day before the Sabbath. They described it as being a wafer with a taste like honey. God does not leave us to starve. God wants to lead us where His joy is deep, His love is full, His peace is abundant, and His glory is manifested through our life.

GETTING TO THE HONEY PATCH

How do we get to the Honey Patch? A vision was given to the prophet Ezekiel. He was shown a scroll and commanded to eat it. Ezekiel said, "Then did I eat it; and it was in my mouth as honey for sweetness" (3:3). The Word of God is the entrance to God's Honey Patch. The Bible says, "More to be desired are they than gold, yea, than much fine gold: sweeter also than honey and the honeycomb" (Psalm 19:10). Well, start right here. The Word of God is the nectar. As we allow the Word of God to be in our mind and heart, we will begin drawing from His Word. Our life will begin to produce spiritual pleasantness. The presence of Jesus Christ will be manifest in our life. There is no other nectar that can make a person who is sour, bitter, and sinful into a joyous soul. But God's Word can! There is no other source that can cause a person to come from despair into the height of joy. But the Word of God can! There is no other source that can take a despondent, broken, and frustrated world, pick it up out of that just-barely-holding-on position, and place its feet on the solid rock. But the Word of God can!

People say, "Well, I'm under another attack from Satan. I'm constantly being bombarded by the enemy." What we need to understand today is that we may be opening the door to Satan's attack. If we will not resist Satan, the Lord is not going to take authority over Satan for us. He has already given us authority over Satan. Jesus said, "And these signs shall follow them that believe; In my name shall they cast out devils" (Mark 16:17). We are to cast the devils out. We are to overcome Satan. We are not to be overcome by evil. We are to overcome evil with good, with God, with His presence, and with His power. We need to understand that we don't have to be constantly defeated by the attacks of Satan. If we make up our mind that we are going to serve God, and the devil knows we are going to serve God, he will flee from us. The reason Satan attacks some people so hard is because he knows they haven't made up their mind. He knows when we're indecisive.

Doesn't the Bible say that a double-minded man is unstable in all His ways? If I say I am going to serve God on Sunday, but on Monday I can't find it in my heart to please Him, Satan is going to attack me because he is waiting on anyone who doesn't have a made-up mind to serve God. We must have a determination to serve God. When this happens, the devil is defeated. He is whipped. Satan cannot come against us to overwhelm us. He will overcome him in every situation. So make up your mind. Be determined. Get in the Book. Stand on the Word of God. Let nothing that Satan says or that people say detour you away from the truth of the Word of God. When you do this, Satan will take his flight.

There are four things we must do if we are going to find and live in this choice place called God's Honey Patch.

LEARN THE DIFFERENCE BETWEEN SATAN'S VOICE AND GOD'S VOICE.

There is a very simple way of doing this. We can know the difference between God's voice and Satan's voice. God's voice will always agree with the Word of God, the Holy Bible. Satan's voice may agree partially, but never fully. Jesus Christ, after 40 days of fasting and prayer in the wilderness was tempted by the devil, who offered Him three good things. The things Satan offered Jesus were not wrong themselves, but they required a deviation from truth in the attitude and action of Jesus if He was to do them. It wasn't wrong for Jesus to turn a stone into bread. It wasn't wrong for Jesus to have all of the kingdoms of this world. And it certainly was not wrong for the angels to bear Him up lest He dash His foot against a stone. But Jesus singled out the error in each of the temptations and said in effect, "But the Bible says, 'Man shall not live by bread alone, but by every word that proceeds from the mouth of the Father. Thou shalt not tempt the Lord thy God. Thou shalt worship the the Lord thy God and Him only shalt thou serve.'" Jesus gave Satan scriptural answers. We must understand the Bible in order to know the difference between the voice of God and the voice of Satan. Discerning the difference between God's influencing us and Satan's influencing us depends upon how much of God's Word we have ingested into our being and how much of it has become a part of our daily life.

LEARN THAT WE CANNOT WATCH PEOPLE IF WE ARE TO SERVE GOD.

We cannot watch people! Each time we get our eyes on people, we begin to lose our walk with God. It matters not how good a preacher is, or how marvelous a saint a person may be, watching people will trip us. Our eyes must be on Jesus. It is very simple, but how powerful it is! We must go beyond people-watching in the church. We must zero in with our vision on Him who is most lovely—specifically Jesus Christ. We must turn our eyes upon Him and keep our eyes upon Him. As long as Simon Peter's eyes were on Jesus, he walked on the water; but when his eyes looked in another direction, he began to sink. People will fail us. Finding God's Honey Patch means keeping our eyes on Jesus and not on people.

WE MUST NOT DEPEND ON AN EMOTIONS, BUT LEARN TO MAKE A COMMITMENT OF OUR WILL.

One of the most difficult problems people face in coming to God is that of making only an emotional commitment to Jesus. When they leave the altar and the tears have dried up, they must face Satan in their daily living. People all around them begin questioning the reality of their experience, and their emotional commitment doesn't last. We must go beyond an emotional commitment; it will take us up one day and let us down the next. It is good when you feel good, and it is bad when we feel bad. It lasts when we have plenty; but when difficulties arise, an emotional commitment will not stand. It's wonderful to have an emotional feeling, but we cannot build our relationship with God on this alone. We must get down to our will, where we make decisions, and sell out completely to God. Make a commitment of your will to Him! Say, *I will* be His child. *I will* do His will.

WE MUST LEARN TO PRAISE GOD REGARDLESS OF CIRCUM-STANCES.

The Honey Patch—this place of blessing, fullness, abundance, joy, strength, and supply—can be found only as we learn to praise God regardless of what we face. Our praise of God could be patterned after that of one of 10 lepers whom Jesus healed. These men were incurably diseased, having no hope of recovery. When Jesus met them on the road, He healed them. "And one of them, when he saw that he was healed, turned back, and with a loud voice glorified God, And fell down on his face at his feet, giving Him thanks: and he was a Samaritan. And Jesus answering said, Were there not ten cleansed? but where are the nine? There are not found that returned to give glory to God, save this stranger" (Luke 17:15-18).

Now please notice with me that this is an example of 10 men gloriously and miraculously healed by Jesus Christ. All of them were healed. As they turned to leave, one wanted more than a healing. He wanted the healer. One of them wanted more than the miracle. He wanted the God who works miracles.

Many are satisfied with an occasional touch of God. They are satisfied with an occasional brush with angels' wings. They are satisfied with an occasional uplift of the power of the Holy Spirit. But there is something sweeter and better. It is coming into His presence and falling down before Him, loving and praising Him. We enter His Honey Patch by praise. This man said with a loud voice, "Glory to God! Thank you Jesus for healing my body." He came and fell upon his face before Jesus and began to worship Him, to honor Him, to praise Him, and to glorify Him. He entered God's Honey Patch. We don't enter by begging. We enter by falling on our face, humbling our heart, bowing our knee, praising the Lord, and worshiping Jesus with all that is within us.

Not only do we find God's Honey Patch through praise; but, just think, 10 of them could have been in His presence. What would you give today to have Jesus standing here physically like that leper who had the opportunity to bow before Him and reach out and touch Him. What would you give? Wouldn't you like to see Him in the flesh? That cleansed leper had the privilege of bowing down and worshiping Him. Have you forgotten how to worship Him through praise? Have you forgotten how to glorify Him? Have you forgotten who healed you? Have you forgotten who cleaned you up? Have you forgotten who dug you out of the dark pit? Have you forgotten? Turn again to the Lord and find that sweet place in the full countenance of His glory. Fall on your face, worship Him, praise Him, glorify Him. When we praise God regardless of circumstances, we are in God's Honey Patch. God's best is when we can praise Him in every situation. The Bible says in "In every thing give thanks" (1 Thessalonians 5:18).

I'm sure Joseph didn't find it so easy when his brothers tore up his coat and threw him in a pit, when Potiphar's wife lied about him and said he tried to come in and abuse her, when he was cast into the prison dungeon, when the butler and baker were given dreams and he revealed the answer to them, and Joseph was forgotten. Surely it was difficult to praise God. Yet he said, "Ye thought evil against me; but God meant it unto good" (Genesis 50:20).

We are to praise God in every circumstance. The Bible says that if we are to mature and to grow to the full measure of a person in Jesus Christ, we must learn how to praise God in every situation. Here is an example of spiritual maturity: "And at midnight Paul and Silas prayed, and sang praises unto God" (Acts 16:25). In the darkest part of the night, with their backs bleeding, Paul and Silas began to praise the Lord.

Jesus was riding into Jerusalem one day on a little colt and people laid coats and palm branches before Him and cried Hosanna to the King! Some said, "Master, rebuke thy disciples." Jesus answered them, "I tell you that, if these should hold their peace, the stones would immediately cry out" (see Luke 19:35-40). God's Honey Patch is available to you through praise.

In another place the Bible says, "And when they had called the apostles, and beaten them, they commanded that they should not speak in the name Jesus, and they let them go. And they departed from the presence of the council, *rejoicing* that they were counted worthy to suffer shame for his name" (Acts 5:40, 41). They found the Honey Patch, for they learned to hear God's voice. They had their eyes on Jesus. They made a commitment of their will. They praised Him regardless of the circumstance. His choice place is the Honey Patch.

We can enter and live in a pleasant place and state of being. We can be successful, prosperous, and blessed. We can know a sweet experience, taste, and position. It is *God's Honey Patch*. Enter it through the Word and live in it by listening to God's voice, by keeping your eyes on Jesus, by making a commitment of your will, and by praising God regardless of the circumstance.

HOW TO KNOW YOU ARE SAVED

R. Edward Davenport

SCRIPTURE: Romans 8:16

INTRODUCTION

Terminology is abundant to describe one's experience with Christ. The terms *saved, born again, New Birth* and others are used often, and many have no real scriptural understanding of their true meaning. Some who have only joined a church or claim a denominational affiliation because of family heritage use these terms thinking that they have obtained eternal salvation. Others continue to live in a manner completely contrary to life in Christ yet emphatically state they are genuinely Christian. The Christian experience and life described by these and other biblical terms are understood only by those who have encountered and accepted Jesus Christ and have become His disciples and students of His Word. It is eternally tragic for anyone to be forever lost, but to use Bible terminology to describe an experience which they falsely feel is theirs is a travesty.

The goal of this message is to cut through denominational vernacular and religious terminology and to go directly to what God's Word has to say about knowing you are born again. Cliches and often quoted words and phrases have a way of losing much (if not all) of their original meaning. Therefore we will sidestep good but misused phrases, words and terms to determine exactly how one may know without doubt they are transformed and divinely prepared to go to heaven at death or our Lord's return. Helping people know for sure about their soul's condition is important. When all jargon and ecclesiastical language has failed, the bottom line is, "If you died today would you go to heaven?" Many say they are saved but have no idea how to deal with this basic question.

Some teach that one can't know for sure about eternity and feel they must take their chances that God will accept them. There is a human need to know for sure and the Apostle John realizing this stated in 1 John 5:13 "These things have I written unto you that believe on the name of the Son of God; that ye may know that ye have eternal life." The Apostle Paul said in 2 Timothy 1:12, "I know whom I have believed, and am persuaded that he is able to keep that which I have committed unto him against that day." There is salvation and security in Christ along with a definite knowledge of both. We now will see how you can know for sure that you would go to heaven if you died today.

THE WITNESS OF THE WORD

The Word of God is foundational. One can know nothing of salvation or spiritual security unless he discovers what the Bible says. One must begin in the Word and from there discover all other sources of knowing about definite eternal life.

In God's Word the plan of salvation is outlined, taught, and illustrated. There are certain steps which must be followed. The steps are the same for everyone although circumstances may be quite different. These steps are as follows: There is first a conviction of sin. This awareness is produced by the Holy Spirit as the Word is preached, taught, or witnessed. In John 16:8 we are told, "When he [Holy Spirit] is come, he will reprove [convict] the world of sin." The undesirable, inescapable feeling of guilt is godly sorrow (2 Corinthians 7:10) which leads to repentance.

The second step is to confess one's sin and ask for forgiveness. One does not have to name all his sins, only confess

261

his guilt. John states in 1 John 1:9, "If we confess our sins, he is faithful and just to forgive us our sins, and to cleanse us from all unrighteousness." God always responds in loving forgiveness to anyone who asks (Romans 10:13).

Confession is then followed by repentance. Repentance means to do an about-face. One's life is to be aimed in a different direction. It has nothing to do with simply saying one is sorry for sin, but calls for the renouncing of sin with a genuine commitment to the Christian life. This is an absolute necessity, and in Luke 13:3 Jesus declares that its absence results in the eternal loss of the soul. This was preached by John the Baptist (Matthew 3:2), Jesus (Matthew 4:17), Simon Peter (Acts 2:38), Paul (Acts 17:30), and is a subtheme of the whole Bible. Repent or perish is more than a cliche; it is fact.

Christ must then be accepted by faith. This faith is pleasing to God and Christ comes into the heart of the individual. This faith experience must be verbalized by the convert. "If thou shalt confess with thy mouth the Lord Jesus, and shalt believe in thine heart that God hath raised him from the dead, thou shalt be saved. For with the heart man believeth unto righteousness; and with the mouth confession is made unto salvation." Confessing publicly is very important. Overcoming strength is the result of sharing the faith one has in Christ. In Revelation 12:11, the Scripture tells us of eventual eternal victory through the word of our testimony. Here is the divine outline from the Word. When followed, the Word of God is the foundational witness of our New Birth.

WITNESS OF THE SPIRIT

The Holy Spirit bears witness with our spirit (Romans 8:16). We recognize this witness through the Word and the divine impression in our spirit being. One of the greatest impressions is that of peace (Colossians 3:15). Listen to the Word as it tells us of this witness: "He that believeth on the Son of God hath the witness in himself" (1 John 5:10). "The Spirit itself beareth witness with our spirit that we are the children of God" (Romans 8:16). "And hereby we know that he abideth in us, by the Spirit which he hath given us" (1 John 3:24). "And because ye are sons, God hath sent forth the Spirit of His Son into your hearts, crying, ABBA, Father" (Galatians 4:6).

Salvation in our heart is wrought by the Holy Spirit. He transforms us and renews our mind. In Romans 8:1-4 is described the impossibility of this experience being acquired by those who walk after the flesh. The good law of God failed because of the weakness of sinful human flesh, but the law of the Spirit of life has prevailed. This spiritual operation is able to change a sinner to a saint of God and liberate from the power of Satan and sin.

Jesus dealt with this subject in John 3. Talking with Nicodemus, Jesus illustrated the Spirit's operation by the wind, and concludes by saying "so is everyone that is born of the Spirit." Ezekiel prophesied to the four winds and this brought revival and renewal in the valley of dry bones. Jesus breathed on His disciples in John 20:19-23 and said, "Receive ye the Holy Ghost." The unseen yet real person of the Holy Spirit witnesses to us about our salvation and security in Christ.

The Holy Spirit has sought us and transformed us into the children of God. He now daily conforms us into the image of his dear Son (Romans 8:29). Dr. Harry Ironside tells a story of the conversion of a Negro man who knew salvation was an act of God alone.

The colored man rose in a meeting to give his testimony to the saving grace of God. He told how the Lord had won his heart and given deliverance from the guilt and power of sin. He spoke of Christ and His work but said nothing of any efforts of his own. The leader of the meeting was of a legalistic turn of mind, and when the man's testimony was ended, he said, "Our brother has only told us of the Lord's part in his salvation. When I was converted there was a whole lot I had to do myself before I could expect the Lord to do anything for me. Brother, didn't you do your part first before God did His?" The other was on his feet in an instant and replied, "Yes, sah, Ah clear done forgot. Ah didn't tell you 'bout my part, did I? Well, Ah did my part for over thirty years, runnin' away from God as fast as evah my sins could carry me. That was my part. An' God took aftah me till He run me down. That was His part." The Holy Spirit woos, wins, and works in our hearts and witnesses of our salvation.

WITNESS OF LOVE

We are taught that God is love. Scripture contains no greater or more profound statement about God. Once convicted we are the recipients and channels of His love. His love is the motivating factor that caused Christ to die for us. Our supposed value or worthiness could never attract God's attention or grace. This love is so great that God commendeth "his love toward us, in that, while we were yet sinners, Christ died for us" (Romans 5:8).

There is first the witness of God's love for us, which is reciprocated by our love for Him after conversion. The knowledge of who He is and what He has done causes a real convert to love in return to the point of commitment, consecration and martyrdom if necessary. Little four-year-old Martha hugged a doll in each arm. She said to her mother, "Mamma, I love them and love them and love them, but they never love me back." In many cases this is true but not in a born-again child of God.

The love possessed after conversion is different. Before conversion one may be physically attracted to another and have a great fondness for that person. After the transformation there is a love from a divine source that loves even when it is not reciprocated or responded to. This is the love Stephen had which evoked the prayer in his dying hour that led to the salvation of Saul of Tarsus. The bright light near Damascus was not the first he ever saw. His conviction began as Stephen died and his conversion culminated near Damascus. God is the only source of this kind of love. John says in 1 John 4:7, 8: "Beloved, let us love one another: for love is of God; and every one that loveth is born of God, and knoweth God. He that loveth not knoweth not God; for God is love." Love for God is followed by love for one's fellow man. The Word says in 1 John 3:11-14, "For this is the message that ye heard from the beginning, that we should love one another. Not as Cain, who was of that wicked one, and slew his brother. And wherefore slew he him? Because his own works were evil, and his brother's righteous. Marvel not, my brethren, if the world hate you. We know that we have passed from death unto life, because we love the brethren. He that loveth not his brother abideth in death." These are some of the most beloved scriptures which witness to this new love. This

264

love is so great a whole chapter is devoted to it in 1 Corinthians 13. Doubts about salvation dissolve like morning fog at sunrise when we realize God has put this love in our heart and we do love each other in Christ.

There is a beautiful Hebrew legend of two brothers who lived side by side on adjoining lands. One was the head of a large family; the other lived alone. One night, the former lay awake and thought, "My brother lives alone, he has not the companionship of wife and children to cheer his heart as I have. While he sleeps, I will carry some of my sheaves into his field."

At the same hour, the other brother reasoned, "My brother has a large family, and his necessities are greater than mine. As he sleeps, I will put some of my sheaves on his side of the field." Thus the two brothers went out, each carrying out his purposes and each laden with sheaves—and met at the dividing line. There they embraced.

Years later, at the very place stood the Jerusalem Temple, and on the very spot of their meeting stood the Temple's altar.

That may be a legend, but this is a fact: When brethren meet in love for each other and faith in God, they can touch God, bar the doors of hell, shake the world, and change the tenor of the times. Greater love hath no man than this, that a man lay down his life for his friends (John 15:13).

This witness of love goes a step further. One will love the unlovely. The power of love will seek to bring men in sin to Christ. Ours is not a closed society which spends its time spit polishing armor hoping to protect it from the corrosion of the evil around us. We will wield the sword and trust the armor as we wade into a loveless world sharing the love of a crucified resurrected king named Jesus. You see, love never fails—tongues and prophesies, yes; but not love! It is a strong witness.

WITNESS OF OBEDIENCE

A new desire fills the heart to obey the Lord Jesus Christ. The law says "do it or else;" but love, like a magnet, draws genuine commitment out of our heart. We are not forced but constrained by the love of Christ to obedience (2 Corinthians

5:14). Those who do not obey have replaced Christ in the heart as their paramount object of love.

John again deals with this witness in 1 John 2:2-5: "And hereby we do know that we know him, if we keep his commandments. He that saith, I know him, and keepeth not his commandments, is a liar, and the truth is not in him. But whoso keepeth his word, in him verily is the love of God perfected: hereby know we that we are in him." It is interesting to note the number of times the word *know* is used. God wants us to know we have eternal life.

All this sounds good but is there any conflict with this commitment? Yes! As long as one lives there will be conflict. The world, flesh, and Satan are always our archrivals. Satan is a relentless adversary. The world's social structure is contrary to Christian philosophy and practice, and the flesh wars against the human spirit continually. Day after day the war goes on. Listen to Paul as he describes this battle: "For that which I do I allow not: for what I would, that do I not; but what I hate, that do I. If then I do that which I would not, I consent unto the law that it is food. Now then it is no more I that do it, but sin that dwelleth in me. For I know that in me (that is, in my flesh,) dwelleth no good thing: for to will is present with me; but how to perform that which is good I find not. For the good that I would I do not: but the evil which I would not, that I do. Now if I do that I would not, it is no more I that do it, but sin that dwelleth in me. I find then a law, that, when I would do good, evil is present with me. For I delight in the law of God after the inward man: But I see another law in my members, warring against the law of my mind, and bringing me into captivity to the law of sin which is in my members. O wretched man that I am! who shall deliver me from the body of this death? I thank God through Jesus Christ our Lord. So then with the mind I myself serve the law of God; but with the flesh the law of sin" (Romans 7:15-25). Close study will show there is a fierce battle but also a blessed victory in Jesus Christ.

In these battles we must hold fast the profession of our faith and be not weary in well doing.

CONCLUSION

The Scripture teaches us that God's will is for all to be

saved (2 Peter 3:9). This knowledge gives us assurance, and this assurance gives us peace of mind and heart. He will not fail us in our dying hour. Paul tells of his security and the fact that nothing can separate believers from God's love. Further in 1 Corinthians 15:54-57 Paul says that God gives us victory to the point that death's sting is erased through knowledge of God's love and keeping power.

One not only realizes that the believer is heaven-bound but also that unbelievers are doomed to hell since they have lived a life of sin. Oliver Cromwell said at his death, "The devil is ready to seduce me, and I am seduced." After a long life of commitment to Christ and a ministry which brought many to Christ and preservation to the church, the Reverend Hiriam Case came near to death. Talking freely of his blessed hope he said, "Hear that singing! They don't have singing on earth like that." As the moment came when he was to separate from this life to a better world he embraced his wife and said "All is well." He went to be with the Lord.

You can know all is well. You can know you would go to heaven if you died today!

GEHAZI'S TRAGEDY

Paul O. Lombard, Jr.

SCRIPTURE: 2 Kings 5:25-27

INTRODUCTION

One of life's great disappointments is unfulfilled promise. In the parable of the talents we are taught that individuals have varying degrees of gifts. We are also told that to whom much is given, much will be expected.

God spoke to Israel through Haggai the prophet saying, "You looked for much, but indeed it came to little" (Haggai 1:9, *New King James Version*). God spoke similar words about unfulfilled promise regarding Israel, His vineyard: "My Well-beloved has a vineyard on a very fruitful hill. He dug it up and cleared out its stones, and planted it with the choicest vine. He built a tower in its midst, and also made a winepress in it; so, He expected it to bring forth good grapes, but it brought forth wild grapes" (Isaiah 5:1, 2, *NKJV*).

The Lord then asks, "What more could have been done to My vineyard that I have not done in it?" (v. 4, *NKJV*).

We could ask a similar question concerning Gehazi, the servant of Elisha: "What more could have been done to prepare him to be a prophet of the Lord?"

Before we look at Gehazi, let us look at Elisha. Elisha had been a trainee or servant of the prophet Elijah. As we observe his apprenticeship to eventually replace Elijah, we see him pouring water on his master's hands (2 Kings 3:11), identified as a disciple (2:3, 5), and fulfilling God's plan for succession (2:15). What a success story when we read, "The spirit of Elijah doth rest on Elisha"!

Who would replace an aging Elisha? Who would be the recipient of that powerful mantle? Who would ascend to this high and holy office?

Gehazi was the obvious candidate. In terms of experience, he was more qualified for the office of prophet than the apprentice Elisha had been.

SCENES OF TRAINING

In 2 Kings 4:8-17, a Shunammite woman and her husband extend kindness and provision to God's prophet. When Elisha seeks to reward their thoughtfulness, *Gehazi* suggests that the barren woman be blessed with the birth of a child.

Gehazi had faith, which was a prerequisite and qualification for this office. Gehazi met this standard.

The child of this Shunammite family grows, but then tragedy strikes. The child dies! Gehazi is trusted by Elisha to carry his staff and lay it on the body of the dead youth. When Elisha arrives, he raises the child; and Gehazi witnesses the miracle. (See 2 Kings 4:18-37).

So, Gehazi was a witness to the most amazing of miracles —the raising of the dead.

Gehazi was also a witness to the unusual healing of Naaman, the captain from Syria's army (2 Kings 5). Gehazi may be the messenger mentioned in verse 10. If so, he bore the message of healing to Naaman. He gave Naaman the instructions for the cure for leprosy as prescribed by the prophet of God.

After Naaman's miraculous healing, the Syrian said to Elisha, "Now I know that there is no God in all the earth, except in Israel; now therefore, please take a gift from your servant" (v. 15, *NKJV*). But Elisha refused a recompense of reward. However, Gehazi pursued the grateful Syrian and fabricated a story to enrich himself.

Gehazi returned with two talents of silver and two changes of garments. Elisha questioned his absence and Gehazi told his second lie. He denied going anywhere, but Elisha said, "Went not mine heart with thee?" Then he pronounced the judgment of Naaman's leprosy upon his disciple.

What a woeful exchange! Naaman came a leper but returned as a disciple; Gehazi left as a disciple and returned a leper. Naaman left behind his disease and money; Gehazi took up his money and disease. Sin bargains hard.

GEHAZI'S TRAGEDY

Where did Gehazi go wrong? Basically, it seems he became ruined by a familiarity with sacred things. No doubt at the beginning he was greatly impressed by the wonders he saw, but the unusual became commonplace to him.

When the wonderful becomes ordinary, when the glory of God becomes entertainment, when the burning bush where we once knelt and removed our shoes becomes a curious spectacle, it's a tragedy! When messages on the baptism of the Holy Spirit become a bore in a Pentecostal church and when sermons on the return of Christ seem outdated to the hearers, it's a tragedy! It is so easy for us faithful churchgoers to become like Gehazi in our attitude toward the three fundamentals of the church: worship, service, and doctrine.

WORSHIP

Pentecostal-style worship can become so familiar to us that we forget that few people on earth know worship as we know it. The worship we offer God is rare, it is distinct, and it is holy.

The tragedy is the present trend of church services, involving spectators (congregation) and performer (preacher). Many of our "Amens" are dying out, and, sadly, many who now fill the pews just sit in silence. There are three words synonymous with Pentecostal worship: *Amen, Hallelujah,* and *Glory to God.* Is it possible they are so familiar that they have lost their meaning to us?

One Sunday morning in Mobile, Alabama, a Catholic boy attended a Church of God service for the first time. After church he told the pastor, "While you were preaching this

270

morning I wanted to lift my hand and shout 'Right on, Preacher!'" If a young man who had been taught only ritualistic, symbolic worship could be moved by the gospel to the point of desiring verbal expression, what about Spirit-filled believers?

Hallelujah is a good worship word. Ten of the psalms are called "hallelujah psalms." Saint Jerome says that the hallelujah psalms were continually heard in the fields and vineyards of Palestine. The laboring plowman chanted these psalms while the reaper, vinedresser, and shepherds sang the songs of David.

At the final overthrow of sin and the exultant victory of the Church, heaven will burst into praises of "hallelujah." "And after these things I heard a great voice of much people in heaven, saying, Alleluia; Salvation, and glory, and honor, and power, unto the Lord our God . . . And again they said, Alleluia. . . . And the four and twenty elders and the four beasts fell down and worshipped God that sat on the throne, saying, Amen; Alleluia" (Revelation 19:1, 3, 4).

If the Church of Jesus Christ loses her "hallelujahs" on earth, we have suffered tragedy.

"Glory to God!" has punctuated thousands of worship services. The Bible tells us that "the heavens declare the glory of God" (Psalm 19:1). Today God's glory is seen in many ways:

Unconsciously:	sun, moon, stars, earth, trees, water
Consciously:	angels, mankind
Silently:	lightning
Audibly:	thunder
By grace:	redeemed souls
By works:	Living sacrifices, Romans 12:1

Spiritual tragedy has diminished the glory of God in the nominal churches to the point that worship often means only lighted candles, dead rituals, and theological creeds. Our living God is seeking true, vibrant worship. Anything less is tragedy.

SERVICE

Service to God becomes drudgery if there is no vision. The endless task of ministry can dull our sensitivities. Human needs are constant, pressures are relentless, and people are fickle.

Look at Gehazi. He performed good deeds, yet this did not save him in the hour of temptation. In John 15:5 Jesus teaches that abiding with Him is critical to the success of our service: "He that abideth in me, and I in him, the same bringeth forth much fruit."

DOCTRINE

"Therefore, brethren, stand fast, and hold the traditions which ye have been taught, whether by word, or our epistle" (2 Thessalonians 2:15).

When Gehazi pursued Naaman for personal gain, he forsook the doctrine taught by Elisha. As a man of God, Elisha knew the danger involved in making merchandise of the gifts of God. Steadfastly he said, "As the Lord liveth, before whom I stand, I will receive none [reward]. And he [Naaman] urged him to take it; but he refused" (2 Kings 5:16).

Contrast this action with Gehazi's. Gehazi said, "As the Lord liveth, I will run after him, and take somewhat of him" (v. 20).

As Christians we must not run after the treasure of this world and return saying that we are rich with goods and have need of nothing else. God's warning to us is found in His message to Laodicea: "Because thou sayest, I am rich, and increased with goods, and have need of nothing; and knowest not that thou art wretched, and miserable, and poor, and blind, and naked" (Revelation 3:17).

Sound doctrine is not in demand because it brings responsibility and discipline. We must look on the doctrines of God's Word as the anchor of our faith. The doctrine taught by the New Testament writers still stands approved of God as the only way to Heaven.

CONCLUSION

Elijah left his spirit with Elisha (2 Kings 2:15). Elisha took his spirit to the grave in his bones (2 Kings 13:20, 21). The man who should have shouldered Elisha's mantle and received double his portion had become a snow-white leper banished from society. What a tragedy!

CLEAN OUT YOUR CLOSET

Howard Hancock

SCRIPTURE: Genesis 35:1-5

INTRODUCTION

"And God said unto Jacob, Arise, go up to Bethel and dwell there: and make there an altar" (Genesis 35:1).

Before Jacob went up to Bethel, he experienced some very discouraging words.

His brother, Esau, had been in pursuit of him since Jacob had stolen his birthright. He had finally caught up with him, and Jacob was not sure whether Esau would endeavor to kill him or accept his gifts of goats, ewes, rams, camels, cows, bulls, and donkeys.

His daughter, Dinah had been molested by the son of King Hamor, the Hivite.

His two sons, Simeon and Levi, retaliated by deceiving King Hamor and Shechum, his son, by agreeing to give their sister in marriage to the king's son provided that all the men be circumcised. The Scripture says that "on the third day, when they were sore, two of the sons of Jacob, Simeon and Levi, Dinah's brothers, took swords and killed all the men.

Jacob then feared that the Canaanites and the Perizzites would revenge the death of those slaughtered and come seeking to destroy him and his entire household.

Now you can understand why Jacob was down and out. Jacob was fearful, Jacob was doubtful; he had lost hope; he had forgotten the promise of God to bless his seed as the sand of the seashore. He had lost his Bethel experience, which was a spiritual experience.

At Bethel he had a glorious experience. He had a vision of a staircase. Angels were ascending and descending. At the top of this staircase was God. God spoke to Jacob and said, "I am the Lord God of Abraham thy father, and the God of Isaac: the land whereon thou liest, to thee will I give it, and to thy seed; And thy seed shall be as the dust of the earth . . . and in thy seed shall all the families of the earth be blessed. And behold, I am with thee, and will keep thee in all places whither thou goest" (Genesis 28:13-15).

Jacob had lost his "Peniel experience." At Peniel he had received a blessed experience. He literally wrestled with God and was blessed with a new name and a new touch. It isn't unusual for men to lose their spiritual experiences. This happens when we forget about our spiritual encounters with God. We forget about our special blessings. The years that come and go cause us to forget those great moments when we wrestled with the Lord for a blessing.

What causes us to forget and lose our commitment and excitement? This is the question!

What is it that we have shut up in our secret closets that we failed to remove. You don't lose out with God without a cause. In the secret chambers of your life are those secrets that are outgrowing your spiritual man. They keep that inner man subdued.

Look into Jacob's family closet. Twenty years had passed since Jacob spent those moments with God at Bethel and Peniel. Since that time, Jacob had married two wives, was blessed with 11 sons and became wealthy in livestock.

But he was not happy! He was happy at Bethel, seeing the glory of God. He was happy at Peniel in the presence of God. But something had happened to Jacob. He wasn't the same now. God was not satisfied with Jacob's gloom. God was not satisfied with Jacob's indifference. God was not satisfied with Jacob's fear.

He said, "Get up Jacob. Go back to Bethel. Build an altar. You need to pray."

What was wrong with Jacob? God appealed to him to return to Bethel. The Lord was saying, "Let's meet again at Bethel. Let's talk your problems over around the altar. Let's remove whatever is creating the distance between us."

Jacob knew his problem. He knew what was wrong. He knew what was bringing spiritual decay into his life. I am convinced when a person begins to lose out with the Lord, they know the cause.

Jacob knew what was wrong. He said, "Let us go to Bethel, and put away the strange gods among you." He knew that stuck away in his closet were some "strange gods." How did they get there? Jacob had been raised from an infant to worship the true God. His grandfather, Abraham, and his father, Isaac, had implanted in his heart that Jehovah was the true and living God.

We must remember that Jacob had spent 20 years with Laban, his uncle. Laban had images he used in worship. Of course, it has never been the will of God for us to merge images with worship. This is what Laban did. When Jacob and Rachel left Laban's house, Rachel stole the images that belonged to her father.

Those images were so much a part of the family that Rachel did not want to live without them. She felt she could not live without them. When her father caught up with them, he searched for his gods among Jacob's belongings; but he found them not for Rachel had placed them in the camel's saddle, and she was sitting on them. Jacob did not know this at the time!

This is happening today! There are those Rachels and Labans who are not willing to clean out their closets of gods. Some folks cannot live without their gods of cigarettes, drugs, obscenities, jealousy, gossiping, and so forth. They feel they cannot live without them; therefore they are unwilling to make the full surrender to the Lord.

It's true that you cannot see some of those gods for they have been brought into the closet of the mind. The mind becomes a closet for evil imagination, for deception, for fables.

Its easy to import into our hearts little gods of pleasure, gods of carnality, gods of jealousy, gods of bitterness, gods of unforgiveness. Nobody will ever know what is hidden, but God knows and he says to you, "Arise, go to Bethel. Arise, build an altar. Arise, let us reason together."

One idol found in the closets of our lives needs to be removed. That idol is *popularity*. We let what people think influence how we talk, where we go, what we do, and how we live. We are so careful to move with the majority. We lean with the crowd. We party with them. We dress like them. We talk like them, we sing like them. We run our business like them. We cheat like them. We deceive like them, we shade the truth like them.

God is searching for people who will arise and be different.

God forbid that we should house the *idol of money* in the closets of our lives. The Scripture says, "The love of money is the root of all evil." Some people let the blessing of wealth become their downfall.

Money itself is not evil. In fact, Jesus encourages us to give it away. He also instructs us to tithe a tenth of our money to Him.

Money talks. Since I was a child I have always heard that "money speaks."

Some folks have been accused of squeezing a nickel until the buffalo grunts. Although I have never heard money talk, I suppose if it could really speak it would say something like this:

To the Christian: "Share me with the Lord and I will bring evangelists to your church to win souls and edify the church. I will build churches; I will feed the poor; I will support a missionary. I will keep the financial wolves away from your church; I will provide Christian literature for children; I will provide transportation for those who don't have a way to church; I will clothe the orphans."

To the Unbeliever: "Worship me and I will make you rich; I will take away the joy of giving; I will make your life miserable.

I will supply you with everything you want if you will take the time to think of those things you need."

Money is simply saying, "I have power to bless you or curse you. Place me in a tithe envelope, drop me in an offering plate, and I will bless you. Hide me in the secret closet of greed and selfishness, and I will destroy you. Where is your treasure? Where your treasure is, there your heart is also."

Money has power. The headlines of a newspaper reads, "Pennies Block Traffic." The article said that in Jessup, Maryland, a treasury truck carrying 4.3 million pennies turned over onto an entrance ramp to the expressway and canvas sacks of pennies went rolling all over the highway. For several hours, traffic was tied up while the police cleared the road. One penny would have never had the power to hold back the traffic, but 4.3 million pennies did. Together they stopped traffic.

Together we can do much!

What is in your closet? Your closet is your "inner sanctum." It must never become defiled with foreign particles of the world. It must never become infiltrated with strange gods that rob you of your desire to please Him, our true God.

When someone says, "I dread to go to church; I have to make myself go." They need to look into their closet and remove that little idol.

When someone says, "I don't have a desire to pray," they need to look into their closet.

Someone says, "The Word does not interest me anymore." Look into the closet. Someone says, "I don't enjoy witnessing; I used to enjoy talking about the Lord, but not anymore." Look into the closet.

Someone says, "I detest clapping my hands unto the Lord." Look into the closet.

"I don't like shouting, why can't people worship silently." Look in the closet.

"I get tired of singing those old church choruses." Look in the closet.

If you and I are not experiencing and enjoying the blessings of God, the reason is that there is something in the closet.

God just doesn't share "closet space" with uncleanness. Clean out your closet and His Word will thrill you. His presence will become felt.

If you are not living in joy and peace in your life, look into your closet.

Those idols which are hidden in the closet of your life will have a spiritual effect upon you. Spiritual decay, deterioration sets in. Death comes. The spiritual man dies. We can't live with bitterness, unforgiveness, criticism, gossiping, greed, carelessness, worldliness. We can't live with idols in our hearts without it affecting us.

Look at what happened to Jacob while he had idols in his closet. He became a foul odor to the people in his land. His family suffered. He suffered and his family suffered.

The same thing can happen to us. We can suffer individually. Our church will suffer collectively if we don't keep our closets clean.

Our church needs to have a church closet inspection. We need to get back to reverencing holy things. Our children need to be trained that the church is no playground. Our balcony is not a social hall. Our pews are not trampolines. Our carpet is not for gum and candy-mint wrappers. Our tithe envelopes are not note pads. Our song book racks are not wastebaskets. Our vestibule and stairwells are not hide-outs. Our musical instruments are not toys designed for weird sounds. Our singing is not for entertainment. Our handclapping is not to be habitual, but is for praise. Our worship is not for spectators, it is for worshipers. We are worshipers.

There are some things we are just going to have to do to retain His blessings. Jacob knew what had to be done. He gathered his family all around him and said, "Look everyone, you have got to put away the strange gods which are among you. You have got to take a bath, wash yourselves and put on new clothes. We are going to Bethel. We are going back to the place where the angels were ascending and descending upon the ladder. We are going back to the place where God's presence was felt."

And Jacob accepted their gods and the women even gave him their earrings and he buried them beneath the oak tree near Shechum. Jacob acted. He did something about their situation and went up to Bethel with the protecting hand of God over them. Shielding them from being attacked by the surrounding cities.

We talk about cleaning out closets, turning over new leaves, making New Year's resolutions, but we fail to do anything. We must act immediately and stop playing games and bury those strange gods that have kept us defeated.

Jacob did what he had to do. It seemed like he was asking a lot, but he knew we must get rid of our idols.

Its not always easy to clean out our temple closets. It was not easy for Jesus to clean the Temple, but it had to be done. He had to use a whip. He turned over tables. He let the turtledoves free. He knew that the needs of the people would never be met as long as these merchant men and money changers were in charge. He drove them out so others could be blessed.

Drive out those idolatrous money changers. Turn the tables over in your soul. Let the Lord help you and you will be blessed.

For 30 years the beautiful Temple of Solomon had been silenced. When Hezekiah became king, his desire was to restore Temple worship. He sent the priest into the inner part of the Temple to cleanse it. They began to clean out loads of filth and had it carted off. Then the song of the Lord was heard.

When Paul was preaching in the synagogue at Ephesus, many of those Ephesians removed the idols from their lives. They made such a clean sweep that they brought their black magic books and charms and burned them at a public bonfire. Someone estimated the value of those books at $10,000. Our young people had a rock record and tape burning some months ago and it was estimated at $3,000.

Total submission and willingness will remove those idols that clog up the channel between you and God.

A little fountain on a farm could not flow until the owner cleaned it out. It was clogged up with cans, bottles, mud, and rocks. When it was cleaned out, it flowed freely. Rivers of living water cannot flow in a life that is clogged up with strange debris. It's time to unlock the doors of our lives and clean out our closets.

MY TIMES ARE IN THY HANDS

H. Loran Livingston

SCRIPTURE: Psalm 31:14-15

INTRODUCTION

God's people appear, at times, to be stumbling through life. Many feel they are being demoted, when, in fact, every step is carefully planned and all circumstances are orchestrated by God.

The scripture for this message is in Psalm 31 and refers to the fact that our times are in God's hand. Never forget that scripture. David was saying in this psalm my life is in Your hand. Your timing is my timing. Your call upon me is according to your calendar, not my watch.

God often moves slower than we do, but God always has us at the right place at the right time. Nothing ever slips out of His hand. Never a moment is wasted when you're in God's hand. You don't lose anything. You forfeit nothing. I want to deal with four persons in this message: Job, Moses, Saul, and you.

JOB

Now to show you how terribly brief life seems to be just

listen to this verse in Job 14:5. Job in a state of panic says, "Seeing his days [referring to man] are determined, the number of his months are with thee, thou hast appointed his bounds that he cannot pass." Have you ever been there like Job when he said, "Time is getting away? I am enclosed in this little box called earth; I have but a limited number of breaths to draw, and I cannot go beyond that. I have to do everything I can while I'm in God's time frame." So sometimes we panic. I talked to a man a few weeks ago who was thoroughly frustrated. He was on the verge of panic because as he said "I'll soon be X-number of years old, and I have nothing to show for it. I have lots of things I want to do; I have lots of talents." And he does. "I have a driving, burning desire to do something for God. But nothing is happening. I am frozen in my tracks. I am stalemated by circumstances. What am I going to do?"

That scripture came to my mind, "My times are in thy hands." You've got to get to the place in your life where you don't panic. You have to trust the providence of God and the timing of your Maker. He has a specific purpose and a beautiful plan for your life. There is something significant you will do before you leave the world, and God will see to it that you accomplish it if you don't panic and go beyond His will. Don't try to work it out quicker and faster than God. That is all-important.

We who feel that the end of time is upon us have a tendency to push things and to force and flail and fight and try to make it happen. But you can't do that. You have to restfully repose in God's providence for your life. When you try to make it happen, when you try to force a birth of something you only create problems for yourself.

MOSES

In Acts 7 we get the picture of a man who tried to make things happen for God. You know the man. He's the most renowned character in the Old Testament. His name is Moses.

I want you to look first at verses 20-22. "In which time Moses was born and was exceeding fair, and nourished up in his father's house three months. And when he was cast out, Pharaoh's daughter took him up, and nourished him for her own son. And Moses was learned in all the wisdom of the Egyptians, and was mighty in words and in deeds."

Here is the picture of a man who had every thing going for him. To start with, when he was born he was exceeding fair. That means he was beautiful to look upon and was endowed with many good characteristics. He was nourished up in his father's house three months. And even though there was trouble in the land and his life was threatened, God had it planned.

Pharaoh's daughter found this little three-month-old baby floating in an ark, and she took him into the palace and arranged for his care. In fact, Moses' own mother nourished him, but later he was exposed to all of the society of Egypt. He was refined; he was cultured. He had more than anybody in the world could possibly have dreamed of having.

"When he was full forty years old, it came into his heart to visit his brethren the children of Israel. And seeing one of them suffer wrong, he defended him, and avenged him that was oppressed, and smote the Egyptian" (vv. 23, 24). Can you see Moses strolling down the spiral staircase of the Egyptian palace? He's going down to see his brothers, the Israelites, who are sunburned, sweaty, rugged, rough, and fierce because they are slaves. Here strolls this well-manicured, beautifully dressed, blessed young man, 40 years old, going down to help these people. He thought he would be a self-appointed messiah.

When Moses saw an Egyptian smiting one of his brothers, he picked up something, cracked the Egyptian in the head and killed him. There he stood clad with gold, jewels, and fine garments, with blood on his hands.

Moses thought that Israel would rally around him. He thought that all the Jewish brothers would say, "This is our man; we elect you as our messiah and our deliverer; get us out of this place." He thought he would be popular. But instead the Israelites turned on him and ran away.

The Bible states in verse 25, "He supposed his brethren would have understood how that God by his hand would deliver them: but they understood not." He thought he knew God's plan. He thought everything was right.

At 40 years of age, Moses had the education, the knowledge, the experience, and the exposure; he thought the time was right. So he decided to do something that would make Israel rally around him. But the Israelites did not understand.

"The next day," according to verse 26, "he shewed himself unto them as they strove, and would have set them at one again, saying, Sirs, ye are brethren; why do ye wrong one to another? " Suddenly his whole world collapsed. The plan he thought was ideal was gone. Pharaoh was now going to take action against him for murdering an Egyptian. The Israelites laughed at Moses. He ran away. He didn't even get a chance to go back and get his clothes. He ran for his life into the wilderness.

In the natural, the plight of Moses didn't make a lot of sense. He was 40, he was bright, everything should have been perfect. But now he had nobody. He had nothing . . . no dreams . . . no hopes. And he was all by himself in the wilderness, isolated from his family, from royalty. He really did not know how to take care of himself—all because he tried to force God's plan too quickly.

Do you know what Moses was now? He was a nobody. He had nobody; he was nobody. He was not royalty. He was not revered; he had no authority. All of his training was for naught. He was not a prince anymore; he was a shepherd. He was not an authority; he was now working, perhaps for minimum wages, at his father-in-law's sheep ranch.

One third of Moses life was spent as a nobody, doing nothing significant without contact with his family, his nation, or the palace. One third of his life was spent on the backside of the desert, trying to figure out what went wrong. For 40 years, from the time he was 40 to the time he was 80, Moses just wasted on the backside of the desert.

I've often wondered how Moses must have felt during those years. Five years pass. Nobody knows him. The Egyptian authorities haven't found him yet. Hopefully, Pharaoh has forgotten about the crime and he isn't hunting him anymore. Many, many times I'm sure, he walked those sheep around to the backside of the mountain and there he sat. He watched them eat and listened to them bleat. He rolled it over and over in his mind, "What did I do wrong? Has God forsaken me? I have wasted my talents. I blew it. What am I going to do now? Am I going to rot in this wilderness? Does anybody know I'm here? Does anybody care? I'm married; I have two children. But what have I really done with my life? What have I done for my generation? What is it that I've done that would cause such a void, meaningless experience in my life on this earth?"

Moses stayed on the backside of the desert so long he didn't even care anymore. A third of his life was wasted, and what's more they were the best years of his life. He watched it go by year after year after year until he was 80 years old. Now to us that seems rather elderly, doesn't it? Who starts a career at 80? Who's making plans at 80? Most people are planning to leave the world at 80. And there he was at that ripe old age and didn't even care anymore.

Even on the day he met God in a bush that would not burn, Moses seemed to have been troubled by the wasted years. God spoke to him and told him what to do; and he responded in a less-than-enthusiastic manner, "Pick somebody else! I don't want to do this. I could have done a good job when I was 40. I could have really made something happen when I was 52. God, go ahead and get somebody else; I don't have the will . . . I don't have the dream. I've lost all my knowledge and my experience. Can you get somebody else? I can't even talk. I'm a stutterer. Pick someone who can speak and someone who wants to do it and somebody who cares because I don't care anymore." But God had chosen him.

The greatest thing Satan would like to do to your mind is make you think that nothing is going to happen, that all of those dreams you had and those impulses to do something big for God were just false feelings. You were in a high state of mind, on an emotional binge, and it's not going to happen. You're just going to sort of fade out of life. You'll contribute nothing. Oh, you'll do a little bit here and there, but you're really never going to be anybody, and you're really never going to do anything. That's Satan's greatest ploy, to make you feel that God can't use you anymore.

But I want to emphasize that while Moses thought his life was being wasted, God was letting him ripen. When Moses thought he was ready to deliver Israel, God said he's just now ready to learn. He had to be a shepherd before he could be a mighty deliverer. He had to understand loneliness with God before he could get in the midst of millions of people and make decisions. The Bible goes on to say in verse 30, "When forty years were expired, there appeared to him in the wilderness of Mount Sinai an angel of the Lord in a flame of fire in a bush. When Moses saw it, he wondered at the sight: and as he drew near to behold it, the voice of the Lord came unto him."

There are long, drawn-out times when you don't hear the voice of the Lord. You don't feel that you're doing anything. Nothing is being accomplished, you're just there on the backside of the desert all by yourself.

But there is a time in your life when God sees that you're ready, when He sees that you're going to hear the voice of the Lord. The doors are then going to open up, and your dreams are going to come to pass. It is never too late when you're in God's hands. Your times are in God's hands. Moses was chosen. And when God chooses you, nobody can disregard you. Nobody can ruin the plan except you. Satan cannot change it. Nobody can take it away.

God's hand is on His people. And He has chosen you to do something for Him!

Chosen, Chosen! That means God laid His hand on you for a specific thing. David said, "Thou hast laid thine hand upon me, and lifted me up" (see Psalm 139:5). When God does that to you, you are chosen. He doesn't just choose preachers. And He doesn't just choose singers. He chooses mothers, and He chooses housewives, and He chooses people in every station of life. You are chosen to do something for God, and it doesn't matter what your career is.

There may be times when God lets you wait it out . . . when you will feel isolated . . . when you will feel like a nobody doing nothing. God just lets you wait. That's the time when you feel least disposed to pray. That is the time when there is no enthusiasm. That is the time you think about another career—something totally out of religion. Don't do it. And don't try to push God's plan. Moses thought he'd do it at 40, but God said it must be done at 80! Moses thought he would do it because he was trained in the palace; God said he wasn't ready until he had been trained in the wilderness.

SAUL

When the Lord struck Paul blind and he was groping to find out where he was and who he was, the Lord spoke to a prophet named Ananias and said, "Ananias, I want you to go find Saul of Tarsus. And I want you to lay your hands on him, and pray for him." And Ananias answered, "Lord, this man is dangerous. He has a reputation for killing Christians. And You want me to go lay my hands on him and pray for him?" The Lord said, "He is a chosen vessel unto Me. I will show him how great things he must suffer for My name's sake. I have chosen him. I have called him to go and preach My name before Gentiles and kings and the nation of Israel. He is My chosen vessel, I chose him to suffer" (see Acts 9:10-16). Moses was chosen to lead. Saul was chosen to suffer and preach. And each man had to go through a time of waiting.

When Saul was converted, he went down into Arabia; and for three and one-half years, he stayed before God, studied the Holy Scriptures, and prepared himself. God allowed him to wait and mature. Then at the appropriate time God brought him out of Arabia, and Paul began to build and establish churches and teach doctrine to the believers. Chosen to suffer! Why? Because his times were in God's hands.

YOU

If you're seeking the Lord, you are right where you ought to be. Right now, your times are in His hands; God has His hand on you.

You may not know where your career is going. You may feel like you missed your opportunity several years ago. You may feel your life is slipping through your fingers and if you don't do something quickly, it won't happen.

But your life is not slipping through your fingers because your life is in God's hands. There are no leaks in the hands of God. There is no weakness in His grip. Your times are in His hand.

Listen to the words of Psalm 139:16, "Thine eyes did see my substance, yet being unperfect; and in thy book all my members were written, which in continuance were fashioned, when as yet there were none of them." That might seem like a long way around saying before you were ever conceived by your parents, God knew you. He had His hand on you, and had already plowed a rut through this world for you. God had a distinct call for you and is not going to leave you. You may not get started or be ready until you're 70 years old. But that's all right; it doesn't matter what people say; we don't go by earthly standards. We go by the standards of an omniscient, all-powerful, all-knowing God, who cares about every single one of us. He cares about the elderly, and He cares about the babies. He still has a plan for everybody's life. You may be 95 years old; God's still got a plan for your life. You may feel like, at the age of 40 you haven't accomplished a thing. God still has a plan for your life. You may feel like you're on the backside of the desert with family gone and nobody understands you or knows where you are. But be assured . . . before long you'll hear the voice of God call you and get you ready for that work which you alone can do in this world.

We should never pattern success after what somebody else is doing. We should not gauge the rightness or the ripeness of the moment by what somebody else did. Before you were formed, before your parents were born, God knew your name. God had his hand on your life. Everything about you was written in the book of God.

When Isaac was looking for a wife, he sent his servant out. The servant here is a man nobody knows about. But when Isaac sent him out to find a wife he did exactly what Isaac told him to do. He said everything to Rebecca's father that Isaac told him to say and he did it well. He accomplished his mission and we don't even know his name.

If that servant had not done his job well, there would really have been no need for Moses to be born. One nameless, humble servant did whate he was supposed to do. God's plan for him was important. "The man bowed down his head, and worshipped the Lord" (Genesis 24:26). Because his master's mission had been accomplished, he was able to worship out of gratitude to God. He wasn't worshiping Isaac, he was worshiping the Lord. He saw that he had done a good job, and now the Lord was going to get all the credit. Where do you think that man is today? He's not in Hebrews 11, listed with all those faithful heroes. We don't know where he is, except heaven! We don't even know his name. But he did God's will. His times were in God's hands. So what if you don't get a name?

CONCLUSION

What if you never get recognized? What if you never get any publicity whatsoever? Does that mean you don't work for God? No! Because nobody's ever supposed to work for God or be faithful to God for the credit we're getting anyway. We're supposed to be serving God just because he's God. We're supposed to be loving God just because He's God . . . not because He heals all our sicknesses . . . not because He forgives all our iniquities . . . not because He supplies our needs daily and loads us with benefits; but we are to love Him and serve Him just because He is God. He is holy, He is good, He is righteous, and that's why we ought to serve Him. Praying people never have to worry about being out of God's will. Your times, your days, your service in the Kingdom are all in God's hands.

THE INVESTMENT OF LIFE

Billy L. Olds

SCRIPTURE: Jeremiah 1:5

INTRODUCTION

God has a plan for every life. He had a plan for Jeremiah's life even before he saw the light of day. He has a plan for your life. He has one for mine. Because of this fact, no one can be supremely happy until he has found God's plan for his life. Somebody wrote a song, "I Was Born to Serve the Lord."

Are you ever discontented, despondent, or miserable? It may be that you have refused to accept His plan and have persisted in following one of your own.

But you ask, "How can I know God's plan?" That I cannot answer. You must decide it for yourself. However, by God's help I may be able to make it easier for you to make a decision.

As a follower of the Lord Jesus Christ you have but one great aim: the advancement of God's kingdom. As a Christian, I say the interests of the kingdom of God become your main object in life. God's work is of paramount importance. Everything else must take a secondary place.

Jesus never entrusted this work to ministers alone. He has laid it upon every Christian man and every Christian woman. Each individual believer has his own particular part in the plan of the Kingdom. God is depending upon you and He is depending upon me. He is depending upon each of us.

If then our aim is to serve the kingdom of God, we should consider the following factors.

SERVICE

Service is the highest motive—not dollars and cents. The man who measures success in life by dollars and cents has not caught the true meaning of success.

There is another standard, vastly higher. Oh, that we might catch the vision of that standard!

Jesus said, "Take heed, and beware of covetousness: for a man's life consisteth not in the abundance of the things which he possesseth" (Luke 12:15).

There lies before each of us a great field of opportunity and responsibility. We have our life to invest. We should desire to invest it as God wishes and according to the greatest need. What help is there for such a crisis? What star will guide us? It seems to me that in the investment of life the place of greatest need has first claim.

THE MINISTRY

Take ministry, for example. How great is the need here? Do you want a field of real service that will yield a rich reward? Then give yourself totally in preparation for this high calling.

Remember, the ministry is made up of common ordinary men, just like you, who have responded to the call of God: "Ye have not chosen me, but I have chosen you, and *ordained* you, that ye should go and bring forth fruit, and that your fruit should remain" (John 15:16). The *Amplified Bible* puts it this way: "But I have chosen you—I have *appointed* you, I have *planted* you—that you might go and bear fruit and keep on bearing."

Paul wrote, "For we are his workmanship, created in Christ

Jesus unto good works, which God hath before ordained that we should walk in them" (Ephesians 2:10).

The *Amplified Bible* translates it this way: "For we are God's [own] handiwork (His workmanship) . . . that we may do those good works which God predestined (planned beforehand)." We read in Psalm 65:4, "Blessed is the man whom thou choosest."

I realize many have made the mistake of measuring success by the standard of dollars and cents. I grant you that very few Church of God ministers will become rich preaching the gospel.

But would you tell me that D. L. Moody was not a success simply because he never became wealthy? that Charles H. Spurgeon's life was a failure because he died a poor man? Success can never be measured in dollars and cents. It can only be judged in terms of service.

If God has spoken to your heart to preach His Word, I urge you to get a good education. Then you need practical training. Be willing to start at the bottom and work up. Ask God for patience in preparing you for the ministry. Be faithful in the place where God has put you.

REMEMBER, TIME IS SHORT.

That calls us to action. Time can be our tool or we can be its slaves. Sit down and write some priorities for your life. Pray for guidance and write down what God speaks to your heart. Your life should be planned.

Although time is running out, this should not make us restless. Even though we believe in the imminent return of Jesus, we should go right on preparing for the work God has called us into.

THE MISSION FIELD

What of the Foreign Missions field? When you look at the conditions existing in the non-Christian world, your heart burns within you as you realize that over two-thirds of the world is still without Christ. In Africa, India, and China, thousands are dying every day who have never heard the name Jesus.

The Savior's command is, "Go ye into all the world, and preach the gospel to every creature" (Mark 16:15).

In the past 1900 years, many have obeyed the voice of God. They have gone to the farthest parts of the world and many have given their lives for the sake of the gospel. Do what you can and God will do what you cannot.

Lillian Thrasher, whom the press once described as "The Greatest American Woman Living Outside the U.S.," ranked high among the missionary heroines of her time. She worked 50 years in Egypt, where she cared for the children, the homeless, the helpless and the blind. They called her, "The Nile Mother." A news reporter asked her about the secret of her success, and what was the greatest thing she ever did. "There isn't any secret," she answered quickly, "I just stayed; I did not quit. I stayed with the work God gave me to do."

May I ask you, What are you going to give the Lord? Money, credit cards, stocks and bonds? Many of us don't have these things to give, but, we can give ourselves.

In Romans 12:1, Paul instructs us, "I beseech you therefore, brethren, by the mercies of God, that ye present your bodies a living sacrifice, holy, acceptable unto God, which is your reasonable service."

Dr. Alexander Duff, that great veteran missionary to India, returned to Scotland to die. As he stood before the General Assembly of the Presbyterian church, he made his appeal. But there was no response. In the midst of his appeal he fainted and was carried off the platform. When he opened his eyes he cried, "Where am I?" He was told by the doctor to lay still, for his heart was very weak. "But," exclaimed the old warrior, "I must finish my appeal. Take me back, take me back!" Dr. Duff struggled to his feet, his determination overcoming his weakness. With the doctors on one side and the moderator on the other side, Dr. Duff was led back to the platform. As he mounted the pulpit steps, the entire assembly rose to do him honor. Then he continued his appeal:

"When Queen Victoria calls for volunteers for India, hundreds of young men respond; but when King Jesus calls, no one goes." Then he paused. "Is it true," he continued, "that Scotland has no more sons to give for India?" Again he paused. "Very well," he concluded, "if Scotland has no more young men to send to India, then old and decrepit though I am, I will go back. Though I can't preach, I can lie down on the shores and die in order to let the people of India know that there is at least one man in Scotland who cares enough for their souls to give his life for them."

In a moment, young men all over the assembly sprang to their feet crying out, "I'll go! I'll go!" After the famous missionary had passed on, many of those same young men found their way to India, there to invest their lives as missionaries as a result of the appeal God had made through Dr. Duff.

Will you go? Will you invest your life in the cause of missions? Have you heard the call? Will you answer, "Lord, here am I, send me!"

Peter asked Jesus, "Behold, we have forsaken all, and followed thee; what shall we have therefore? And Jesus said unto them . . . and every one that hath forsaken houses, or brethren, or sisters, or father, or mother, or wife, or children or lands, for my name's sake, shall receive an hundredfold, and shall inherit everlasting life" (Matthew 19:27-29).

Moses made an investment: "Choosing rather to suffer affliction with the people of God, than to enjoy the pleasures of sin for a season; Esteeming the reproach of Christ greater riches than the treasures of Egypt: for he had respect unto the recompense of the reward" (Hebrews 11:25, 26).

Paul also made an investment. He seems to reflect on what he could have been: "But what things were gain to me, those I counted loss for Christ. Yea doubtless, and I count all things but loss for the excellency of the knowledge of Christ Jesus my Lord: for whom I have suffered the loss of all things, and do count them but dung, that I may win Christ" (Philippians 3:7, 8).

Paul wasn't a quitter. He made an investment and it paid off. Paul's last testimony was this: "I have fought a good fight, I have finished my course, I have kept the faith: Henceforth there is laid up for me a crown of righteousness, which the Lord, the righteous judge, shall give me at that day: and not to me only, but unto all them also that love his appearing" (2 Timothy 4:7, 8).

There are many who say, "It's my money, my talent and my life; so I will do as I very well please." It would be well to remember the words of the preacher in Ecclesiastes 11:9: "Rejoice, O young man, in thy youth; and let thy heart cheer thee in the days of thy youth, and walk in the ways of thine heart, and in the sight of thine eyes: but know thou, that for all these things God will bring thee into judgment."

The same writer said, "Remember now thy Creator in the days of thy youth, while the evil days come not, nor the years draw nigh, when thou shalt say, I have no pleasure in them" (12:1). It would be well to have precious memories of a life you had spent in the service of the Lord.

REMEMBER, GOD HAS A PLAN FOR YOUR LIFE!

You will face untold pressure as you invest your life in the service of the Lord. You will need inside braces against outside pressures.

The first brace is God's Word: "Thy word have I hid in mine heart, that I might not sin against thee" (Psalm 119:11).

God told Joshua, "This book of the law shall not depart out of thy mouth; but thou shalt meditate therein day and night, that thou mayest observe to do according to all that is written therein: for then thou shalt make thy way prosperous, and then thou shalt have good success" (Joshua 1:8).

The second brace is God's peace: "And the peace of God, which passeth all understanding, shall keep your hearts and minds through Christ Jesus" (Philippians 4:7).

One can actually have peace during the storm. In Acts 27 we find the story where they were shipping a preacher. The storm was so severe—there was no sun by day and no moon by night. God dispatched an angel to speak to Paul. The apostle was then able to stand on the deck of the ship, with the peace of God in his heart, and state, "Brethren, I believe God."

The third brace is love. In 1 Corinthians 13 it speaks of love contrasted . . . love analyzed . . . love defended as the supreme gift. Regardless of the gifts man may claim, it is stated loud and clear that without love "it profiteth [us] nothing." If you are going to be successful in whatever ministry —teacher, minister or missionary—you must have the *love* of Christ flowing through you (John 13:35).

294

CONCLUSION

There is only one life and it will soon past; only what's done for Christ will last!

So invest your life well. Invest it for the services of the Lord.

In Psalm 126:6 we are promised a reward, "He that goeth forth and weepeth, bearing precious seed, shall doubtless come again with rejoicing, bringing his sheaves with him."

THE "I WILLS" OF CHRIST

Kenneth R. Looney

SCRIPTURE: Revelation 3:20

INTRODUCTION

The promises of our Lord are steadfast and sure. It is God's will for men and women to receive His righteous promises, for He is not willing that any should perish, but that all should come to repentance. When one repents of his sins and accepts Christ Jesus as his Savior, he is able to receive the exceeding great and precious promises of the Lord.

Christ does not deal in alternatives, for His promises and commandments are clear and direct. The Bible declared, "[Abraham] staggered not at the promise of God . . . but was . . . fully persuaded that, what he had promised, he was able also to perform" (Romans 4:20, 21). Also, "no good thing will he withhold from them that walk uprightly" (Psalm 84:11).

Throughout the Gospels and the Book of Revelation, we observe the life and ministry of Jesus Christ, the teachings and sayings of Christ. His words were not empty words, but as adequately stated, "The people were astonished at his doctrine: For he taught them as one having authority, and not as the scribes" (Matthew 7:28, 29).

In the words Jesus spoke, men find deliverance and hope. Christ said, "The words that I speak unto you, they are spirit, and they are life" (John 6:63). The Apostle Paul confirmed this in his own life by saying, "For to me to live is Christ, and to die is gain" (Philippians 1:21).

On a number of occasions, Christ in His sayings and promises used the expression, "I will." This very affirmative statement denotes assurance and dependability in all He has promised. These "I wills" of Christ are given to all believers and will ultimately be received by those who are faithful.

Everyone uses the expression "I will," and we intend for the most part to keep the promise. Take for instance, one may say to another, "*I will* see you tomorrow at 3 p.m.," or a grandmother may say to her grandchild as they are conversing on the phone, "*I will* bring you a gift when I come to see you." These individuals may have every intention of fulfilling their promise ("I will"), but because of some unfortunate or unforeseen circumstance, they may be unable to do so. Man is limited and can be prevented from carrying out his planned activities or commitment.

In comparison to Christ, who is all truth, Satan is a liar and the father of liars. He tries to mimic all that God has done for the good of mankind, and his ultimate goal is deception.

Before his great fall, Lucifer used the same expression, "I will" to perpetrate his evil intentions:

"How art thou fallen from heaven, O Lucifer, son of the morning! how art thou cut down to the ground, which didst weaken the nations! For thou hast said in thine heart, I will ascend into heaven, I will exalt my throne above the stars of God: I will sit also upon the mount of the congregation, in the sides of the north: I will ascend above the heights of the clouds; I will be like the most High. Yet thou shalt be brought down to hell, to the sides of the pit" (Isaiah 14:12-15).

Five times in those scriptures Lucifer used the expression "I will" ("I will ascend", "I will exalt", "I will sit", "I will ascend," "I will be"). He actually believed he could bring rebellion to pass. It is possible he still believes he can succeed in this rebellion. His sin can be summed up in two words: pride and rebellion.

Satan's "I wills" are based on deception and falsehood. His "I wills" are death and destruction. "The thief cometh not, but for to steal, and to kill, and to destroy" (John 10:10).

THE PROMISES AND "I WILLS" OF CHRIST ARE FOR REAL

The promises and "I wills" of Christ are given to every born-again believer who has accepted His free grace. "Faithful is he that calleth you, *who* also will do it" (1 Thessalonians 5:24). Christ said, "Behold, I stand at the door, and knock: if any man hear my voice, and open the door, I *will* come in to him, and will sup with him, and he with me" (Revelation 3:20). It is up to man to open the door of his heart before Christ can perform His word.

Note some of the "I wills" which Christ spoke as He ministered on earth. To the leper He said, "*I will*: be thou clean" (Luke 5:13). To all who believe, He said, "And this is the will of him that sent me, that every one which seeth the Son, and believeth on him, may have everlasting life: and *I will* raise him up at the last day" (John 6:40). And in His prayer for His disciples, He prayed, "Father, *I will* that they also, whom thou hast given me, be with me where I am" (John 17:24).

THE FIRST SPECIAL "I WILL" IS TO ALL BELIEVERS

There are many "I wills" that Christ spoke to the disciples and unto all who will believe on His name. These special "I wills" give a solid foundation for our Christian faith, for they provide comfort, consolation, strength, and hope.

The first special "I will" of Christ for the believer is given in Matthew 4:19: "And he saith unto them, Follow me, and *I will* make you fishers of men." He is saying, "Give Me your life as a yielded vessel and *I will* make you what I desire you to be."

There was a song that came out a few years ago, and the lines went something like this: "He's still working on me, to make me what I ought to be. It took Him just a week to make the moon and the stars, the sun and the earth, Jupiter and Mars. How loving and patient He must be, He's still working on me."

There's a lot of truth to that song, for after we are saved, we are still but a rough copy of what the Lord plans for us to be. After his conversion, the Apostle Paul was far from being all that God planned for him to be. If we will but follow Christ, He will make us what He wants us to be. "But grow in grace, and in the knowledge of our Lord and Savior Jesus Christ" (2 Peter 3:18).

After one accepts Christ as Lord and Savior, the road to heaven is a process. This was especially the case with the Apostle Peter, who was prejudiced against the Gentiles, until the Lord gave him the great vision on the housetop in Joppa (Acts 10:14).

It was not an easy thing for a Jew to go and preach to the Gentiles, but our Lord made Simon Peter a willing messenger to the household of Cornelius. Paul wrote: "Being confident of this very thing, that he which hath began a good work in you will perform it until the day of Jesus Christ" (Philippians 1:6).

Christ will perform His work in us so that we may be able to conform to the image of the inner man (Jesus Christ). "For we are his workmanship, created in Christ Jesus unto good works, which God hath before ordained that we should walk in them" (Ephesians 2:10).

THE SECOND SPECIAL "I WILL" RELATES TO HIS CHURCH

The next marvelous "I will" Christ uttered is found in Matthew 16:18: "And I say also unto thee, That thou art Peter, and upon this rock I will build my church; and the gates of hell shall not prevail against it."

The Lord is saying two important things: "I will build my church," and "the gates of hell shall not prevail against it."

The Church is ordained by Christ to be the Body which bears His identity and carries His light. This body of believers will be the vehicle to take the gospel to all nations. "Unto him be glory in the church by Christ Jesus throughout all ages, world without end" (Ephesians 3:21). "Husbands, love your wives, even as Christ also loved the church, and gave himself for it . . . That he might present it to himself a glorious church, not having spot, or wrinkle, or any such thing; but that it should be holy and without blemish" (Ephesians 5:25, 27).

Christ did not say the gates of hell would not come against the Church, but that the gates of hell will not prevail against it. She (the Church) will be lied on, maligned, persecuted, hated, intimidated and tried; but the Church lives on.

How many governments, kingdoms, organizations, and powers have risen and fallen since our Lord made the statement, "The gates of hell shall not prevail"; but the Church lives on. She has been through the flood, she has been through the fire, but one of these days the Church is going to move up higher. Yes, Christ will present unto Himself a glorious church.

The word *church* in the New Testament is taken from the Greek word *ekklessia*, which means "called-out ones." "They are not of the world, even as I am not of the world" (John 17:16). The Church is that bright light beaming the message of Christ who is the life of the Church itself.

THE THIRD SPECIAL "I WILL" RELATES TO HIS PRAYER TO THE FATHER

The next "I will" of Christ is to equip believers to do His work on earth efficiently. Christ said, "And I will pray the Father, and he shall give you another Comforter, that he may abide with you for ever" (John 14:16). There is no greater consolation for the child of God than Christ's promise to all believers that they can be filled with the Spirit.

The Lord also said, "If ye love me, keep my commandments. And I will pray the Father, and he shall give you another Comforter, that he may abide with you for ever; Even the Spirit of truth; whom the world cannot receive, because it seeth him not, neither knoweth him: but ye know him; for he dwelleth with you, and shall be in you. I will not leave you comfortless: I will come to you" (John 14:15-18).

The disciples were told they would enter a new dimension in the Spirit's work. The Spirit had been with them, but in a few days He would be in them to perform the work of Christ.

It seems inconceivable that Christians would overlook the promise of the baptism of the Holy Ghost, for the Word declares, "Nevertheless I tell you the truth; It is expedient for you that I go away: for if I go not away, the Comforter will not come unto you; but, if I depart, I will send him unto you" (John 16:7).

While He was on earth with His disciples, Christ was their strength, consolation, and comfort. He told them He would go to the Father, and "I will pray the Father, and he shall give you another Comforter, that He may abide with you forever." The term *Comforter* in the original means "one who walks along beside us." The strength of Christ is in the heart of every Spirit-filled believer and this is the will of Christ.

Jesus said, "Ye are the light of the world" (Matthew 5:14). The Lord was going to endow the believers with the ability to continue to shine brightly in a darkened world. He would finish the work He began by the power of the Holy Ghost who would fill the believer with divine enablement to complete this task. "But ye shall receive power, after that the Holy Ghost is come upon you: and ye shall be witnesses unto me both in Jerusalem, and in all Judea, and in Samaria, and unto the uttermost part of the earth" (Acts 1:8).

The Bible speaks of the power of the Holy Spirit. It is recognized in the life of Jesus Christ: "How God anointed Jesus of Nazareth with the Holy Ghost and with power: who went about doing good, and healing all that were oppressed of the devil; for God was with him" (Acts 10:38).

Wherever Christ went He faced difficulties or crises. However, He could minister only in one place at a time. He healed the sick, raised the dead, calmed the sea, fed the multitude, and preached to those around Him.

He was concerned about mankind and was thinking of those who would be born in ages to come. This world of which He speaks, He mentions 32 times in John 15, 16, and 17.

The work of Christ must be carried on by Spirit-filled believers. Imagine Christ living on earth today as He was before His crucifixion, wanting to minister to each individual. It would take Him 10,000 to 12,000 years to get around to every person, not to mention all those who have lived since mankind begun.

He left this task to the believer and would empower the Spirit-filled believer to continue His work, for "howbeit when he, the Spirit of truth is come, he will guide you into all truth: for he shall not speak of himself; but whatsoever he shall hear, that shall he speak: and he will shew you things to come" (John 16:13).

The Holy Spirit is blessing men and women everywhere throughout the world, and it was prophesied that this would happen, "And it shall come to pass in the last days, saith God, I will pour out of my Spirit upon all flesh: and your sons and your daughters shall prophesy" (Acts 2:17).

Jesus is ministering to the diseased, the sick, the infirm, to those in darkness, and to all who will receive His blessings. He is using men and women that have been baptized in His spirit to bring this to pass. It is so marvelous that this can be done through the power of the Spirit in the life of the believer, all because Christ promised, "I will pray the Father, and he shall give you another Comforter."

THE LAST GREAT "I WILL" OF CHRIST RELATES TO HIS COMING AGAIN

The final "I will" of Christ that is so wonderful to all believers, is found in John 14:1-3: "Let not your heart be troubled: ye believe in God, believe also in me. In my Father's house are many mansions: if it were not so, I would have told you. I go to prepare a place for you. And if I go and prepare a place for you, I will come again, and receive you unto myself, that where I am, there ye may be also."

It is prophesied over 318 times in the Bible that Christ will come again. There are two stages of Christ's coming: (1) First He comes in the clouds to rapture the living and dead saints to meet Him in the air; (2) then He comes back to earth to rule and reign with those same saints He has raptured.

When Christ comes in the clouds to catch away the living saints and those who have died in Christ, in what is commonly called the rapture of the Church, the saints of God will have their vile bodies changed to a glorified body. Christ will not set foot on earth at this first phase of His coming, the Rapture, at which moment only the saints of God will see Him (1 Thessalonians 4:13-18). But at the end of the Tribulation, He will descend very slowly to earth and every eye shall see Him (Revelation 1:7). Christ and the saints of God will reign on the earth for one thousand years, in a reign of righteousness and peace.

Most Christians talk more about the rapture of the Church when one speaks of the second coming of Jesus Christ. The Bible plainly declares, "And every man that hath this hope in him purifieth himself, even as he is pure" (1 John 3:3); also, "Wherefore comfort one another with these words" (1 Thessalonians 4:18). Living and looking for Christ to return in the clouds is the great comfort of the redeemed of God.

The world is filled with sadness, gloom, darkness, and death; but the church of Jesus Christ is ready to rise up in power, redemption, righteousness, resurrection and rapture. Our Lord Jesus said, "Because I live, ye shall live also" (John 14:19).

CONCLUSION

Thank God for our Lord's "I wills." He desires for us to enjoy the fullness of joy and to live victoriously in His name. "I am come that they might have life, and that they might have it more abundantly" (John 10:10). "For it is God which worketh in you both to will and to do of his good pleasure" (Philippians 2:13).

His "I wills" are forever comforting and reassuring to all who believe in His immutable power. In the Book of Revelation, chapters 2 and 3, Jesus said "I will" 28 times: "I will give thee a crown of life," "I will come unto thee quickly," "I will give him the morning star," "I will not blot out his name out of the book of life," "I will confess his name before my Father, and his angels," "I will write upon him a new name." These are but a brief number of the many references to His "I wills" in those chapters.

If we will but hear the Word, believe and receive the "I wills" of Christ into our heart, then are we persuaded that He is able to perform His will in our life. His purpose is to sup with each of us.

Hallelujah! He has promised, "To him that overcometh will I grant to sit with me in my [Father's] throne" (Revelation 3:21). The "I wills" of Christ relate to every one who believes, including me.

WALKING IN THE WILL OF GOD

Guy P. Duffield

SCRIPTURE: Ephesians 5:17

INTRODUCTION: One of the wisest things in all of life is to know and walk in the will of God. I am not a fatalist, but I do believe that God has a plan for the life and service of each of His children.

Jesus said to His disciples, "Ye have not chosen me, but I have chosen you, and ordained you" (John 15:16). In Psalm 37:23 we read, "The steps of a good man are ordered by the Lord." One of the most asked questions of young Christians to their spiritual advisers is, "How can I know the will of God for my life? Is it really possible to know the will of God?" Our text assures us that it is. Paul says, "Be ye not unwise, but understanding what the will of the Lord is" (Ephesians 5:17).

HOW CAN YOU KNOW THE WILL OF GOD?

A. Get to the place where you really want to know His will and are willing to do it.

1. Many times we have preconceived ideas as to what we should do, and we want God to agree with us.

   2. Come to the place where you can freely say, "Lord, I want Your will even if I do not want it."

B. Find out what the Word of God says about the matter.

   1. God's will is revealed in His Word.

   2. It is never God's will to go contrary to His Word.

C. Look for and yield to the leading of the Holy Spirit. Jesus promised, "When he, the Spirit of truth, is come, He will guide you into all truth" (John 16:13).

D. Recognize the providential leadings of the Lord.

   1. Sometimes the Lord will lead through circumstances.

   2. Wait until the Word, the Spirit, and circumstances are in agreement.

E. Be patient.

   1. This is one of the most important principles. (Isaiah 30:18; 49:23).

   2. If it is not clear what you should do, do nothing. "Be thou there until I bring thee word" (Matthew 2:13).

F. Have confidence that God will lead you, not merely others.

   1. Jesus said, "My sheep hear my voice" (John 10:27).

   2. These are the words of the Shepherd, not the sheep. Ask Him to prove it to you.

THE IMPORTANCE OF WALKING IN HIS WILL.

Speaking of the wicked man, the writer of Proverbs says, "He speaketh with his feet" (6:13). The ungodly tell what is in their heart by the way they walk. Likewise the Christian reveals, by his walk, just what kind of life he has.

A. If two are going to walk together, they will both have to go in the same direction.

   1. This means yielding ourselves to the will of God.

   2. God is certainly not going to change the direction in which He is going.

B. If you are going to walk with God, you must keep step with Him.

1. You cannot say you are walking with God if you lag behind.

2. If you are going to walk with God, you are going to have to learn to take big steps.

C. If you are going to walk with someone, you have to be in agreement.

1. This is more than following God—it is walking with Him. This means fellowship.

2. You must be in harmony with Him.

"Can two walk together, except they be agreed?" (Amos 3:3).

GOD IN THREE PERSONS

E. J. Reynolds

SCRIPTURE: Luke 3:21, 22

INTRODUCTION: Christians believe in God the Father, God the Son (Jesus Christ), and God the Holy Spirit. The Christian doctrine of one God eternally existing in three persons cannot be discovered by reason. However, God in three persons is clearly revealed in the Bible and must be accepted by faith.

At the baptism of Jesus by John the Baptist, there was a divine revelation of the three distinct persons of the Holy Trinity. God the Father spoke His approval of His Son, Jesus Christ. As the Father spoke and God the Son stood in the water, God the Holy Spirit descended upon the Son in the form of a dove. This revelation of the three persons of the Godhead is a good place to begin with an examination of the biblical doctrine of the Trinity.

PERSON DEFINED

A. Since we speak of *persons* in the Godhead, it is important for us to understand the meaning of *person*.

B. Any rational being who can say, "I am" or "I act" is a person. A person has a conscious, rational life.

C. A person has a personality—a consciousness of one's self as a rational being, able to communicate with other persons.

D. Thus we say that humans are persons, angels are persons, and God is person. In fact, all persons derive their personhood from God—the supreme person.

E. God the Father, the Son, and the Spirit are all persons and are capable of personal communion with mankind.

THE FATHER, HE IS GOD

A. The Christian confession is this: "To us there is but one God, the Father, of whom are all things" (1 Corinthians 8:6).

B. Christians believe in the God revealed in the Old Testament as the Almighty, the Creator of all things.

C. Christians believe in the God revealed in the New Testament as the heavenly Father (Matthew 6:9; Ephesians 1:3; 2:18).

D. So Christians offer this confession: I believe in God the Father Almighty, Creator of heaven and earth, the God and Father of Jesus Christ (John 20:17).

JESUS THE SON, HE IS GOD

A. In numerous passages of Scripture, the New Testament leaves no doubt that Jesus Christ is the Son of God.

B. This title, "Son of God," clearly means that Jesus Christ is God—equal with God (John 5:18-23).

C. The Bible teaches that Jesus Christ is equal with God, but humbled Himself to become a man (John 1:1-3, 14; Philippians 2:5-7).

D. Christians make this confession: I believe in Jesus Christ, God's only Son, our Savior and Lord—"who is the image of the invisible God" (Colossians 1:15).

THE HOLY SPIRIT, HE IS GOD

A. The Holy Spirit is not merely a force or power. The Spirit is a person of the Godhead, as indicated by the personal pronouns used in Scripture to speak about Him (John 14:16, 26; 15:26; 16:7, 13; Acts 13:2).

B. The Holy Spirit is God, equal with the Father and the Son (Acts 5:1-4). The Holy Spirit is the Spirit of God and the Spirit of Christ (Romans 8:9-11).

CONCLUSION: All three persons of the Holy Trinity are personally involved in our salvation from sin and our Christian living (see the Apostolic Benediction, 2 Corinthians 13:14).

VALUE OF TRIALS

Ray H. Hughes

SCRIPTURE: 1 Peter 4:12

INTRODUCTION: Not until a Christian understands the purpose and value of trials will he attain to the life of an overcomer. Christians through the ages have asked, "Why do Christians have to bear afflictions and face trials?" This is especially true of young Christians. Some have despaired because they did not know the answer and could not understand.

SOURCES OF TRIALS

    A. One's own faults and failures (1 Peter 2:20)

    B. From Satan by permissive will of God (Job 2:3-6)

    C. Directly from God

        1. Providential (Philippians 1:12, 13)

        2. Appointment of God (1 Thessalonians 3:3)

PROPER ATTITUDE TOWARD TRIALS

    A. God understands (Job 23:10).

        1. Knows your load limit (1 Corinthians 10:13)

        2. Helps to bear it

B. The biblical pattern

　　1. The prophets (James 5:10, 11)

　　2. Christ (1 Peter 2:21)

C. Understanding God's purpose in trial

　　1. Common to man (1 Corinthians 10:13)

　　2. Not strange to Christians (1 Peter 4:12)

　　3. His grace sufficient (2 Corinthians 12:9)

REASONS FOR TRIALS (Those whom God uses most are usually tried the most.)

A. Brought upon ourselves (1 Peter 2:20)

B. To test our faith (Genesis 22:1)

C. To work patience (Romans 5:3, 4; James 1:2, 3)

D. Partakers of His sufferings (1 Peter 4:13)

E. Disciplinary action (Hebrews 12:10)

RESULTS OF TRIALS

A. Brings us into conformity with Him (Hebrews 12:6)

B. Brings happiness in Christian experience (Job 5:17)

C. Yields fruit of righteousness (Hebrew 12:11)

D. Glorifies God (1 Peter 4:16)

E. Produces praise, honor, glory (1 Peter 1:7)

CONCLUSION: When the Christian comes to the realization that this world is not his portion and that the sufferings of this present time are not worthy to be compared with the glory which shall be revealed in Him, then he is in position to have the right outlook on life. Christ did not say that Christians would not have afflictions, but He did teach that "our light affliction, which is but for a moment, worketh for us a far more exceeding and eternal weight of glory" (2 Corinthians 4:17).

FRESH OIL

Harold O. Downing

SCRIPTURE: Psalm 92:10

INTRODUCTION: David was a man who greeted life with a positive note. He was confident in his belief concerning God's faithfulness; therefore we are not surprised to hear him say positively, "I shall be anointed with fresh oil."

We need not read far in the Psalms until we are convinced David believed in the ever-living and all-sufficient God. We will also find as we draw near to God we will move into a region of positive certainty. While we depend upon man, we are in the realm of "maybe" and "perhaps." When we trust in God, we are removed from everything that is of chance and conjecture.

Our God is a God of truth and righteousness.

THE CONFIDENCE OF DAVID WAS ONE FULL OF MEANING. What did he mean when he said, "I shall be anointed with fresh oil"?

    A. He meant his strength would be renewed.

    B. He was assured of divine favor.

    C. He would be qualified for office.

    D. He would have new cause for delight.

THE CONFIDENCE OF OUR TEXT IS WELL GROUNDED UPON GOD.

A. David's expectation of fresh anointing rested in God.

B. We can be sure of a fresh supply because of our union with Christ.

   1. We are hidden with Christ in God (Colossians 3:3).

   2. We are the branches; He, the vine (John 15:5).

C. The Holy Spirit dwells in us.

   1. Our bodies are temples or vessels of His Spirit.

   2. There can be no famine in our souls while He dwells there.

D. We possess God's promises.

E. The experiences of God's people in all ages verify it.

THIS CONFIDENCE OF A FRESH ANOINTING BANISHES OUR FEARS.

A. The fear of poverty

B. The fear of temptation

C. The fear of backsliding

D. The fear of bereavement

CONCLUSION: When we wisely put our trust in the great "I Am" and rest securely in His love and provision, we need never fear the rich supply of His grace will run out. As David, we can rely on the refreshing of God's Spirit, face each new day with assurance, and be confident of fresh anointing in times of need.

DAN, A PRODIGAL RETURNED HOME

Robert M. Varner

SCRIPTURE: *Luke 15:11-24; Genesis 49:16-18*

THEME: God's amazing grace can recover and restore any prodigal. The history of the Israelite tribe of Dan is an excellent example of God's ability to restore a prodigal.

HISTORY OF THE TRIBE OF DAN

A. *Jacob* (meaning "supplanter, deceiver") had his name changed to *Israel* (meaning "prince of God"). God removed Jacob's identity as the deceiver (Genesis 32:28).

B. Israel (Jacob) had 12 sons (Genesis 35:22-26). Dan, from whom the tribe of Dan descended, was the fifth son of Israel. His mother was Bilhah, Rachel's maid.

C. According to the census of Israel taken just before Israel entered the land of Canaan, the tribe of Dan, with 64,400 men over 20 years of age, was the fourth largest tribe (Numbers 26:43).

D. However, in the genealogies of Israel listed in 1 Chronicles 2:3 through 9:44, the tribe of Dan is omitted. And in the list of the tribes of Israel given in the Book of Revelation (7:4-8), the tribe of Dan is omitted.

WHY WAS THE TRIBE OF DAN OMITTED?

A. There is a prophetic answer to this question in the blessing Jacob (Israel) pronounced upon Dan (see Genesis 49:16-18, the Old Testament text for this sermon).

B. Notice the three aspects of the prophetic blessing pronounced upon Dan:

1. He would judge his people. Samson, of the tribe of Dan, was one of the great judges of Israel (Judges 13:5; 16:30, 31).

2. He would be a serpent by the path. He would have a nature like his father Jacob—a deceiver.

3. He would be redeemed, restored by the salvation of the Lord.

C. The second part of this prophetic blessing was fulfilled in several ways:

1. The tribe of Dan failed to drive out the Amorites from the land of Canaan (Judges 1:34, 35).

2. The tribe of Dan was cowardly rather than valiant for the Lord (Judges 5:17).

3. The tribe of Dan committed idolatry, corrupting the worship of Jehovah by making and bowing down to images (Judges 17:7-13; 18:26-31; 1 Kings 12:28-30).

D. From this we conclude there were two major reasons the tribe of Dan was omitted from the later genealogies of Israel:

1. The tribe of Dan was unreliable. They could not be counted on to obey the Lord.

2. The tribe of Dan persisted in committing idolatry. Dan was a prodigal tribe.

RESTORATION OF DAN

A. The last part of Jacob's prophetic blessing upon Dan expressed confidence that the Lord's saving grace would restore the tribe of Dan.

B. Long after the time of Jacob, the prophet Ezekiel (chapters 40-45) had a vision of the future glory and restoration of Jerusalem. (At the time, Jerusalem lay in ruins, having been destroyed by the Babylonians.)

C. In his description of the restored Jerusalem, Ezekiel said each of the three gates on the four sides of the city would be named in honor of a tribe of Israel.

D. On the east side, the most honored position, a gate is named for the tribe of Dan (Ezekiel 48:32). Here, Dan is included along with Joseph (a type of Christ), and Benjamin, Jacob's much loved youngest son.

CONCLUSION: The biblical record regarding the tribe of Dan illustrates the fact that by God's grace prodigals can be restored. Today, God's grace is sufficient to restore any prodigal. By grace those who have failed God and wandered from Him can be restored.

THE MARK OF A BLESSING

Victor Pagan

SCRIPTURE: *Genesis 32:22-32*

INTRODUCTION: We frequently hear this kind of expression from our pulpits: "Last night's blessing is over. Let us get a new one tonight." Such expressions reflect a wrong concept of God's blessings. We should be marked by His blessings.

JACOB WAS MARKED

A. His background
1. In terms of his father
2. With his mother
3. With his brother

B. The experience in Bethel (Genesis 28:10-22)
1. The revelation
2. The promise

C. The experience in Peniel (32:22-32)
1. The fight
2. The mark

A YOUNG MAN WAS MARKED (John 9)

A. His background (born blind)

B. The miracle of healing (the mark)

C. His testimony (before the Pharisees)

PAUL WAS MARKED (Acts 9)

A. His background

1. Religious

2. Academic

3. Political

B. The Damascus Road experience

1. The light

2. The voice

3. The commitment

C. Paul's testimony before Agrippa

D. Paul's ministry: the mark of Jesus on his body

CONCLUSION: We can't come to church and be filled tonight but be empty tomorrow. Our experience with God should be deeper. His blessings should remain with us. We should be marked.

DIVINE BLESSINGS THAT CAN BE LOST

Joel Hobbs

SCRIPTURE: Judges 16:15-21

INTRODUCTION

1. The question of security: Can divine blessings be lost?
2. The Bible records many spiritual blessings that men receive from the Lord that can be lost.

SAMSON LOST HIS POWER WITH GOD

"And he awoke out of his sleep, and said, I will go out as at other times before, and shake myself. And he wist not that the Lord was departed from him" (Judges 16:20).

A. His call and ministry (Judges 13:24, 25)

B. The causes of his fall

    1. He broke his separation—consorted with God's enemies.

    2. He frustrated God's will for his life.

    3. He failed to use God's power to perform God's work.

    4. He sinned through presumption.

    5. He yielded to fleshly desires.

321

DAVID LOST THE JOY OF HIS SALVATION

"Restore unto me the joy of thy Salvation, and uphold me with thy free spirit" (Psalm 51:12).

A. David's joy in the Lord—return of the ark to Jerusalem (1 Chronicles 16:7-36)

B. His sin of adultery and murder

C. Christian joy is full (John 15:11); unspeakable (1 Peter 1:8); exceeding (1 Peter 4:13).

PETER LOST HIS BOLDNESS AND TESTIMONY FOR THE LORD

"Peter sat down among them. But a certain maid beheld him as he sat by the fire, and earnestly looked upon him, and said, This man was also with him. And he denied him, saying, Woman, I know him not" (Luke 22:55-57).

A. He boasted.

B. He followed afar off.

C. He sat with wrong associates.

D. He lacked courage.

THE EPHESIANS LOST THEIR FIRST LOVE

"Nevertheless I have somewhat against thee, because thou hast left thy first love" (Revelation 2:4).

A. Notice Christ's knowledge of them: "I know thy works . . . labour . . . patience . . . canst not bear them which are evil . . . have tried false apostles, nevertheless . . . Remember . . . from whence thou art fallen" (2:2, 4, 5).

B. Consider the greatness of this church as expressed by Paul in the Epistle to them: They were blessed . . . chosen . . . predestinated unto the adoption of sons . . . were made accepted . . . received redemption . . . revelation . . . and inheritance . . . sealed with the Holy Spirit (see Ephesians 1:3-14).

C. Essence of true religion is love for Jesus Christ.

MULTITUDES WILL LOOSE THEIR SOULS IN ETERNAL DARKNESS

"Then shall he say also unto them on the left hand, Depart from me, ye cursed, into everlasting fire, prepared for the devil and his angels. . . . And these shall go away into everlasting punishment: but the righteous into life eternal" (Matthew 25:41, 46).

A. The reality of the soul (Hebrews 4:12).

B. The soul can be destroyed (Matthew 10:28).

C. The soul can be saved (Hebrews 10:39).

CONCLUSION: Where do you stand today? Are you conscious of God's power and presence in your life? Are you daily delighting in the Lord? Is your love warm and vital toward the Lord . . . His people . . . the lost? Is your testimony clear and bold? Are you sure, beyond doubt, that you are saved?

It is essential to us as true believers that we come by the "Spirit into the temple," for it is only then that we will see God and express true worship to the triune God.

THE SPEECH OF THE NEW MAN

B. L. Kelley

SCRIPTURE: Colossians 4:2-6

THEME: The new man in Christ, and how he talks in front of a watching world

INTRODUCTION: (Please use some personal experience or pertinent anecdote to introduce subject or theme of the sermon.)

THE SPEECH OF PRAYER (4:2)

A. Prayer is the most important speech your mouth will ever utter.

B. Continue in prayer. Paul is not saying to start praying but to stay at it.

"Pray without ceasing" (1 Thessalonians 5:17).

The apostles gave themselves "continually to prayer" (Acts 6:4).

"Praying always" (Ephesians 6:18).

"Be careful for nothing; but in every thing by prayer and supplication with thanksgiving let your requests be made known unto God" (Philippians 4:6).

C. Always be conscious of God.

Continual means to be steadfast and courageously persistent (Luke 18:1-8).

D. Watch with thanksgiving. What am I thankful for?

1. God's presence (Psalm 75:1)

2. God's promise (Ephesians 1:3, Philippians 4:19)

3. Salvation (Romans 6:17)

4. Victory (1 Corinthians 15:57; 2 Corinthians 2:14)

THE SPEECH OF PROCLAMATION (4:3)

A. God will open unto us a door of utterance.

B. Paul did not pray for physical help but that his mouth would have an utterance, literally—"a door for the Word."

THE SPEECH OF PERFORMANCE (4:5)

A. What you are should add credibility to what you say. Walk comes before talk.

B. Walk in wisdom—to properly evaluate circumstances and make godly decisions. Wisdom is setting your lifestyle by the Word of God.

THE SPEECH OF PERFECTION (4:6)

A. Speak what is spiritual—wholesome, kind, sensitive, complimentary; not bitter, abusive or vindictive.

B. Add a little salt.

1. Salt stings when put in a wound—after that, it heals.

2. Salt prevents corruption (Ephesians 4:29).

3. The Greeks had another idea—salt symbolized wit. Wit is the ability to say just the right thing at the right time.

CONCLUSION: Let us walk in wisdom before a watching world to bring glory to our Lord.

WALKING IN THE SPIRIT

Alex Thompson

SCRIPTURE: Ephesians 5:18; Galatians 5:16

INTRODUCTION: On one occasion, flying in a jet when the air-conditioning malfunctioned, I truly did pull down the mask, just as the stewardesses always instruct, place it over nose and mouth, and breathe normally.

What a relief!

Without oxygen we can't make it. The highest experience of the believer is the call to "walk in the Spirit—to dwell, live, move and have our being in the atmosphere of the Spirit. God created an atmosphere in which His creation could enjoy life. He has done it again in the Spirit, so that the new creatures may enjoy spiritual life.

THE BREATHING OF AIR HELPS FEED US.

A. Only 25 percent of our nourishment comes from the food we eat.

B. Oxygen does the rest.

C. Along with the Word, dwelling in the Spirit plays a large role in our spiritual health.

ATMOSPHERIC PRESSURE IS IMPORTANT.

A. At 15 pounds to the square inch, it is important that the same pressure be within us as that which is around us.

B. It is the same in the spiritual realm (Ephesians 5:18; Galatians 5:16).

ATMOSPHERE PROTECTS.

A. The meteor becomes dust by the action of the atmosphere.

B. The fiery darts of the enemy are quenched by Holy Spirit-inspired faith (Ephesians 6:16).

ATMOSPHERE TRANSMITS.

A. It is the atmosphere that carries the sound waves which enable us to hear the music and the message.

B. John was in the Spirit on the Lord's Day and he heard.

ATMOSPHERE REFLECTS.

A. It enables us to see.

B. It breaks down the rays of the sun.

C. In the Spirit, Simeon, Stephen, and John saw (Luke 2:27-30; Acts 7:55-57; Revelation 1:10-20).

D. The Holy Spirit shall receive of Christ and show it unto us (John 16:14).

CONCLUSION: Have you heard about the water spider? He takes a bubble of air under his body down into the water, where he puts it under a root or rock. Then he surfaces to get another, and another, and so creates a little world of air beneath the water in which he can live.

Taking the atmosphere of God's presence with us, from the prayer closet into the world, enables us to walk in the Spirit and enjoy all the benefits and blessings He has provided.

REAL CHRISTIANITY

David M. Griffis

SCRIPTURE: Acts 11:19-26

INTRODUCTION: The early Christians *dared, cared,* and *shared.* They were excited about Jesus and were convinced that Calvary meant salvation, the resurrection meant eternal life, and the world was a ripe field for the planting of the Gospel.

PERSECUTION MADE THE EARLY CHURCH A *DARING* CHURCH

  A. Some react as Elijah—under persecution he sat under the juniper tree of self-pity (2 Kings 19:4).

  B. Some react as Simon Peter—he tried to disassociate himself from the church (Luke 22:54-61).

  C. Real saints react under fire.

   1. Daniel prayed "as he did aforetime" (Daniel 6:10).

   2. The three Hebrews refused to bow" (Daniel 3:12).

   3. Paul and Silas sang in prison (Acts 16:25).

   4. Stephen preached while the crowd gnashed their teeth (Acts 7:54).

LABORERS TOGETHER WITH GOD

J. Ralph Brewer

SCRIPTURE: 1 Corinthians 3:9

INTRODUCTION: In this brief statement the great Apostle Paul focuses upon three important aspects of the work and ministry of the church. First, he focuses upon people. Second, he focuses upon the importance of cooperate action, and third, he focuses upon the assurance of divine involvement.

FOCUS UPON PEOPLE ("We")

A. Paul understood the value of every person (abilities, skills, undeveloped potential).

B. Every person has a certain achievement level (business and industry concerned with efficiency and productivity).

C. Maximum success is not achieved by one man doing the work of twelve, nor twelve men doing the work of one, but every man striving to reach his maximum potential.

D. Jesus chose twelve disciples—they changed the course of history and the destiny of nations.

FOCUS UPON COOPERATE ACTION ("We are laborers together")

A. Paul said, "I have planted, Apollos watered, God gave the increase." (I Corinthians 3:4)

B. God is not only interested in our participation in his plan of grace, but also in His plan of service.

C. The term *unity in* scriptural context refers to the harmonious function of the body of Christ in fulfilling the will of God on the earth.

D. The phrase "one accord" is found in the Book of Acts on at least 10 different occasions, emphasizing the active demonstration of the spirit of unity in the early church. (See also Ephesians 4:3.)

FOCUS UPON DIVINE INVOLVEMENT ("With God")

A. As spiritual leaders we must be cognizant of God's presence and the availability of spiritual power for a spiritual task.

B. What a marvelous truth that when we go, we do not go alone; when we work, we do not work alone. All the power, blessings, and resources that are resident in God are available to us.

CONCLUSION: "And they went forth, and preached everywhere, *the Lord working with them,* and confirming the Word with signs following" (Mark 16:20).

PROPHECY TODAY

A. A. Ledford

SCRIPTURE: 2 Peter 1:19-21

INTRODUCTION: One of the most thrilling episodes recorded in the Bible is the Transfiguration of Jesus (Matthew 17). One of those in attendance was Peter, and he wanted to build three tabernacles and stay there. Later, while reviewing that scene in verses 16 through 18 of the first chapter of his second epistle, he states abruptly that we have something more sure than what he saw. Seeing Jesus changed before their eyes, hearing the voice from heaven, as well as seeing Moses and Elijah paled in his perspective when considering the "sure word of prophecy."

THE RELEVANCE OF PROPHECY TODAY

A. God wants us to know (Amos 3:7, 8).

B. God has always shared his plans (Genesis 15:13, Jeremiah 25:11).

C. This generation rather than "these" is used, signifying immediacy (Matthew 24:34).

THE WITNESS OF HISTORY

A. Abraham's message gave the length of captivity in Genesis 15:13, a fact proven by history.

B. Jeremiah's witness of Babylonian Captivity (25:11) is also a matter of recorded history.

C. Of Daniel's 70 weeks, 69 weeks have been fulfilled, covering 483 years up to the crucifixion of Jesus. If 483 are fulfilled, the other 7 years (yet to come) will also be fulfilled. Revelation, chapters 5-19 cover that period.

THE SURE WORD OF PROPHECY

A. Not one word of Scripture will fail (1 Kings 8:56, Psalms 89:34, 119:89).

B. Our future is wrapped up in the faithfulness of God (Numbers 23:19).

C. Jesus emphasized prophecy (Matthew 24, Luke 21, Mark 13), as well as New Testament writers.

CONCLUSION: Several times we have the word "know" presented to us relative to prophecy. When his disciples asked him, "Wilt thou at this time restore again the kingdom to Israel?" (Acts 1:6), they were told, "It is not for you to know the times or the seasons."

But Paul writes to us in 1 Thessalonians 5:1, 2, "For yourselves know" and in 2 Timothy 3:1, "This know" and in Romans 13:11, "And that knowing the times." Obviously we cannot know the "day and hour" but we can know the "generation of his coming." It appears from Scripture this is the generation of the Lord's coming!

LAYING HOLD OF THE KINGDOM OF HEAVEN

William A. Reid

SCRIPTURE: *Matthew 11:7-15*

TEXT: "From the days of John the Baptist until now, the kingdom of heaven has been forcefully advancing, and forceful men lay hold of it" (Matthew 11:12 *New International Version*).

INTRODUCTION: Recorded in the eleventh chapter of Matthew's Gospel is the incident of John the Baptist sending his disciples to inquire of Jesus, "Art thou he that should come, or do we look for another?"

This was while John was in prison. Jesus was at the height of His popularity. John evidently was looking for a political Messiah and could not understand why Jesus was not taking proper action toward that end. Indeed he had begun to wonder if there was not a mistake somewhere.

Jesus' answer indicated that He considered His miracles as sufficient evidence of His Messiahship. Notice that John's doubt did not lower him in Jesus' estimation. There had not risen a greater, said Jesus.

JOHN THE BAPTIST

A. Born in the city of Abraham

1. Reared in daily view of Mt. Nebo from whose heights Moses had viewed with longing eyes the Promised Land and spoke of the promised Messiah.

2. Overlooking the Jordan where Joshua had crossed, and Jericho whose walls had fallen at Joshua's blast.

3. Same region where Amos had pastured his flocks and had dreamed of the coming Davidic King who would rule all nations.

4. Often visited the brook of Cherith where Elijah had been fed by the ravens.

5. Meditated deeply on the history that was now heading to its climax and waited for the called of God.

B. Called to be an Elijah-like prophet (Malachi 4:5; I Isaiah 40:3; Mark 1:3; Matthew 3:4).

C. His call came.

D. He had a great role in preparing the way for the Messiah.

JESUS COMMENDS JOHN THE BAPTIST

A. He was a firm, resolute man and not a reed shaken in the wind (Ephesians 4:14; Matthew 11:7)

B. He was a self-denying man and mortified to this world.

C. He was a prophet.

D. The least saint is greater than John the Baptist.

E. John prepared the people for the kingdom of heaven.

F. "The kingdom of heaven has been forcefully advancing" (Matthew 11:12, NIV).

G. "And forceful men lay hold of it" (Matthew 11:12, NIV).

CONCLUSION: Satan is unleashing his last barrage. The Bible says that when Satan comes in like a flood, the Spirit of God will raise up a standard against him. The kingdom of God is advancing today. Forceful men lay hold of it—men like Jacob when he wrestled with an angel, Daniel in the lion's den, Joseph in an Egyptian prison, Peter on the day of Pentecost, and Paul throughout his ministry.

CHRISTIAN EVIDENCES

R. B. Thomas

SCRIPTURE: Matthew 3:1-10

Sometimes Christians feel threatened when someone says, "Show me." We should not be so defensive. I have always felt that we were too harsh on Thomas for his honest doubt. Jesus did not seem to be offended by his "show me" request, and there is no reason we should. As a matter of fact we ought to search our own lives for evidence that we are genuinely Christian.

THERE SHOULD BE EVIDENCE OF OUR FAITH (James 2:14-24).

A. "Show me thy faith without thy works, and I will show you my faith by my works" (v. 18). "Even so, faith if it hath not work is dead, being alone" (v. 17).

B. Abraham was a man of faith but did not become one until after his faith produced works.

C. Rahab believed what the spies told her, but this meant nothing until she proved her faith by her action.

D. James condemns the religionist who says to the naked, "The Lord will clothe thee," but gives the naked no clothes or money; and to the hungry, "The Lord will feed thee" but gives him no food.

THERE SHOULD BE EVIDENCE OF OUR LOVE (1 John 3:16).

A. There is no way to show love other than by sacrifice.

B. Many of today's Christians have never practiced sacrifice. We do not know what it is to suffer for His name's sake.

C. The greater the persecution of the saints, the stronger they become.

THERE SHOULD BE EVIDENCE OF DISCIPLESHIP (John 8:31).

A. To be a disciple of Jesus is more than just to be impressed by His teachings.

B. To be a disciple of Jesus is more than a mere attempt, or temporary effort, to live His words.

C. To be a disciple of Jesus is more than being an authority on His teachings.

D. Genuine discipleship is to know and do the teachings of Jesus.

THERE SHOULD BE EVIDENCE OF OUR UNION WITH CHRIST (John 15:5).

A. Jesus is saying that those who are in union with Him *will* bear much fruit.

B. Jesus also tells us what will happen to those who cease to bear fruit. They shall cease to be united with Him. He will sever them from His fellowship.

C. Christian fruitfulness is not optional—it is the natural outgrowth of being in Christ.

THERE SHOULD BE EVIDENCE THAT WE HAVE RECEIVED GOD'S GRACE IN OUR SOUL (Titus 2:11,12).

A. The grace of God insists on an inseparable connection between creed and character, between life and doctrine.

B. The grace of God is a discipline, enforcing self-restraint in a world where sin is the normal thing.

C. You cannot possess the grace of God and be soft on sin at the same time. You cannot follow the course of sin in your own life and posses His grace.

D. It is not just the church that demands holiness, the grace of God does.

GENUINE SALVATION

Ted Gray

SCRIPTURE: Acts 4:12

PURPOSE: To show that genuine salvation is found only in and by Jesus

INTRODUCTION: There is a counterfeit for almost everything —money for sure! Just as there are people who make and market the counterfeit money, designer clothes, and such like, so there is Satan who works at passing out a counterfeit salvation.

GENUINE SALVATION DOES NOT JUST COVER UP THE SINFULNESS OF MAN.

    A. The counterfeit says this:

        1. Start doing better.

        2. Become educated and enlightened.

        3. Adopt a new code of ethics.

    B. The Bible teaches this:

        1. We were all born in sin (Psalm. 51:5).

        2. We all have sinned (Romans 3:23).

3. We are all under the curse of death (Romans 6:23).

   a. Sin will cause man to be cast into hell for eternity.

   b. Sin is absolutely and totally condemned by God.

GENUINE SALVATION DOES NOT IGNORE THE HOLINESS OF GOD.

A. The counterfeit says this:

   1. Just do your best . . . especially on Sunday.

   2. "The Man upstairs" knows and understands that man is just clay.

B. God spoke often of His holiness (Leviticus 11:45).

C. Angels declare God's holiness in a special way (Isaiah 6:3).

D. God's holiness is illustrated in two wonderful events:

   1. The Holy of Holies in the tabernacle (Leviticus 16).

   2. The sinless life of Christ.

E. God's holiness must be our standard for living (Hebrews 12:14).

   1. In Christ we measure up to this standard (1 Corinthians 1:30).

   2. Our life is to be a witness of our holiness in Christ.

GENUINE SALVATION DOES NOT MINIMIZE THE SACRIFICIAL DEATH OF JESUS.

A. Paul made the Cross—death of Christ—his central theme (1 Corinthians 2:2; Galatians 6:14).

B. Some people fail to appreciate this major truth (1 Corinthians 1:23).

   1. Jews—because of their religion

   2. Greeks—because of their learning

C. This central theme is the sum total of our salvation (Galatians 3:13).

GENUINE SALVATION DOES NOT SUBSTITUTE THE ACT OF FAITH.

A. The counterfeit says this:

   1. Good works is what you need.

   2. Good morals is what you need.

      3. A good name is what you need.

   B. But the Bible teaches this:

      1. Man's goodness cannot save him (Isaiah 64:6; Titus 3:5).

      2. Faith alone in Christ saves us (Ephesians 2:8, 9; Romans 5:1; John 3:16).

CONCLUSION: Thank God for genuine salvation. It works for time and eternity.

THE POISON OF A BITTER SPIRIT

Richard D. Dillingham

SCRIPTURE: Hebrews 12:11-15

INTRODUCTION: I know of nothing more counterproductive to the human spirit than bitterness and resentment. These enemies of man have ruined more lives than all the dictators who have paraded across our planet. Countless families have been broken apart because of bitterness. Successful people who achieve the top spot in the business world have been plummeted back to the bottom by bitter spirits. Ministers and churches have been stymied by it and the Kingdom suffers loss because of it.

WOUNDS OF THE SPIRIT—THE ROOTS OF BITTERNESS ARE UNIVERSAL.

A. Autobiographies and biographies of great people reveal that all have been wounded.
  1. Kings
  2. Statesmen
  3. Ministers
  4. Athletes
  5. Jesus Christ

B. All Christians are hit by the devil's warfare.

 1. Persecutions

 2. Criticisms

 3. Misunderstandings

BITTERNESS IS COUNTERPRODUCTIVE TO CHRISTIAN LIVING.

A. There is not one positive thing to be said about bitterness.

 1. It never healed a broken heart.

 2. It never built a church.

 3. It never cemented family relationships.

 4. It never inspired a rebellious child.

B. Bitterness stops the flow of God's blessings.

 1. Joy and peace are swallowed up by it.

 2. It's poison spills over to others.

SPIRIT LIFE IS A MATTER OF CHOICE.

A. You choose to live self-centered lives.

 1. Holding on to hurts

 2. Living in self-pity

B. You choose to live Christ-centered.

 1. Taking on His characteristics

 2. Setting your affections on things above

 3. Letting the exhortations of the Word be the key to living

CONCLUSION: Joseph is considered the most Christ-like man in the Old Testament. His brothers accused him. Some wanted to kill him and they finally reached a compromise by selling him. He was taken into a foreign country and sold like a common slave.

Years later, as his brothers stood before him for judgment, he could have wiped them off the face of the earth. He did not. He went the second and third and fourth mile in restoring broken fellowship. Joseph was a great and brilliant man. He knew that a dungeon cannot break a man; but a bitter spirit can.

CHRIST ABOVE ALL

Orville Hagan

SCRIPTURE: John 3:31

INTRODUCTION: As the sun is greater than a candle, as the ocean is greater than a drop of water, as a tornado is greater than a ladies fan, so is Jesus Christ above all.

CHRIST IS ABOVE ALL IN HIS BIRTH.

   A. A prophesied birth (Micah 5:2)

   B. A virgin birth (Luke 1:30-35)

   C. A startling statement (Genesis 3:15)

CHRIST IS ABOVE ALL IN HIS NAME.

   A. An exciting name (Philippians 2:9)

   B. Salvation only in His name (Acts 4:12)

   C. Ask in prayer in His name (John 16:23)

CHRIST IS ABOVE ALL IN POWER AND AUTHORITY.

   A. Taught with authority (Matthew 7:29)

   B. Spoke with authority (Matthew 28:18; *New International Version*)

CHRIST IS ABOVE ALL IN HEALING.

    A. He heals all diseases (Psalm 103)

    B. He heals the soul, mind and body.

CHRIST IS ABOVE ALL IN FORGIVENESS.

    A. Forgave the thief on the cross

    B. Forgave those who crucified Him

CHRIST IS ABOVE ALL IN DEATH.

    A. He was made alive (Acts 1:3)

    B. He destroyed man's last enemy.

CONCLUSION: There will never be another Jesus Christ! He is the incomparable One. There may be another Einstein, de Vinci, and so forth, but never another Christ. He is above all.

STRESSED OR BLESSED?

E. M. Abbott

SCRIPTURE: Joshua 1:7

INTRODUCTION: A recent ad in the Southwest Times of Pulaski, Virginia, was promoting a scheduled seminar on stress at the Radford Community Hospital. It stated of stress, "Everybody has it, everybody talks about it." Sometimes it seems that way.

STRESS HAS BEEN WITH US SINCE MAN SINNED (Genesis 3).

A. Stress is basically based on fear.

B. When Adam and Eve sinned, not only did they lose their innocence, but stress entered the human family.

C. They were fearful God would find them out.
1. They covered their nakedness.
2. They hid from God.
3. They felt guilt.
4. The serpent was blamed.
5. They became accusatory toward each other.
6. They even blamed God.

D. Stress and anxiety entered the peaceful, cool, lovely, and blessed garden.

JOSHUA FOUND HIS LIFE FILLED WITH STRESS (Joshua 1).

A. His respected leader, Moses, had died.

B. He was grieving over the loss of a dear and close friend.

C. He was feeling the pressures of his new role as leader of Israel.

D. He was feeling the weight and responsibility of being the spiritual counselor and guide to a stiff-necked, hard-headed people.

WE HAVE BUILT STRESS INTO OUR MODERN SOCIETY.

A. Ours is a competitive structure.

B. Winning is everything.

    1. Parents press children into being "A" students.

    2. College and professional sports have become mega-buck enterprizes.

    3. The stress of winning at any cost has led to drugs, alcohol, steroids, cheating, and so forth.

WHAT ARE SOME FACTORS CONTRIBUTING TO STRESS?

A. Loneliness—feeling unloved and unwanted

B. Fear of being rejected

C. Low self-esteem

    1. Afraid of not being "good" at something

    2. Afraid of not being accepted by our peers

    3. Dread of failure

HOW DO WE LIVE THE BLESSED LIFE?

A. Begin by thinking positively (Philippians 4:8).

B. Believe someone does love you—in fact, many do.

C. Look around you—there are people who care and want to give you support and help.

D. Raise your faith level (confidence) (Romans 10:17).

E. Accept your position in God and know He is with you (Joshua 1:9).

    1. To give you Direction

2. To give you Protection

3. To Reward you

4. To Encourage you

5. To Uphold you

CONCLUSION: If you want a blessed life, instead of a stressed life, look to Jesus.

Someone once said, in order for life to be happy and fulfilling, everyone needs three things: someone to love, something worthwhile to do, and something to hope for.

We have all three needs met in Jesus Christ. We can love Him, serve Him, and look forward to being in His Presence forever. As God's child you are BLESSED!

TO BE CRUCIFIED

Jim O. McClain

SCRIPTURE: Galatians 2:20

INTRODUCTION: According to the late Dr. A. W. Tozer, a young believer approached an older Christian with the question, "What does it mean to be crucified?" "To be crucified," replied the mature believer, "means three things: (1) The man on the cross is facing only one direction; (2) he is not going back; and (3) he has no further plans of his own."

Think about these. Too many Christians are trying to face two directions at the same time. They are divided in heart. They want heaven, but they are in love with the world. Like Lot's wife they are running one way, but they are facing another. There is finality to crucifixion. The person who is crucified with Christ is not going back to the old life. And a crucified person has no plans of his own. He is not dreaming of a bigger house or a better car. He is finished with this life. Its chains are all broken; its charms are all gone.

Are you crucified?

THE MAN ON THE CROSS IS FACING ONLY ONE DIRECTION.

A. He set His face toward Jerusalem (Luke 9:51).

B. He looks neither to the left nor to the right (Luke 23:46).

C. Forgetting, reaching, pressing (Philippians 3:13, 14)

D. Looking up, redemption draws nigh (Luke 21:28)

HE IS NOT GOING BACK.

A. Elisha burned his plows (1 Kings 19:21).

B. If any man puts his hand to the plow and looks back, he is not fit for the Kingdom (Luke 9:62).

C. Lot's wife looked back (Luke 17:32).

HE HAS NO FURTHER PLANS OF HIS OWN.

A. He has died to his own desires (John 12:24).

B. He dies daily (1 Corinthians 15:31).

C. He is crucified unto the world (Galatians 6:14).

D. His desire is to do the will of the heavenly Father (John 4:34; Luke 22:42).

A SPIRITUAL ANSWER TO NEGATIVE ATTITUDES

Larry Hess

SCRIPTURE: 2 Corinthians 6:1-10

THEME: The grace and power of God shall not fail.

INTRODUCTION: All of us can look back over our past and see things that we wish had been different. We can think of things we wish we had done differently, said differently, and decided differently. We know that we cannot change what has already happened. What we can do is learn from the past and neutralize the negatives in our lives. We tend to become programmed for negative thinking. In order to change our lives we must change the program we have put into our minds. Life is determined by the attitudes and principles we live by.

SPIRITUAL LAWS TELL US HOW TO LIVE.

A. The law of RECIPROCITY (Luke 6:38)

B. The law of PERSEVERANCE (Matthew 7:7)

C. The law of UNITY (Matthew 18:19-20)

D. The law of MIRACLES (John 14:12)

E. The law of DOMINION (Matthew 16:18)

354

BUILD LIFE ON FAITH IN GOD AND HE WILL HELP YOU FACE YOUR TRAGEDIES.

A. Guard against your vulnerabilities through prayer.

B. Program your thinking through personal prayer.

C. Discipline your desires through spiritual development.

D. Stabilize your relationships by congruent, holy living.

E. Strive to be consumed by the power of God so you can overcome anything.

THE CORINTHIAN CHURCH FACED A LOT OF NEGATIVES.

A. They were confused on doctrine.

B. They were carnal in their habits.

C. They sinned and excused it.

D. They were confused about the meaning of marriage.

E. They were corrupting the spiritual gifts.

F. They didn't understand what it meant to be a Christian.

PAUL INSTRUCTED THEM, IN 2 CORINTHIANS 6, HOW TO DEAL WITH THESE NEGATIVE ATTITUDES.

A. Learn to maintain an optimistic view of life (6:1-3).
   1. You can trust in the reality of Jesus and His grace.
   2. Jesus has called you and He will not fail you.
   3. You are not dependent on this world.
   4. You live in a Kingdom beyond this world.
   5. What is optimism? It is to anticipate the best possible outcome in every circumstance.

B. Learn to live by encouragement and commendation (6:4).
   1. We must submit our will to the will of God.
   2. We must believe in ourself.
   3. We must build a healthy self-image which is seeing ourself as God sees us—no more and no less.
   4. We measure our life by what God says we are in Him.
   5. We learn to live beyond our limitations.

C. Learn to live by principles of contentment (6:10).

1. Conditions are always changing, therefore, we must not be dependent on conditions.

2. Whatever happens we must let God work His will in us.

CONCLUSION: When we are at our weakest, the Bible speaks the strongest. The grace and power of God will never fail to lift us up. The Lord will sustain us through anything if we turn to Him. Let us see our present circumstances as only temporary experiences preparing us for the consumation of our eternal life with Christ.

YOU CAN HAVE A MIRACLE

Fred G. Swank

SCRIPTURE: John 6:5-13

INTRODUCTION: This is a simple story, and a wonderful story of the miracles. It is recorded in all four gospels. It is the only miracle that Jesus performed that is recorded in all the gospels. I think that is significant.

MIRACLES WERE FOR THE PURPOSE OF TEACHING.

A. Like the parables, God wants us to learn from them.

B. This miracle is recorded so we might know how miracles happen.

C. They can happen in our lives

LET US LOOK AT THIS STORY A LITTLE CLOSER.

A. Consider the crowd (5,000).

B. They had a desperate situation (a hungry crowd).

C. Jesus had fed them spiritually, but now they are exhausted, hungry and a long way from home.

D. Let me tell you what happened.

CONSIDER THE ABUNDANCE OF JESUS (12 Baskets left).

A. His miracle-working power always gives more than we need.

B. Consider the prodigal son

   1. He needed and asked for forgiveness.

   2. His father not only forgave him, but he gave him a ring, a robe, slippers, a feast and sonship.

C. A man asked Jesus for healing (Mark 2:9-11), and received pardon for his sins too.

D. Jesus works miracles to provide what we ask for and need.

WE HAVE A MIRACLE-WORKING GOD.

A. He wants to solve the problems in your life.

B. The disciples were saying, we have a problem.

   1. Christ wanted them to believe that together they could solve it.

   2. What if they had said we can not solve this problem?

   3. Man's extremity is God's opportunity.

FAITH IS THE TRIGGER (Mark 9:23).

A. Look at the healing of the lame beggar (Acts 3).

   1. He expected to receive something of them.

   2. He had positive expectancy. (Shoot at nothing and you will always hit your target.)

WHAT DO YOU NEED?

A. Is it salvation? (The greatest miracle in the world is the salvation of a soul.)

B. Is it healing?

C. Is it deliverance from a physical habit or a mental fear?

D. The name of Jesus is the key.

E. Matthew 9:29 contains the uncompromising measure "according to your faith, be it unto you."

WINNING THE BATTLE OVER SATAN

Mike Chapman

SCRIPTURE: Various Texts (Topical Message)

INTRODUCTION: The New Testament clearly presents the theme of the Christian life as a battle. In this spiritual warfare it is important that we understand the methods of our archenemy, Satan, and our strategy for victory.

THE PAST OVERTHROW OF SATAN (Twofold Event)

A. Satan's fall from heaven (Isaiah 14:12-15)

 1. He was cast from one realm to another realm.

 2. Immediately, we see his work on the earth (for example the temptation of Eve).

 3. This indicates that his overthrow was yet an unfinished task.

B. Satan's defeat at the Cross
 1. Hebrews 2:14

 a. *destroy* (Greek *katargeo*): "to make of none effect"

 b. This destruction was not in the sense of doing away with.

 c. It carries the idea of "putting in one's place"

2. 1 John 3:8
   a. *destroy* (Greek-*luo*): "to break"
   b. On the Cross, Jesus broke the power of Satan.
3. Colossians 2:15
   a. Three key words: *spoiled, exposed, triumphed*
   b. The Cross stripped Satan of his power, openly exposing Him, and was the ultimate triumph over him.
   c. As a result, believers stand in this deliverance (Colossians 1:13).

SATAN'S PRESENT OVERTHROW

A. His present overthrow is based on the permanency of his past defeat.
   1. His defeat did not remove him from the scene.
   2. Yet, he is a defeated and dominated foe, made subject unto the authority of Jesus.
B. Satan is overthrown when believers learn the truth that their enemy is a defeated foe (Luke 10:18-20).
C. Steps to victory over Satan:
   1. Establishing a good defense
      a. Give no room for the Devil (Ephesians 4:27).
      b. Be sober and watchful (1 Peter 5:8).
      c. Resist the Devil (James 4:7).
   2. Applying the Principle of Calvary
      a. We must be totally yielded to Christ.
      b. We must die to self, taking up Christ's cross.
      c. The only person who cannot be bought out is the one who's already sold out.
      d. This is the principle of Revelation 12:11.
   3. Exerting our Authority
      a. Jesus gave us authority over the power of the enemy (Luke 10:19).
      b. The dynamics of this power rests in proclaiming the Word of Christ and performing the works of Christ.
   4. Entering the Future Victory Now

    a. The ultimate overthrow is based on the blood of the Lamb and our testimony (Revelation 12:11).

    b. Our present victory is gained by appropriating the merits of Calvary and by our spoken affirmation of the testimony of God's Word.

SATAN'S FUTURE OVERTHROW

A. Satan's destiny is sure.

B. He is bound for the bottomless pit forever (Revelation 20:10).

    1. This will occur following Christ's reign upon the earth.

    2. Hell was created to be his eternal abode (Matthew 25:41).

CONCLUSION: Satan has been overthrown and knows it. Yet, he tries to get believers not to believe it. He wants your destiny to be the same as his. However, we have the victory through the Cross!

THE THINGS GOD KNOWS ABOUT YOU THAT YOU DON'T KNOW

J. David Stephens

SCRIPTURE: Psalm 139:1-6

INTRODUCTION: As we read the first two verses of Psalms 139 we realize that God has taken time to search us and know us. In verses 3 and 4 the psalmist emphatically declares that God knows everything about us, and in verses 5 and 6 he proclaimed that God knows us better than we know ourselves. God knows you better than you know yourself. There are many times when we do not understand ourselves, but never a time when He doesn't. I want to share with you three very important things that God knows about you that you don't know yourself.

GOD KNOWS YOUR POSSIBILITIES.

A. He knows what you are made of (Psalm 139:15, 16).

B. He knows what you can become, what you can accomplish, and what you can handle.

C. God knew Esther's, Joseph's, and David's possibilities when friends and family had given up on them.

D. The best thing you will ever do for yourself is put your

life and future into God's hands so He can lead you to become what He knows you can (Proverbs 3:5-8).

GOD KNOWS YOUR LIMITATIONS.

A. All of us are different, and so are our load limits.

B. He knows what you can't do and what you can't handle.

C. He has made you a very important promise in 1 Corinthians 10:13.

D. Your God will never fail you, if you'll follow Him.

GOD KNOWS YOUR NEED.

A. None of us always knows what we need because of man's fall in the garden.

B. Even Christians do not have perfect understanding in every situation (Romans 8:22, 23; 1 Corinthians 13:12).

C. Our faith is not in what we understand, but in what our God knows (Psalm 139:5, 6; Matthew 6:8).

D. You can trust your God with all your needs (Romans 8:26-28).

CONCLUSION: As the favorite old hymn declares: "Only Trust Him." Be assured that God knows who you are, where you are, and what you need. You may not understand what is happening or why things are the way they are, but trust Him. Put your possibilities, your limitations, and your needs in His hands.

HOLY GROUND

Danny L. May

SCRIPTURE: Acts 7:17-33

INTRODUCTION: Just before Stephen, one of the first deacons, was stoned to death, he preached a masterful sermon, recorded in the Book of Acts, chapter 7. He recounted the history of Israel, which included Moses being invited by God to stand on *Holy Ground*! Is there still Holy Ground? Does God invite any to stand on Holy Ground in our day? If so, how do we get there? Where is it? Let's follow Moses and see what happens.

A PLACE CALLED "HOLY GROUND"

    A. Not a short or easy journey

    B. Means you must lose sight of self

    C. Realize you are not sufficient

        1. Your abilities can never find holy ground.

        2. Moses slew an Egyptian, but his abilities failed.

WHERE HOLY GROUND IS FOUND

    A. Holy ground requires going farther than we have ever been.

1. Moses 40 Years (Acts 7:30)

2. Moses had been all over this mountain, but never this far.

B. What holy ground is

   1. A place we can "see" (Acts 7:31; Job 42:5; Matthew 5:8; John 14:19; Isaiah 6:1), as illustrated by John on Patmos

   2. A place you can "approach" (Acts 7:31; James 5:8; Psalm 73:28; Hebrews 10:22)

   3. A place where you can "stand" (Acts 7:33)

HOLY GROUND IS A SACRED PLACE.

A. God's presence (Exodus 3:11-14)

B. Miracles (Exodus 4:1-9)

C. Brotherly agreement (Exodus 4:10-17; Exodus 4:27-28)

D. Refreshing (Exodus 17:1-7)

E. Family reconciliation (Exodus 18:1-12)

F. God's Word (Exodus 19:1-6)

G. God's glory (Exodus 24:15-18)

H. Renewed Calling (1 Kings 19:1-18)

I. Revealed glory (2 Chronicles 5:11-14)

J. Requested glory (Exodus 33:1-23)

K. Completed glory (John 1:1-18)

CONCLUSION: Jesus is our revelation of "holy ground." His glory (Luke 9:32), is the glory of the Father (John 17:5). See also 1 Timothy 1:17, Philippians 4:19, Colossians 3:4; 1 Peter 1:11; 5:1.

THRONGING OR TOUCHING

S. Lane Sargent

SCRIPTURE: Matthew 19:16-22; Mark 5:24-34

INTRODUCTION: We all have a choice when it comes to Jesus —either to throng about Him or to intimately touch Him. A thronging person is one who stands in the crowd just to see what is happening. A touching person moves beyond the crowd and into a personal encounter.

THRONGING (Matthew 19:16-22)

    A. Dissatisfied (v. 16)

        1. He came running.

        2. He kept the law, but was not happy.

    B. Disappointed (vv. 21, 22)

        1. Terms

           a. Go and sell

           b. Commitment to follow

        2. Tragedy

           a. Close to Jesus

           b. Went away sorrowful

    C. Denied

1. Now a life of joy and peace

2. Eternity—a life in heaven

TOUCHING (Mark 5:24-34)

A. Distressed (vv. 25, 26)

   1. Twelve years of suffering

   2. Many different physicians

   3. Broke

   4. Getting worse

B. Determined (vv. 27, 28)

   1. Heard of Jesus

   2. Faith in her heart

   3. Went to where He was

   4. Touched Him

C. Delivered (vv. 29-34)

   1. Instantly healed

   2. Jesus recognized a touch of faith

CONCLUSION: Flesh presses against Jesus; faith always touches Him. He knows the difference between the jostle of a curious crowd and the touch of faith of a soul in need.

BETWEEN TIMBRELS AND ELIM

H. B. Thompson, Jr.

SCRIPTURE: Exodus 15:20-27

INTRODUCTION: Israel was now an unpursued nation, and yet the road was still difficult. Review briefly Chapter 14, and emphasize the "Song of Moses." There are three distinct emphases in Chapter 15.

REJOICING AT THE RED SEA (vv. 20-27)

A. What a time and reason they had to rejoice!

B. The "Song of Moses" summarizes graphically what the Lord had done.

C. Interspersed in the song and providing a dynamic conclusion was the dance of Miriam and the playing of the timbrel.

D. And well they should rejoice.

    1. They had no might to repel Pharaoh, yet the army was destroyed.

    2. They could see no hope for survival, much less continuation, and God gave them both.

E. At this point doubt was unthinkable, discouragement

impossible, and defeat incomprehensible. (Don't we love to live in such places and under such circumstances?)

RESOURCES OF ELIM (v. 27)

A. Another divine benefit that came a few days later—an oasis with 12 wells and 70 palm trees.

B. Plenty of water and beauty in the midst of a wilderness

C. A pleasant place to camp—a marvelous divine provision —in the middle of dryness and desert, God placed an Elim to refresh and rest Israel.

D. The resources were not only adequate but abundant—not only beautiful but bountiful.

E. A pause that refreshed, but the journey must continue —Elim was a great place to camp but not one to colonize.

REALITIES OF MARAH (vs 22-25)

A. Right between victory and refreshing came frustration, disappointment, and distress.

B. Three days after the "Song of Moses" they came to a place of bitterness (Marah—meaning "bitterness').

C. Here are the realities:
   1. Thirst was unbearable.
   2. Water was undrinkable.
   3. Complaining was uncontrollable.

D. The people quickly forgot the Red Sea rejoicing and were unaware of the nearness of Elim.

E. They became disgruntled, disappointed and disillusioned.

F. But another reality surfaces here—prayer became unresistible.
   1. Moses didn't panic—he prayed.
   2. Prayer will bring God's power, provision and pleasure to us.

G. And God showed Moses a tree that would change things.
   1. Type of tree is not revealed.
   2. The source or reason for the bitterness is not revealed.

373

H. God is not in the diagnostic business. He is in the deliverance business.

I. Final reality is that the power was unlimited—not by revelation but by application.

CONCLUSION: We can rejoice over the victory at the Red Sea. We can repose in the shade of Elim, but somewhere in between may be Marah. That's where we live, and that's where we need the Lord's help more than any other place. The song of the Red Sea may lose its rhyme and the pleasantness of Elim may lose its appeal; but the power of God to provide what we need never changes!

CONVICTION, A GENUINE NEED

T. David Sustar

SCRIPTURE: *"No man can come to me, except the Father which hath sent me draw him" (John 6:44).*

INTRODUCTION: To some, *conviction* is an old-fashioned term, a word obsolete and seldom used. Legally it means "judged guilty," but morally it means "inner persuasion." If we are to have the revival the church needs and the world should experience, we must have a renewing of the convicting power of God's Holy Spirit.

CONVICTION IS A WORK OF THE TRINITY

A. By the Father (our text)

B. By Christ himself—"And I, if I be lifted up from the earth, will draw all men unto me" (John 12:32).

C. By the Holy Spirit—"And when he is come, he will reprove the world of sin, and of righteousness, and of judgment" (John 16:8).

CONVICTION IS A WORK OF THE HEART (SOUL)

A. More than wakened sentiments (Luke 17:32; Acts 24:25)

B. More than a stir of the emotions

C. More than a desire to escape hell

D. Conviction grips the soul, something never to be forgotten.

    1. It produces unrest (Psalm 32:3).

    2. It brings a burden to the soul (Psalm 38:4).

    3. It causes misery (Psalm 51:3).

    4. It stings the conscience (Acts 2:37).

THE OBJECTIVE OF CONVICTION IS SALVATION

A. The sinner feels the exposure of sin and confesses God's works (Psalm 139:7-14).

B. He realizes the truth of God (Romans 3:23).

C. He receives a sense of personal responsibility for sin (Psalm 51:4).

D. He awakens to a desire to be delivered from sin (Isaiah 1:18).

CONCLUSION: Conviction is essential to salvation. It is the objective of preaching and the burden of Christian prayers (Zechariah 12:10; Revelation 22:17).

3. Jesus does not judge in this life (John 12:47).

   a. Judas is proof of that; Jesus taught him, prayed with him, washed his feet, discerned that he was "of the devil," but never judged.

   b. The wheat and tares (Matthew 13:24-30)

B. Cast not (Matthew 7:6).

   1. "Cast not" means discerning your action in relation to someone else.

   2. Test questions for each teaching to prove its truth or error

      a. Theological—Is Jesus Lord (1 Corinthians 12:3; 1 John 4:2)?

      b. Spiritual—Does the Spirit bear witness with our spirit (Romans 8:16)?

      c. Biblical—Does it square with the whole Word (2 Timothy 3:16)?

      d. Moral—What kind of life and fruit does it produce (Matthew 7:15, 16; Galatians 5:22, 23)?

      e. Practical—Does it edify (1 Corinthians 14:14-26)?

WHAT ABOUT THE ADULTERER IN 1 CORINTHIANS 6?

A. That was a matter of church discipline.

   1. Discipline is only for those under your authority.

   2. Discipline is to be done by the church and not by a single individual.

   3. It must not be done harshly or condemningly.

   4. It must always aim toward restoration.

B. Three important distinctions

   1. Judge no man.

   2. Discern all teachings and spirits.

   3. Discipline only those over whom you have authority.

CONCLUSION: When you hear teaching about which you are concerned, apply the five questions previously mentioned. When you find the teaching in error, you still must leave the teacher alone unless you are in authority over him. We will find our load lighter when we stop trying to do more of God's work than He intended for us to do.

THREE SINS WHICH BESET CHRISTIANS

Julius Roberts

SCRIPTURE: Hebrews 12:1; Colossians 2:6, 7; Galatians 5:26; Psalm 126:6

INTRODUCTION: Perhaps we should use some word other than "sin" for our subject, since some do not like a reference to sin when it comes to Christians; but these three things to which I wish to refer are really sins which have become "respectable" in that most all of us are guilty.

THE SIN OF INCONSISTENCY (James 1:5-12; Hebrews 10:22, 23; Colossians 2:6, 7)

A. Inconsistent in devotion (Colossians 4:2; Luke 18:1; Psalm 19:7)

B. Inconsistent in disposition

C. Inconsistent in convictions (Mark 14:72; Luke 15:21; 18:13)

D. Inconsistent in our talents (Matthew 25:15-25)

E. Inconsistent with our tongues (James 3:5, 6; Ephesians 5:1-4; 15-17)

THE SIN OF JEALOUSY (Song of Solomon 8:6, 7)

A. Jealousy is shown in the Book of Isaiah—the "I wills" of the devil (Isaiah 14:13, 14).

B. Saul was jealous of David (1 Samuel 18:8; 19:1).

C. Jonah was jealous and angry at God (Jonah 4:1-11).

D. Two kinds of jealousy

1. Divine (Exodus 20:5; 34:14; Deuteronomy 4:24; 29:20; 1 Corinthians 10:22)

2. Human (Genesis 37:4; Judges 8:1; 1 Samuel 19:10; Matthew 20:12; Luke 15:28)

THE SIN OF NO COMPASSION FOR THE LOST

A. The wise man wins souls (Proverbs 11:30).

B. Woe to those at ease in Zion (Amos 6:1; Mark 13:32-37).

C. Indifference (Isaiah 47:8; Matthew 22:5; 24:12)

CONCLUSION: The Great Commission is to "go ye therefore, and teach all nations, baptizing them in the name of the Father, and of the Son, and of the Holy Ghost: Teaching them to observe all things whatsoever I have commanded you: and, lo, I am with you alway, even unto the end of the world. Amen" (Matthew 28:19, 20).

THE BATTLE OF THE MIND

Billy L. Olds

SCRIPTURE: Philippians 2:5

INTRODUCTION: To move a man to action you have to influence his thinking. Sometime you must change it. A little leaven changes the whole character of the bread. So a little thought or an attitude can start changes in motion that will affect one's entire destiny.

THE AGITATED MIND (2 Thessalonians 2:12; Isaiah 26:3)

A. Don't dwell on the world's conflicts.

B. Don't get wrapped up in personal problems.

C. Keep your mind on Christ.

THE GULLIBLE MIND (Philippians 4:8)

A. Careful of the music we listen to

B. Careful of what we read

C. Careful of the television programs we watch

THE LAZY MIND (Acts 17:11)

A. Read the Bible.

B. Study the Bible (private, group).

C. Listen to the Word.

THE TOLERANT MIND (Romans 1:28; 1 Timothy 4:2; Isaiah 5:20)

A. One who gives excuses for evil

B. One who takes no stand against evil

THE WARPED MIND

A. Child abuse (Ephesians 6:4)

B. Spouse abuse (Ephesians 5:33)

C. Parent abuse (Ephesians 6:2)

THE SECRET OF VICTORY

A. Keep your mind on Christ (Matthew 22:35-37).

B. Christ in you (Philippians 2:5)

C. Be diligent (Hebrews 12:3).

D. Ask the Lord for help (Psalm 139:23, 24).

CLOSING SCRIPTURE: "For God hath not given us the spirit of fear; but of power, and of love, and of a sound mind" (2 Timothy 1:7).

WHY WORRY WHEN YOU CAN TRUST

David S. Bishop

INTRODUCTION

A. Worry is a counterproductive activity.

ILLUSTRATION: A panel of psychologists recently concluded that 40 percent of the things people worry about
never happen. Thirty percent of worry is about past
events about which we can do nothing. Ten percent
deals with trifles. Only about 8 percent of what we
worry about is related to legitimate concerns.

1. Worry brings stress.

2. Worry dilutes effort and saps energy.

QUOTATION: George Lyos once said, "Worry is the interest paid by those who borrow trouble."

B. There is a good biblical remedy for worry.

1. The next time you feel you are falling apart, that
things are not working right, and you're about to
lose hold of self-control through fretting, turn to
Psalm 46.

2. The theme of this psalm is God's adequacy for every
demand of life.

        a. The psalm was written to keep people from falling apart.

        b. The psalm says that when the mountains of life are shaking with trouble, God will see His children through.

"Therefore will we not fear, though the earth be removed, and though the mountains be carried into the midst of the sea" (v. 2).

C. Let us look at the background of the psalm.

    1. Many Bible scholars feel this psalm was written by King Hezekiah to commemorate God's great victory over Sennacherib (2 Kings 18, 19; Isaiah 36, 37).

        a. The Assyrian King thought he had Hezekiah caught in Jerusalem like a bird in a cage.

        b. But Hezekiah prayed.

        c. God gave hope through the prophet Isaiah.

        d. The enemy was devastated through God's intervention.

           (1) In one night, the angel of the Lord slew 185,000 enemy soldiers.

           (2) The succinct postscript of scripture was "And when they arose early in the morning (those that had not been slain), behold they were all dead corpses" (2 Kings 19:35).

THE DESTRUCTION OF SENNACHERIB

"The Assyrian came down like the wolf on the fold,
And his cohorts were gleaming in purple and gold;
And the sheen of their spears was like the stars
   on the sea,
When the blue wave rolls nightly on deep Galilee.
Like the leaves of the forest when summer is green,
That host with their banners at sunset were seen:
Like the leaves of the forest when autumn hath
   blown,
That host on the morrow lay wither'd and strown.
For the Angel of Death spread his wings on the blast,
And breathed in the face of the foe as he pass'd;
And the eyes of the sleepers wax'd deadly and chill,

And their hearts but once heaved, and forever grew
    still!
And there lay the steed with his nostrils all wide,
But through it there roll'd not the breath of his pride;
And the foam of his gasping lay white on the turf,
And cold as the spray of the rock-beating surf.
And there lay the rider distorted and pale,
With the dew on his brow, and the rust on his mail:
And the tents were all silent, the banners alone,
The lances unlifted, the trumpet unblown.
And the widows of Ashur are loud in their wail,
And the idols are broken in the temple of Baal;
And the might of the Gentile, unsmote by the sword,
Hath melted like snow in the glance of the Lord!"

D. This psalm makes some great affirmations—let's look
at them.

AFFIRMATION ONE: I WILL NOT FEAR BECAUSE I HAVE A REFUGE FOR STRENGTHENING.

"God is our refuge and strength, a very present help in
trouble. Therefore will not we fear, though the earth be removed, and though the mountains be carried into the midst
of the sea; Though the waters thereof roar and be troubled,
though the mountains shake with the swelling thereof. Selah."
(Psalm 46:1-3).

A. He is our refuge to hide us.

1. He does not hide us to pamper us.

    a. Too often we want to be escapists—to run away!

    b. We are not to be spared the challenges of life
    when the challenges are really what we need to
    make us men and women of faith.

2. There *are* times when we need to flee to Him!

    a. David said, "Deliver me, O Lord, from mine ene-
    mies: I flee unto thee to hide me" (Psalm 143:9).

    b. No matter the situation, you can flee to the Lord
    by faith and He will welcome, shelter, and
    strengthen you.

3. How do you flee to Him?

    a. By reaching out to Him (it may mean shutting
    yourself up with Him for a time).

      b. By trusting the promises in His Word.

      c. By claiming His promises in prayer and confession.

B. He is our energizer to strengthen us.

  1. When He hides us, He does so to prepare us to go back and face life.

  2. He plugs us into His strength so we can make it by His power and not our own.

      a. "The Lord is my light and my salvation; whom shall I fear? The Lord is the strength of my life; of whom shall I be afraid?" (Psalm 27:1).

      b. "The Lord is my strength and my shield; my heart trusted in him, and I am helped: therefore my heart greatly rejoiceth; and with my song will I praise Him. The Lord is their strength, and he is the saving strength of his anointed. Save thy people, and bless thine inheritance: feed them also, and lift them up for ever" (Psalm 28:7-9).

      c. "Not by might, nor by power, but by my spirit, saith the Lord of hosts" (Zechariah 4:6).

  3. We can trust Him to take care of what He has committed Himself to do.

  ILLUSTRATION: A man walked into a telegraph office one day and handed a message to the operator to send. As he did so he said, "This goes to a little town up in the Northwest, and I hear they have been having lots of bad weather up there lately. I suppose a snowstorm has blocked all of the roads in that area. Very likely the message will never get through to the man I am sending it to. What do you think? Do you suppose the message will get through all right?" The operator looked up impatiently. "I'm not running both ends of this telegraph line," he said, "I'm only responsible for this end. I am sure that there is someone at the other end of this line who probably knows his business, and he will get the message to the person for whom it is intended. There is no point in my trying to carry his responsibilities for him. I'll do my part on this end and leave the rest to him." Friend, we need to do the same with God.

AFFIRMATION TWO: I WILL NOT FAINT BECAUSE I HAVE A RIVER.

"There is a river, the streams whereof shall make glad the city of God, the holy place of the tabernacles of the most High. God is in the midst of her; she shall not be moved, God shall keep her, and that right early. The heathen (Gentile nations) raged, the kingdoms were moved: he uttered his voice, the earth melted. The Lord of hosts is with us; the God of Jacob is our refuge" (Psalm 46:4-7).

A. Rivers were important to ancient cities.

    1. Look at the great cities of history.

        a. The great cities of Egypt drew from the Nile.

        b. Nineveh was built on the Tigris.

        c. Babylon was built on the Euphrates.

        d. Anicent Antioch of Syria was built on the Orontes.

        e. Damascus was situated upon the Abana.

    2. But Jerusalem was one of the few great cities of ancient times not built on a river.

        a. This made the city . . .

            (1) Free from floods.

            (2) Vulnerable to siege (Sennacherib was sure their lack of water would make them easy prey).

        b. Unknown to Sennacherib, Hezekiah had built an underground system.

            (1) It was 1,777 feet long (one of the engineering marvels of ancient time).

            (2) It was built through solid rock.

            (3) It connected the spring of Gihon to the Pool of Siloam.

            (4) It can still be walked through today.

B. But Hezekiah and his people had a greater river than that—"There is a river, the streams whereof shall make glad the city of God." (v. 4).

    1. God was their source from which to drink deeply for strength.

        a. He *sustained* them.

        b. He *overflowed* the enemy.

"When the enemy shall come in like a flood, the Spirit of the Lord shall lift up a standard against him" (Isaiah 59:19).

2. We, too, have a river.

   a. Jesus said, "If any man thirst, let him come unto me, and drink. He that believeth on me, as the scripture hath said, out of his belly shall flow rivers of living water. (But this spake he of the Spirit, which they that believe on him should receive)" (John 7:37-39).

      (1) The river flows out from Him.

      (2) The river flows to us, through us, and out to bless others.

   b. Jimmy Swaggart said it well in his song, "There Is A River."

      "There is a river that flows from deep within,
      There is a fountain that saves the soul from sin.
      Come to the waters, There is a vast supply,
      There is a river, that never shall run dry."

      There Is a River © copyright 1969 by David and Max Sapp

3. All nature depends upon hidden resources.

   a. Plants and trees send roots to hidden "rivers."

   b. The believer must do the same (Psalm 1:3).

      ILLUSTRATION: J. Hudson Taylor, founder of the China Inland Mission, learned how to depend upon this resource. When hearing of uprisings in other parts of his work where safety of workers, were threatened, he began to sing, "Jesus, I am resting, resting, in the joy of what Thou art; I am finding out the greatness of thy loving heart." He was criticized by associates for his seeming carefree attitude. He replied, "Would you have me anxious and troubled? That would not help them, and would certainly incapacitate me for my work. I have just to roll the burden on the Lord, and God intervenes."

4. He also intervened for Hezekiah and He'll do it for you when you trust Him.

AFFIRMATION THREE: I WILL NOT FRET BECAUSE I HAVE A REVELATION.

"Be still and know that I am God: I will be exalted among the heathen, I will be exalted in the earth" (Psalm 46:10).

A. There is no need to fret.

    1. Fretting is a common sin.

        a. We tell friends we are not worried—only burdened or concerned.

        b. The truth is, we're plainly fretting.

    2. The meaning of fretting.

        a. The Hebrew means "to be hot, to be angry."

        b. The English root means "to eat up, to consume."

            (1) Fretting does that.

            (2) Fretting eats up peace, joy, and robs of blessings.

B. How does one avoid fretting?

    1. Know that God wants to reveal Himself—prepare yourself for it.

    2. Be still before Him.

        a. The words "Be still" literally mean "take your hands off. Relax!"

        b. We are so prone to try to do "everything"—or at least all we can.

        c. There are times when God wants us to know, "Relax, I can handle it."

    3. Receive the revelation.

        a. Hezekiah let God reveal Himself to him.

            (1) He took the threatening letter he had received from the enemy and laid it out before the Lord (2 Kings 19:14).

            (2) He asked God to help: "Now therefore, O Lord our God, I beseech thee, save thou us out of his hand, that all the kingdoms of the earth may know that thou art the Lord God, even thou only" (2 Kings 19:19).

        b. Let God reveal Himself to you.

            (1) He may do it through His Word.

      (2) He may do it through a word of encouragement or wisdom communicated to your spirit.

      (3) He may do it through an inspired word from others.

          CAUTION: To be sure that you are receiving God's revelation, be sure that it agrees in all aspects with the Word and ask God to confirm it. It is a principle in both testaments of the Bible that "in the mouth of two or three witnesses shall every word be established" (2 Corinthians 13:1; see also Deuteronomy 17:6; 19:15).

   c. The ultimate revelation is this—HE IS GOD! Let Him be that to you.

  4. Let God be God.

   a. Don't scheme your way out of a situation.

   b. Seek divine guidance and let Him have control.

CONCLUSION

A. Here, then, are three great affirmations.

  1. I have a refuge and strength—I will not fear.

  2. I have a river—I will not faint.

  3. I have a revelation, He is God—I will not fret.

B. Can we depend on Him?

  1. The Bible says this:

   a. "Fear thou not; for I am with thee: be not dismayed; for I am thy God: I will strengthen thee; yea, I will help thee; yea, I will uphold thee with the right hand of my righteousness" (Isaiah 41:10).

   b. "When thou passest through the waters, I will be with thee; and through the rivers, they shall not overflow thee: when thou walkest through the fire, thou shalt not be burned; neither shall the flame kindle upon thee" (Isaiah 43:2).

  2. Your experience says this:

   a. When you look ahead, you sometimes feel, "There's no way!"

   b. When you look back, you realize He has done it again.

    C. Look at the psalm.
       1. If the psalmist had written, "The God of Abraham is our refuge," we would be discourged.
         a. Abraham was a great man of faith—sometimes we are not.
         b. But Jacob (v. 7) was like us, sinful at times, prone to his share of failures—but repentant.
       2. No wonder Martin Luther was inspired by Psalm 46 to write "A Mighty Fortress Is Our God."
    D. Indeed, God is adequate for you in any situation—why worry when trusting is so good?

THE DIMENSIONS OF PRAYER

David S. Bishop

INTRODUCTION

A. *ILLUSTRATION*: I recently read of a cotton-factory worker
who was new on the job. Over her machine there was
a card which read, "If your threads get tangled, send
for the foreman." One day her threads got tangled and
rather than show her ineptness in handling the machine
she tried to untangle them. Soon they were hopelessly
tangled and then she called for the foreman. When he
came he asked, "You've been working on these, haven't
you?" She said, "Yes, I did my best." He said, "No, you
did not do your best. Your best is to call for me."

How much this illustration has to say to us about how
we need to turn situations over to God in prayer.

B. What is prayer?

1. It is more than my talking to God.
2. It is a two-way communication with God—the most
important part of which is God's talking to me.
3. "Prayer is that spiritual exercise by which I bring
myself into such communion with God until I become

possessed with God's will, God's passion, and God's plan for the world."—selected.

4. There are many kinds of prayer.

a. Prayer can be conversation (sharing together).

b. Prayer can be communion (heart-to-heart).

c. Prayer can be petition (asking of God).

d. Prayer can be intercession (to come in between—to stay God's wrath or judgment).

e. Prayer can be praise and worship (adoration).

THE PROMISES OF PRAYER

A. To read the Bible's teachings on prayer brings a quickening of expectancy in our hearts and a rising of faith in our spirits. Notice just a few of them.

1. Matthew 7:11—"If ye then, being evil, know how to give good gifts unto your children, how much more shall your Father which is in heaven give good things to them that ask him?"

2. Matthew 21:22—"And all things, whatsoever ye shall ask in prayer, believing, ye shall receive."

3. Mark 11:22-24—"And Jesus answering saith unto them, Have faith in God. For verily I say unto you, That whosoever shall say unto this mountain, Be thou removed, and be thou cast into the sea; and shall not doubt in his heart, but shall believe that those things which he saith shall come to pass; he shall have whatsoever he saith.

Therefore I say unto you, What things soever ye desire, when ye pray, believe that ye receive them, and ye shall have them."

4. John 14:12-14—"Verily, verily, I say unto you, He that believeth on me, the works that I do shall he do also; and greater works than these shall he do; because I go unto my Father.

And whatsoever ye shall ask in my name, that will I do, that the Father may be glorified in the Son.

If ye shall ask any thing in my name, I will do it."

5. John 15:7—"If ye abide in me, and my words abide

in you, ye shall ask what ye will, and it shall be done unto you."

B. Of such lavish scriptural promises one scholar has said, "To make such outlandlishly extravagant claims about prayer, Jesus was either a madman or He is truly God." For those of us who know Him personally, there is no question—He is God!

THE PERSPECTIVES OF PRAYER

A. Prayer reaches up.

1. This is a beautiful thought—but it is very true!

   "And this is the confidence that we have in him, that, if we ask any thing according to his will, he heareth us:

   And if we know that he hear us, whatsoever we ask, we know that we have the petitions that we desired of him" (1 John 5:14, 15).

2. The truth is, you reach heaven when you pray.

   a. *ILLUSTRATION*: A church member was candidly asked one day, "What size preacher do you people like over there in your church?" The man thought for a moment and then answered earnestly, "It really doesn't matter, as long as he's big enough to reach heaven when he's on his knees." Not only is that the size preacher we need in the pulpits of America, but that is the size members we need on our pews.

   b. *ILLUSTRATION*: Remember the old Gospel song we used to sing many years ago, "Down on your knees, you're taller than trees"? That is ever so true!

   c. *ILLUSTRATION*: Prayer is like a powerful telescope. By prayer we can fix our gaze above the frustrations and disillusionments of life and zero in on the heart of God. What a change that makes. As the chorus says, ". . . and the things of earth will grow strangely dim, in the light of His glory and grace."

3. Yes, prayer reaches up. Wherever God is—that is

how far prayer reaches upward. It touches the heart of God.

B. Prayer reaches in.

1. Prayer not only reaches up, but it effectually draws the power of God into our souls.

ILLUSTRATION: As a little boy rummaging around in my grandmother's things, a lad came across a most marvelous little instrument. It was a magnifying glass. Someone showed me how to catch the rays of the sun in that magnifying glass and to focus them upon a piece of paper. If you could make the dot small and intense, soon the paper would burst spontaneously into flame. One day I was out on the front steps of our old porch burning my initials in the wood, when my mother came out. I was proud—she was aghast. In any event, prayer is that spiritual magnifying glass by which I catch the rays of love that stream from the heart of my heavenly Father. Through prayer I can focus those rays of love upon my own heart and it sets my spirit on fire for God.

2. Prayer unleashes power in the life of the person who prays.

a. ILLUSTRATION: A motto found on many walls says, "Prayer Changes Things." That is true, of course. Prayer does change things. But I would like to suggest another motto, "Prayer Changes the One Who Prays."

b. Prayer has great power to change the individual —but I want to speak about that a few minutes later.

C. Prayer reaches out.

1. There is no limit to how far—or how fast prayer reaches out.

ILLUSTRATION: They tell me that light travels at the rate of 186,000 miles in one second. That is an incredible statistic. I have no way of comprehending such speed. Yet, I can tell you of something that is faster—and reaches farther. Because we are mortal, we are bounded in our concepts by time and space. Time and space are really convenient inventions of the finite mind of man to help him cope with the thought of immensity and eternity. God doesn't need such devices. When you pray, the message goes immediately to God (wherever that may be) and when accompanied by faith, the answer is immediately sent on its way with no time delay because of distance. How amazing when you realize that you may be praying in Washington to God in heaven about a need in Africa and the answer is activated even as you reach out to God. What an incredible dimension prayer affords in ministering to the needs of those who are beyond our physical reach.

    2. How many times have you known God to minister to those for whom you were deeply moved when you prayed, and even though you could not be there, you knew that He was there in answer to your prayer?

D. Prayer reaches through.

    1. There are no barriers or obstacles that can withstand the powerful thrust of prayer.

    2. When you are faced by situations for which there seems to be no hope or resolution, remember that prayer reaches through—no matter the difficulty.

ILLUSTRATION: "Got any rivers you think are uncrossable?

Got any mountains you can't tunnel through?

God specializes in things thought impossible?

And He can do for you what no other power can do."

THE POWER OF PRAYER

A. The fact of its power.

    1. This is an age of power.

        a. We call this the nuclear age—and so it is.

        b. *ILLUSTRATION*: The power generated by one atomic bomb is awesome. Think of the power generated by a 100 megaton bomb, and these are small by today's potentials. Yet, that is like having a Hiroshima every day for 13 years. Awesome and tragic!

       c. But this is nothing compared to the power potential of prayer.

   2. What makes prayer such a powerful force?

      The Creator and sustainer of a hundred million universes is saying, "If you will pray, I will work." "Call unto me, and I will answer thee, and shew thee great and mighty things, which thou knowest not" (Jeremiah 33:3).

   3. Prayer does not release some power in man but makes man available so that God can flow His power through him.

B. The manner of its power

   1. When we pray for situations

      a. God, who is the Master Controller of all things, works in ways we could never design . . . or even comprehend.

      b. For this reason, it is not always wise to try to tell God *how* He is to answer prayer. His way is always best anyway.

      c. Sometimes answers will be immediate—at other times God will work through a process.

         (1) He knows what He is doing.

         (2) Leave it with Him.

   2. When we pray for others

      a. God answers prayer offered for others.

      b. God immediately gets involved when you pray for others.

         (1) No matter how it looks, trust Him.

         (2) If it has to do with something that involves the other person's will there are some vital things to remember.

            (a) Understand that when God is dealing with the will of another person, He does not violate the will but brings pressure to bear.

               (1b) This is not a guarantee that a thing may be done.

ILLUSTRATION: While it is God's will that none should perish, He does not force all to accept His salvation.

(1a) This takes time.

(b) Accept the fact that God has pressures at His disposal that you don't have and He knows best when and how to use them.

(c) When you begin to pray for another person and God begins to put pressure on them, they may react negatively.

(1a) Don't become alarmed.

(1b) Know God is working.

(1c) Understand that there has to come a breaking of the will before the thing can be accomplished, so be aware of what this may mean.

(1d) Continue to "keep the faith" while all of this is in process.

3. When we pray for ourselves.

a. This is the area where we have the greatest concerns.

(1) We want answers NOW!

(2) We want answers without personal difficulty or complications.

b. We need to understand, however, God's ways are not always man's ways—and again He knows the best way.

c. God answers many of our prayers through personal growth and spiritual development.

(1) We pray for patience—and God sends those who tax us to the utmost. Why? Because "tribulation worketh patience" (Romans 5:3).

(2) We pray for submission—and God sends suffering. Why? Because we "learn obedience by the things we suffer" (Hebrews 5:8).

(3) We pray for love—and God allows unlovely people into our lives. Why? So that we may learn to love through His strength and not our own (Galatians 2:20).

(4) We pray for victory—and the things of the world sweep down on us in a storm of temptation and adversity. Why? For "this is the vic-

tory that overcometh the world, even our faith" (1 John 5:4).

(5) We pray for intimate union with Jesus—and God severs natural ties and lets our friends misunderstand or become indifferent. Why? So we can learn to depend on the intimacy of the One who loves us and cares for us like no one else ever could (John 15:9, 10).

(6) We pray for quietness—and everything within and around us seems to be confusion. Why? That we may learn that when He giveth quietness, no one can make trouble.

d. For the things that happen that we cannot understand, know that God is still on the throne and He is working (Romans 8:28).

e. Remember James' words, "But let patience have her perfect work, that ye may be perfect and entire, wanting nothing" (1:4).

THE PRACTICE OF PRAYER (How Then Should We Pray?)

A. Approach God confidently in prayer.

"Let us therefore come boldly unto the throne of grace, that we may obtain mercy, and find grace to help in time of need" (Hebrews 4:16).

1. As His child, you have a right to come to the Father . . . you have a ready audience.

2. Do not come with hesitancy, a sense of unworthiness, or fear . . . come boldly.

B. Pray in faith believing.

"And all things, whatsoever ye shall ask in prayer, believing, ye shall receive" (Matthew 21:22).

1. God is touched by the feelings of our infirmities . . . but He is moved by our faith.

2. Childlike faith moves the hand of God!

C. Be definite when you pray.

1. Most people make it impossible for God to give a definite answer because their prayers are too general.

ILLUSTRATION: Some pray the impossible prayer. They cry out for God to save the lost or heal the sick when all the lost are not going to be saved or all the sick healed. We need to care enough to carry a burden and then get down to business with specifics and pray: "God, save my next door neighbor," or "Lord, heal my boss at the office."

ILLUSTRATION: A little fellow bowed beside his bed to say is nighttime prayers. It was Christmastime. Among special favors for others, he asked for one for himself—a two-wheeled bike. His father, who heard his son's prayer, asked him about his request the next morning saying, "Son, you didn't mean a bicycle; you're too small. Surely, you must mean a tricycle." With that, the little fellow said with determination, "Nope! I asked God for a two-wheeler and that's just exactly what I'm going to get!"

    2. When you get definite with God, you can expect a definite answer.

D. Give yourself unto prayer.

    1. The devil can wear down a person's resources—but he is defeated by the one who prays.

    2. *ILLUSTRATION*: What better epitaph could be put upon the headstone of any believer's grave than this: "Here lies one who daily exercised the privilege of prayer."

CONCLUSION

A. But all that we may say about prayer is of little consequence unless we put it to use.

QUOTATION: "Prayer is one of those subjects about which there is much talk and little practice"—anonymous.

B. God has devised prayer as a means of . . .

    1. communication.

    2. communion.

    3. petition.

    4. intercession.

    5. worship.

C. Prayer is also the gateway to power with God.

QUOTATION: One saint has said, "Prayer and power make up a simple equation: little prayer, little power —much prayer, much power."

ILLUSTRATION: Consider Jonathan Edwards, the American herald of the Great Awakening. When Jonathan Edwards preached, men cried and clung to the columns of the church for fear they would slide into an eternity without God. This man was not a preacher. He wore thick glasses, read most of his sermons, and had awkward gestures. What most do not know, however, is that he often spent 10, 12, sometimes 15 and 18 hours on his knees in prayer before he preached. That made a difference.

D. Be honest with God.

1. Rebuild damaged or severed lines of communication with God.

2. Ask Him to change "attitudes of prayerlessness" to "habits of prayerfulness."

3. Let God work a transformation in your life that will testify to a renewed power connection between you and God.

HOW TO PRAY FOR OTHERS TRIUMPHANTLY

David S. Bishop

SCRIPTURE: Ephesians 1:15-23; cf. 3:17-20

INTRODUCTION

A small Kentucky town had two churches and one whiskey distillery. Members of both churches complained that the distillery gave the community a bad image. Besides, the owner of the distillery was an atheist. The churches tried civic means of shutting the distillery down but were unsuccessful. At last they decided to hold a joint Saturday night prayer meeting to ask God to intervene. Saturday night came and all through the prayer meeting a terrible electrical storm raged. To the delight of the church members, lightning struck the distillery and it burned to the ground. Next morning, the sermons in both churches centered on "The Power of Prayer."

The fire insurance adjuster promptly notified the distillery owner they would not pay for his damages because the fire was classed as being caused by an "act of God." The adjuster pointed out that coverage for "acts of God" was excluded from the policy. Whereupon the distillery owner sued all the church members, claiming they had conspired with God to destroy his building. At that point, the defendants denied vehemently that they had done anything to cause the fire. The trial judge wryly observed after the preliminary presentations: "I find one thing about this case very perplexing," he said. "We have a situation where the plaintiff—an atheist—is professing his belief in the power of prayer, and the defendants—church members—are denying that there is any power in prayer at all."

A. How much do we really believe in prayer?
1. I guess one thing about prayer will always seem like a paradox to me.
   a. The people who say they believe in it . . . but don't believe.
   b. The people who say they don't believe in it . . . but really do believe (just let them get into trouble).
2. We, however, are people of prayer because we believe in its exercise and its results.

B. A basic expectation for any consideration of prayer is that it be effective.
1. We want results from our petitions.
2. We want to know how to pray for others effectively.

C. Paul's prayers should be a model for such praying.
1. He was a man of prayer.
2. He planted a lot of churches.
3. He had a lot of people on his prayer list.

D. For our focus in this discussion, let us note how Paul prayed for others in his opening prayer in his letter to the Ephesians.

THE OCCASION OF THE PRAYER (v. 15)

A. The prompting of it
   NOTE: The reasons Paul gives for praying for these saints are unusual when compared with much current practice.
   1. Their faith was authentic.
      a. It was not based on hearsay, superstition, learning, or legend.
      b. It was based "in the Lord Jesus."
   2. Their faith was active.
      a. If faith is authentic, it will be manifested in good works.

406

b. The greatest of all good works is the showing forth of love.

"By this shall all men know that ye are my disciples, if ye have love one to another" (John 13:35).

c. The Ephesians' faith was demonstrated by their "love unto all the saints."

(1) Their love was God's love released in them by faith.

(2) Their love touched all the saints—the unlovely as well as the lovely.

B. The suggestion of it

1. Paul's prayer was prompted by positives, not negatives.

a. Most people do not pray for others until there is a need (negatives).

b. Paul's prayer is offered in view of their faith and love (positives).

NOTE: The practical section of the book (chapters 4-6) would indicate the Ephesians had needs, but Paul does not refer to them as the stimulus for his prayers.

2. Paul's prayer indicated a systematic exercise rather than a sporadic one.

THE MANNER OF THE PRAYER (v. 16)

A. He was consistent.

1. Paul told the Ephesians that in prayer and thanksgiving for them, "I . . . cease not."

2. Paul was indicating to the Ephesians that His remembrance of them was as sure as clock work.

B. He was proper.

1. He began with thanksgiving.

a. Thanksgiving is the proper atmosphere for prayer.

"Enter into his gates with thanksgiving" (Psalm 100:4).

b. Paul looked for the virtues in their lives for which to give thanks.

(1) A pervasive negativism in our culture encour-

ages many people to look for flaws in others rather than virtues—but Paul didn't practice this.

(2) A perfectionist attitude will tend to magnify inadequacies in others at the expense of positive qualities—but Paul didn't do this.

2. He proceeded to petition.

THE CONTENT OF THE PRAYER (vv. 17-22)

NOTE: Paul makes only two basic petitions as far as the Ephesians are concerned. The fulfillment of these two petitions, however, would pretty much provide all other things they might have need of.

A. Spiritual enlightenment—in three areas (vv. 17, 18)

1. That they might have the spirit of wisdom and revelation.

a. Paul is not praying for them to be baptized with the Holy Spirit.

b. Paul is praying that the Holy Spirit, who dispenses wisdom and gives revelation, may be free to administer these in their lives.

(1) They need spiritual *wisdom* to know how to apply scriptural knowledge to daily life and experience.

(2) They need *revelation* in the deep, intimate things of God to know God's will and pleasure.

(a) This is revelation from God—not manipulated daydreaming.

(b) This is *rhema* that flows from the *logos* —not impulse based on desire.

ILLUSTRATION: It was a sense of the revelation of God's pleasure and will that gave Luther his great boldness in prayer. In 1540, Luther's great friend and assistant, Frederick Myconius, became sick and was expected to die within a short time. On his bed he wrote a loving farewell note to Luther with a trembling hand. Luther received the letter and instantly sent back a reply: "I command thee in the name of God to live because I still have need of thee in the work of reforming the church. . . . The Lord will never let me hear that thou art dead, but will permit thee to survive me. For this I am praying, this is my will, and my will be done, because I seek only to glorify the name of God." The words are almost shocking but they were words born of revelation of the will of God. When Luther's letter arrived at Myconius's bedside, he had already lost the ability to speak, but in a short time he revived. Myconius recovered completely, and he lived six more years to survive Luther himself by two months.

2. That they might have enlightenment concerning their hope.

   a. The great hope of the believer is the appearing of Christ in glory.

     "Looking for that blessed hope, and the glorious appearing of the great God and our Saviour Jesus Christ" (Titus 2:13).

   b. The hope Paul speaks of here is the "hope of his calling" and is a hope inspired by the personal call of God.

     (1) It inspires and includes a confident expectation of eternal blessedness.

     (2) It lets us know . . .

       (a) He has an interest in us (ministry).

       (b) We have an inheritance in Him (hope).

3. That they might have an awareness of their rich inheritance.

ILLUSTRATION: Recently a gem enthusiast bought a rough piece of stone at a garage sale for $10 that was really a rare gem stone. The newspaper reported that the new owner plans to have it professionally cut and mounted and expects it to bring between $2 and $5 million dollars. Somewhere there must be a very sick garage-sale entrepreneur. He had an extremely rich inheritance but he let it go because he was not aware of its true value. This loss is nothing compared to the potential loss of one who fails to appreciate his inheritance as a believer in Christ.

   a. It is only natural that Paul would underscore the need for true awareness of the believer's inheritance as he had already listed several aspects of it in the 14 verses preceeding this prayer.

(1) We are blessed with all spiritual blessings in heavenly places in Christ (v. 3).

(2) We have been chosen in Him before the foundation of the world (v. 4).

(3) We have been predestinated unto the adoption of children (v. 5).

(4) We have been accepted in the Beloved (v. 6).

(5) We have been redeemed through His blood (v. 7).

(6) He has abounded toward us in all wisdom and prudence (v. 8).

(7) He has made known unto us the mystery of His will (v. 9).

(8) We have obtained an inheritance in Him (v. 11).

(9) We have been sealed with the Holy Spirit of promise (v. 13).

(10) We have already been given an earnest of our inheritance (v. 14).

b. Our inheritance in Christ Jesus is a two-sided inheritance.

(1) Our inheritance in Him (which is beyond comparison with earthly wealth)

(2) His investment in us (making us a treasure unto Himself)

B. Fullness of power

1. The direction of it (v. 19)

a. Power of such magnitude is not for everyone.

b. Power of such magnitude, however, *is* promised for believers—"to us-ward who believe."

2. The greatness of it (vv. 19-22)

a. Paul qualifies the power as, "exceeding greatness of his power."

b. Paul measures the power by its "working . . . in Christ."

AMPLIFICATION: The Greek word *energia*, which is used here for "working," is a word which is used only in reference to superhuman power, whether of God or the devil (Thayer). As

410

such, it is active and not latent—a divine power working on behalf of the believer.

(1) It raised Christ from the dead.

(2) It set Christ at God's right hand in the heavens.

(3) It put all things under Christ's feet.

(4) It positioned Christ to be the Head over all things to the Church.

    (a) All things are in submission to Him in the Church.

    (b) All things are under Him (as to authority) outside of the Church.

3. The surety of it (v. 23; cf. 2:1-10)

    a. Paul mentions here that the Church is Christ's body, "the fulness of him that filleth all in all."

    b. Paul tells the Ephesian brethren in chapters 2 and 3 that they are a part of that Body and, as such, have been the recipients of that same power's working.

    (1) If Christ has been raised from the dead, we are also partakers with Him.

        (a) Though dead, we have been made alive in Christ.

"And you hath he quickened, who were dead in trespasses and sins" (2:1).

"Even when we were dead in sins, hath he quickened us together with Christ, (by grace ye are saved)" (2:5).

        (b) Made alive in Christ, we shall experience resurrection from the dead, even as Christ did—"because I live, ye shall live also" (John 14:19).

"But if the Spirit of him that raised up Jesus from the dead dwell in you, he that raised up Christ from the dead shall also quicken your mortal bodies by his Spirit that dwelleth in you" (Romans 8:11).

"But now is Christ risen from the dead,

and become the firstfruits of them that slept" (1 Corinthians 15:20).

(2) If Christ has been seated at God's right hand, we are also seated with Him.

(a) It is our present *position* in Him.

"And hath raised us up together, and made us sit together in heavenly places in Christ Jesus" (2:6).

(b) It is our future *heritage* in Him.

"That in the ages to come he might shew the exceeding riches of his grace in his kindness toward us through Christ Jesus" (2:7).

"To him that overcometh will I grant to sit with me in my throne, even as I also overcame, and am set down with my Father in his throne" (Revelation 3:21).

(3) If all things have been placed under Christ's feet, they are under ours as well, since we are members of the body of Christ.

ILLUSTRATION: One fellow was projecting his low sense of self-esteem by saying, "I'm a nobody in the body of Christ." He went on to elaborate, "I am the least of the least. I'm nothing more than a part of the bottom of the foot in the body of Christ." The truth is, however, if one were not more than a freckle on the bottom of the little toe of the body of Christ, Satan and his imps would still be under, for He "put all things under his [Christ's] feet."

CONCLUSION

A. One cannot properly conclude this prayer without looking ahead to the fulfillment Paul desires for the Ephesians as a result of his prayer.

B. In the closing of the doctrinal part of the book in the last part of chapter 3, Paul expresses himself as desiring for them that "Christ may dwell in [their] hearts by faith," so that they may *comprehend* and *experience* . . .

1. His incomparable love (3:17-19)

    a. Its dimension

        (1) Breadth—broader than the heaven with its septillions of stars

        (2) Length—longer than the minutes in eternity's day

        (3) Depth—deeper than the deepest chasm in the mighty Atlantic

        (4) Height—higher than the farthest star . . . reaching even to the throne of God

2. His boundless power (3:20)

    a. Its degree

      Able to do. . .

        do. . .all

        do. . .above all

        do. . .abundantly above all

      do exceeding abundantly above all. . .

    b. Its extent

        (1) "that we ask or think. . ."

        (2) "according to the power that worketh in us"

          (a) The power of the resurrected Christ

          (b) The power that is over all

"Now unto him that is able to do exceeding abundantly above all that we ask or think, according to the power that worketh in us."